Communities of the Qur'an

Communities of the Qur'an

Dialogue, debate and diversity in the twenty-first century

Edited by Emran El-Badawi
and Paula Sanders

ONEWORLD
ACADEMIC

Oneworld Academic

An imprint of Oneworld Publications
Published by Oneworld Academic, 2019

ISBN 978-1-78607-392-1
eISBN 978-1-78607-393-8

Typeset in Adobe Jenson by Hewer Text UK Ltd, Edinburgh
Printed and bound in Great Britain by Clays Ltd, Elcograf S.p.A.

Oneworld Publications
10 Bloomsbury Street
London WC1B 3SR
England

Stay up to date with the latest books,
special offers, and exclusive content from
Oneworld with our newsletter

Sign up on our website
oneworld-publications.com

Contents

Note on Transliteration

Arabic and Persian transliteration are based on the transliteration system used by the *International Journal of Middle Eastern Studies* (*IJMES*). The simplified transliteration system does not mark letters with dots below or macrons. The *ta' marbuta* is rendered *a* not *ah* (e.g. *Sura, umma*), and it is rendered as *at* in the construct state (e.g., *Surat al-ikhlas*). Vowels are limited to *a, i, u.* The *'ayn* is rendered as a single open quote ('); the *hamza* is rendered as an apostrophe (').

Urdu, Gujurati, Indonesian and Javanese transliterations follow the standards set by the authors.

Foreword

It is said that when 'Umar b. al-Khattab, the brash, young Qurayshi elite who would become the second caliph of the Muslim community after the death of the Prophet Muhammad, first heard the words of the Qur'an, he was so astonished at their power and elegance that he abandoned his tribe and his status and immediately converted to Muhammad's movement.

As the story goes, 'Umar had discovered that one of his sisters had become a follower of Muhammad and was planning on killing her for it. He raced to her house, sword drawn, to avenge the honor of his family and tribe. Before he could strike her down, however, he heard the Qur'an being recited from within. All at once, he dropped his sword and began to weep, transformed by the beauty of the words, and ready to give up everything for them.

For centuries, Muslims have pored over the pages of the Qur'an, trying to discern its multiple layers of meaning. For some, the Qur'an is a source book of law and morality; for others, it is a secret message to humanity from God himself. There is simply no other text – secular or sacred – that compares with it. The Qur'an represents the height of the Arabic language. It could, in fact, be argued that the Qur'an created what we now know as Arabic. As I have written elsewhere, the Qur'an is to Arabic what Homer is to Greek and what Chaucer is to English.

But of course, unlike the works of Homer and Chaucer, the Qur'an is also holy scripture. For most Muslims, it is quite literally the direct speech of God. For some it *is* God, in-so-far as the principal of *tawhid*, or strict monotheism, forbids separating God's attributes – e.g. God's speech – from God's self. As the direct speech of God, the Qur'an is infused with divine power. That is why its words are inscribed on mosques and tombs, etched onto cups and bowls, or made into talismans.

Yet it is precisely this unique, elevated status that has made the Qur'an such a difficult text to study in a non-devotional context. Indeed, the same process of literary and historical criticism that has been applied to the Bible for more than two centuries is barely in its infancy when it comes to Qur'anic studies.

That is not to suggest that there have not been profound arguments over the meaning and message of the Qur'an throughout the last fifteen centuries of Islam. From the very beginning there were deep disagreements among Muslims over how to read and interpret the sacred text, to what degree it has been affected by the cultural norms of the society in which it was revealed, and whether historical context and independent reasoning should have a role in its interpretation. It's just that the unique properties of the Qur'an, and the unique role it has had in the Muslim community, has, for the most part, excluded a large swath of Muslim voices from this fifteen-century debate.

This collection aims to remedy that situation by bringing together a diverse array of textual scholars who are engaging the Qur'an from perspectives that have been sorely lacking in Islamic scholarship for far too long. The inclusion of, for example, African-American, female, LGBTQ, Ahmadi, and even Baha'i voices to the centuries-long conversation about the meaning of the Qur'an is vital to ensuring the viability of this extraordinary text in the twenty-first century. Most importantly, by prioritizing engagement and disagreement, rather than the pretense of forced unity, this book is symbolic of the increasingly diverse Muslim community itself.

Reza Aslan

Acknowledgments

Contributing something this important to the study of the Qur'an and to intrafaith dialogue has been both fruitful and challenging. Completing this book would not have been possible without a sensitive and scholarly vision shared by both its editors. As much of our world moves towards populist nationalism, there is an urgency behind preserving the values of religious tolerance and cultural literacy.

As scholars based in Houston, we made full use of the resources at our academic institutions. First and foremost we share our deepest thanks and appreciation with the Boniuk Institute for Religious Tolerance at Rice University for hosting the Communities of the Qur'an conference in 2016. Likewise we are indebted to the College of Liberal Arts and Social Sciences at the University of Houston for a generous book subvention. Of course, the completion of this book was possible because of collaboration between both institutions, as well as individuals.

Our thanks go to Dr. Milton and Mrs. Laurie Boniuk for their leadership, philanthropy and compassion over the years. Our thanks also extend to Imam Feisal Abdul Rauf, Rabbi-Professor Reuven Firestone and Dr. Zahra Jamal for helping shape the conference, and therefore this book. We also thank Kate Eubanks and Laura Johnson for their precision and coordination during various stages of this project. We share our heartfelt gratitude with the contributors of this book, who demonstrate the importance of both scholarship and service. This book also came to fruition through various presentations and intellectual exchanges, namely those at: the Centre for Islamic Theology in Münster, Germany (2018); and Sam Houston State University in Hunstville, Texas (2017).

Finally, we would like to thank Professor Reza Aslan for his commitment, and also professors Karen Bauer and Mohammad Hassan Khalil for their feedback on this book's introduction. We are grateful for their thought-provoking critiques and intellectual generosity. Last but not least, we are indebted to Oneworld for publishing this book.

Emran El-Badawi and Paula Sanders
Houston

Introduction

Emran El-Badawi and Paula Sanders

The *Communities of the Qur'an* project evolved from a conference into a book. The purpose of this essay is to introduce the ten communities selected, and to connect their twenty-first-century dialogue, debate and diversity with that of the Qur'an's first audience. This book investigates the dialectical relationship between a single scripture and its multiple communities of interpretation. Our examination begins with the Qur'an itself.

DISPUTE AND DIVERGENCE WITHIN THE QUR'AN

The Qur'an is the first Arabic book in history. It appeared in seventh-century Arabia, at once and with unprecedented eloquence and power.[1] Its sound, text and message captivated its audience through the new 'clear

---

[1] There is no precedent for Arabic literature prior to the Qur'an. The genres of pre-Islamic poetry (*shi'r jahili* or *mu'allaqat*) and battle folklore (*ayyam al-'arab*) were preserved orally, then committed to writing and subjected to editing and embellishment well over a century after the Qur'an itself. Alternately, the growing body of late antique Arabian epigraphy, while a valuable primary source, largely preserves short, dedicatory inscriptions and graffiti in disparate scripts, not a fully developed form of Arabic literature. See further *EQ*, s.v. 'Arabic Language' (Herbjørn Jenssen).

Arabic tongue,' deliberately surpassing the prestige of older religious texts in Aramaic, Greek and Persian. The text's audience of believers – its first **community of the Qur'an** – was for the most part literate, at least reading and writing business contracts (Q 2:282). At the same time, this audience was likely bilingual at a time when Arabic was evolving into a language of religious writing (Q 16:103; 68:1). Finally, this audience was able to access the doctrines and laws of the Christian patriarchs and Jewish rabbis (e.g. Q 3:79; 5:48; 6:91; 20:133; 87:19).

The text appeared among quarreling religious sects and competing empires. The Middle East in the seventh century was divided by perpetual warfare between the Persians and Byzantines. The cities and oases of Arabia lay at the frontier between these two empires. Arabia served as a safe haven for prophets, missionaries and pious men and women fleeing imperial conflict and worldly temptation. The Qur'an emerged in a world where sectarianism and conflict were the norm, and where divine salvation was to be found in both new revelations as well as ancient customs. The Qur'an – both its content as well as reception – was not always a source of unity, but rather served as a source of significant dispute and divergence.

The text explicitly differentiates between 'believers' and 'Muslims' (cf. Q 49:14). It also mentions 'assemblies who have splintered and disputed' (Q 3:105); different Jewish groups; Nazarene-Christians; people of the Gospels (Q 5:47); people of the scripture; Gentiles (Q 62:2); Sabians (Q 5:69; 22:17); Zoroastrians (Q 22:17); puritans/ Hanifs (cf. Q 22:31); polytheists/associators; hypocrites; and rebels. We learn that the rebels live in 'complacence and factionalism' (Q 38:2). Among them are 'those who say that God is Christ the son of Mary' (Q 5:17, 72) or 'the Third of Three' (Q 5:73). Splinter groups existed even among the believers as reference is made to: sects (*firaq*; esp. Q 2:75; 146; 100–1; 3:23, 78, 100; 5:70; 19:73; 23:109; 34:20); groups (*tawa'if*, e.g. Q 33:13; 49:9; cf. Q 61:14); units (*fi'at*; Q 3:13, 69–72; 4:81; 7:87); parties (*ahzab*; Q 5:56; 58:18–22); and protectors (*awliya'*; e.g. Q 8:34). To these may be added the 'brethren in religion' (Q 9:11) and allied subjects (Q 33:5). Similarly, Q 5:48 teaches that different religious groups possessed different laws and customs. The enmity of the Jews and the friendliness of Christians found in Q 5:82 is also worthy of note in this regard. Q 60:7–8 cautions the believers that 'God may cause friendliness between them and those whom they antagonize,' and that they should deal honestly and equitably with 'those who have not fought them in religion nor expelled them from their homes.' The point is that the Qur'an makes ample reference to the sectarian landscape from which it emerged.[2]

Salvation, therefore, does *not* depend on one's religious group or sect, but rather on one's personal beliefs and actions. The text declares that its believing audience – the very first community of the Qur'an – was *not* Muslim, *nor* Arab, *nor* one religion. It states, rather:

> Those who believe, the Jews, the Christians and the Sabians – whoever believes in God and the last day and does good works – they will have their reward, so no fear is upon them, nor will they be saddened. (Q 2:62)

Moreover, in cases where one's personal salvation is in question, the Qur'an does *not* call for their punishment, *nor* excommunication, *nor* any worldly consequence. It states, rather:

> Those who believe, the Jews, the Christians and the Zoroastrians, and those who associate [gods with God], God will surely decide between them on the day of resurrection. God is indeed witness over all things. (Q 22:17)

The very first 'community' (*umma*) of the Qur'an was *not* the majority of society, *nor* did they agree on matters of religion. The community was a microcosm of humanity – *divided*. So on the one hand it addresses them directly: 'this is indeed your community – a single community – and I am your Lord so serve me' (Q 21:92; 23:52), adding:

> You are the best of communities brought forth for humanity: you command virtue, forbid the contemptible, and you believe in God.

---

[2] See further El-Badawi, *The Qur'an and the Aramaic Gospel Traditions*, pp. 3–5.

> And if the people of the scripture believed it would be better for them. Among them are believers, but most of them are corrupted. (Q 3:110)

On the other hand, the text acknowledges the diverse and divided nature of humanity:

> For humanity was but one community then they disputed, and if it were not for a word decreed by your Lord, then a settlement would be found between them concerning what they disputed. (Q 10:19; cf. 2:213; 43:33)

The text adds elsewhere:

> And if God so willed He would have made you one community. However, He guides whoever He wills and leads astray whoever He wills. And you will surely be asked about what you used to do. (Q 16:93; cf. 11:118; 42:8)

Numerous passages demonstrate the inherent diversity and inevitable divergence of humanity along religious lines. According to the text, what is the fundamental cause of humanity's religious dispute and divergence? The Qur'an itself!

The text states unequivocally that divine revelation, the final manifestation of which is believed to be these Arabic 'recitations' (qur'an), is the root cause of dispute among its audiences:

> For even if a recitation (qur'an) made the mountains crumble, the earth split asunder, or the dead speak, the matter belongs all to God. Have not those who believe given up? For if God so wills, he would guide all humanity. And those who reject remain afflicted by disorder because of their actions or desecration near their homes until the promise of God arrives. Surely God does not renege on his promise. (Q 13:31)

The text adds elsewhere that their dispute came only *after* its call to 'submit' to God:

> Surely the religion near to God is submission (*islam*). And the people of the scripture did not dispute until after [its] knowledge came to them, [causing] animosity between them. And whoever rejects the signs of God, surely God is swift in taking account. (Q 3:19; cf. 42:24)

It adds further that God deliberately created multiple communities, laws and customs, to test humanity:

> And We revealed the scripture [i.e. the Qur'an] in truth, affirming what is before it from the scripture [i.e. the Hebrew and Christian Bibles], overruling it. So judge between them according to what God revealed, and do not follow their whims over the truth that has come to you. To each of you We have prepared a law and custom. And if God so willed He would have made you one community. However, he tests you with that which has come to each of you. So hasten towards good works. To God is your return – all of you – where he will inform you concerning what you used to dispute. (Q 5:48)

All this is to say that the Qur'an itself did not lead to greater unity and religious conformity, but rather contributed to further sectarian dispute and divergence. Humanity does not know which of its communities is the 'best', nor can people settle religious disputes or judge individuals in this life. According to the text, only God has this authority. What humanity learns is that religious dispute is a predetermined 'word decreed' by God. In response to this inevitability the very first community of the Qur'an had recourse to a 'common word' (Q 3:63) – a process of negotiation and compromise – and calling others to the faith 'through wisdom and good advice' (Q 16:125). Spreading the faith *exclusively* through a campaign of violence – which is a fact of certain episodes in medieval and modern history – is nevertheless unfounded in the text. That being said, violence plays an integral role in the exodus, retaliation and overall shaping of the community. There is an undeniable tension, on the one hand, between the text's punitive treatment of unbelievers who break peace treaties – unless they repent, observe prayer and charity (Q 9:1–15) – and its overall reluctance to coerce or penalize any individual based on religious beliefs alone.[3]

It is worthy of note that the text states: 'there is no compulsion in religion' (Q 2:256) and 'the truth is from your Lord, so whoever desires may believe and whoever desires may reject' (Q 18:29). For each soul is only responsible for itself (Q 17:15; 35:18; 39:7; 53:38), and we must ultimately await the judgment of God about our religious differences – including those who reject the prophecy of Muhammad and the veracity of the Qur'an (Q 7:87). The text states some two dozen times that the majority of the Qur'an's audience and Muhammad's society were *not* believers (e.g. Q 2:100). Like the prophets of the Hebrew Bible before him, Muhammad was mocked as a madman, a sorcerer and a liar (e.g. Q 38:4; 40:24; 51:39–52). Society's rejection of him grieved Muhammad to the point of suicide (Q 18:6; 26:3). Yet the Qur'an prohibits him from forcing his religious views upon others:

> And if God so willed surely everyone on earth would believe. Will you compel humanity until they become believers? For it is not possible for a soul to believe except by the will of God. (Q 10:99–100)

Elsewhere the text repeats that Muhammad is merely a messenger, not a strongman or a watchman over people's religious affairs (Q 6:107; 39:41; 50:45).

If the Qur'an ordains diversity, mandates religious tolerance and largely defends individual freedom, why is Islam today frequently

---

[3] The subject of violence in the Qur'an is beyond the scope of this chapter. However, suffice to say that the text's general mantras are: 'fight in the way of God those who fight you, but do not transgress; God does not like the transgressors' (Q 2:190); 'whoever kills one soul it is as though they have killed all humanity' (Q 5:32). That being said, Q 9:29 stands in stark contrast as fighting 'those who do not believe in God, nor the Last Day, nor forbid what God and His messenger have forbidden, nor follow the religion of truth' becomes embroiled in the breaking of political alliances, holding tribute and full-scale warfare. See further, Afsaruddin, *Striving in the Path of God*, pp. 277–8.

associated with religious intolerance and extremism? More directly, why is there a disconnect between Muslims on the one hand and the Qur'an on the other? These questions have undergone thorough and thoughtful investigation in the works of intellectuals and reformers.[4] However, the problem of associating the Qur'an on the one hand with modern religious extremism – terrorism – is one addressed in this project as well. The purpose of covering both the positive as well as negative considerations of the Qur'an today is to refine the boundaries of our investigation, and attempt to offer a greater scope of critical analysis. Instead of rehashing fourteen centuries of Islamic sectarianism, how would focusing precisely on the interaction between the ancient scripture and its modern communities make for a fresh and fruitful investigation? It is to this task that we turn next.

DEBATING THE QUR'AN

What are the different approaches to reading and understanding the Qur'an? How do different kinds of Muslims, especially, understand their scripture, and how does this understanding shape their communities? With approximately 1.7 billion adherents, the global Muslim community (*umma*) is anything but monolithic – but is it a single community at all? Some attempts to answer these questions have had recourse to discourses on 'sectarianism', 'ancient hatreds' and Sunni–Shia conflict. Such discourses are superficial, often political, and fundamentally naive. A deeper, more systematic and critical theory is needed to explain the culturally diverse and even fractured nature of the global Muslim community.

A more systematic exploration takes one through classical exegesis, modern hermeneutics and arrives at literary theory, especially reception and reader response criticism, and the idea that the text is shaped – physically changed even – by the community that reads it, no matter what community it may be. Like other scriptures conceived within a framework

---

[4] See generally Siddiq, *Hal qara'na al-qur'an*; Shahrur, *The Qur'an*.

of collective devotion, the Qur'an has meaning only when interpreted by the community into which it was received, and it is informed by that community's cultural assumptions.[5] This idea resonates with the famous tradition ascribed to 'Ali b. Abi Talib (d. 40/661) addressing the Khawarij, stating 'as for this Qur'an, it is but writing between two covers and it does not speak, but it is men who speak through it.'[6] Since the Qur'an is interpreted in different ways by different communities it has – to quote the renowned American literary scholar, Stanley Fish – 'many different communities of interpretation.'[7]

At its heart, *Communities of the Qur'an* investigates the dialectical relationship between the Qur'an and its communities of interpretation. How is the relationship between community and scripture mediated? Can a better understanding of each community's reception, hermeneutics and cultural assumptions bring about a better understanding of the Qur'an for the twenty-first century? It is, then, about both intellectual inquiry and religious dialogue. This project also seeks to revive the 'ethics of disagreement' (*adab al-ikhtilaf*) found in classical Islam. The Qur'an interpreters, jurists and theologians of medieval Baghdad, Cairo and Cordoba serve, for the most part, as examples of peaceful coexistence and tolerance in the face of vehement disagreement.[8] On numerous occasions, the historical record shows that Muslims from different legal schools or denominations, as well as Christians, Jews, Zoroastrians and others, agreed to disagree. The point here is not to fall into the trap of romanticizing the past, but rather to be inspired by the fact that it was once commonplace among religious schools to utterly disagree on matters as central as the Qur'an, Islam and God's role in the universe. Most Muslim majority societies do not enjoy this freedom today. Even in modern times, authors have explored the limits of the ethics

---

[5] On constructing the meaning of the Qur'an, and its embeddedness in patriarchy, see Wadud, *Inside the Gender Jihad*, pp. 158–86.

[6] Among Sunni variants, see the Shia version by Ibn Babawayh al-Qummi, *Risalat al-i'tiqadat*, p. 77.

[7] Cf. Fish, *Is There a Text in this Class?*, esp. pp. 171–3.

[8] The intellectuals and politicians did, nonetheless, have their share of religious persecution, including for example the Mihna (833–48 CE) or Almohad dynasty (1121–1269 CE). These episodes, however, represent an aberration rather than the norm of life in classical Islamic civilization.

of disagreement, but only within traditional forms of Islam forged centuries ago.[9]

Recent literature on 'Islamic communities of interpretation' demonstrates how feminist discourses and traditionally conceived theological reforms have made some progress.[10] However, framing the dialectical relationship, as this book does, between disparate communities and a single scripture accommodates even greater diversity. Similarly, *Communities of the Qur'an* maps out new territory by including groups typically outside the pale of traditional (or neo-traditional) Islam: the Baha'is (a distinct nineteenth-century development out of traditional forms of Islam from Iran); the Ahmadis (a twentieth-century Islamic sect from South Asia, excommunicated by the World Muslim League in 1974); African-American communities, including the Nation of Islam, Five Percent Nation, Moorish Science Temple and others considered beyond 'mainstream' Islam; the Ismaili Shia; and LGBTQ groups, including those who have recently established 'gay mosques,' altogether rejected by traditional mainstream Muslims.

Why should a project like *Communities of the Qur'an* cast such a wide net? Because the circumstances of the twenty-first century demand it. The challenges of today's political climate are greater than those of our predecessors. The religious, social and cultural diversity of the imagined global Muslim community, known as the 'umma,' and the richness of its people's cultures, are under threat by extremist fundamentalism. It is Muslims themselves who have paid the greatest price for the twenty-first century warfare and 'sectarianism' undertaken in the name of Islam. The discourses surrounding the so-called 'war on terror' on the one hand, and Islamic fundamentalism on the other, which have spread in the wake of the September 11, 2001, attacks, and the Arab uprisings of 2011, have polarized members at both extremes of the debate. As a result, the Qur'an, Islam's sacred scripture and a monument of world literature, has become the subject of abuse and misunderstanding. More than ever before, leaders from within and without the imagined global Muslim community

---

[9] Cf. the work of Alalwani, esp. *Adab al-ikhtilaaf fi al-islam.*
[10] See Daftary, 'Diversity in Islam.'

have the opportunity to protect the diversity of Islamic civilization and promote religious tolerance, as well as peaceful coexistence broadly speaking.

SELECTING THE COMMUNITIES OF THE QUR'AN

Despite the broad scope of our project, enumerating, let alone including, every single community in our world today that experiences or finds inspiration in the Qur'an is nearly impossible. At the very least, their numbers far surpass the seventy-three Muslim sects prophesied in the tradition ascribed to Muhammad.[11] Future research may yet refine our examination. The limited sample of communities included in this project is, nonetheless, broad in representation. The process of selecting a limited number of communities that was globally representative – as this project has aimed to do – was a major challenge. A meeting of minds was necessary to interrogate the process and criteria for selection, along with our investigation of the communities of interpretation themselves. This is why an academic conference was convened.

The Communities of the Qur'an conference took place March 10–11, 2016, on the campus of Rice University in Houston, Texas. Hosted by Rice's Boniuk Institute for the Study and Advancement of Religious Tolerance, the conference brought together notable academics and leaders of faith communities. The participants who presented are both secular and religious in background. A number of them are both trained scholars in the academic study of religion as it is practiced in American and European universities, and trained within religious traditions. Conference presentations were made by eight international speakers (in order of presentations: Dr. Ingrid Mattson, Dr. Sajjad Rizvi, Dr. Ali Asani, Dr. Ahmed Subhy Mansour, Dr. Amina Wadud, Counselor Mujeeb Ur Rahman, Dr. Todd Lawson, and Dr. Aminah Beverly Al-Deen), three panel chairs (Dr. Hina Azam, Dr. David Cook and Dr. Emran El-Badawi), welcoming remarks by Boniuk director, Dr. Paula Sanders, and parting words by philanthropist,

---

[11] Tirmidhi 40:2641.

Dr. Milton Boniuk. Together with the eight conference papers now transformed into chapters, two chapters were solicited: one on the LGBTQ reception of the Qur'an by Dr. Scott Kugle, and another on popular-Sufi Qur'an reception in rural Indonesia by Ms. Lien Fina and Dr. Ahmad Rafiq. The contributors to this book belong to a wide spectrum of confessional, scholarly and reformist communities who developed in the shadow of the Qur'an, one way or another.

This book took a number of important concerns into consideration. First was ensuring that each contribution demonstrated the dialectic relationship between an ancient scripture – the Qur'an – and a modern community of readers. Each chapter expresses, therefore, how the respective community 'wrestles with scripture,' so to speak.[12] Do modern readers connect with the Qur'an through communal musical performance, social activism, deeply personal experience, medieval commentaries, or any number of other ways?

Second, this book acknowledges, and was indeed partly motivated by, the imbalance of power and representation afforded to some communities over others. The sheer dominance of Sunni, and in some cases Imami Shia, orthodoxy is problematic. Consequently, the blind authority granted medieval tomes – especially works related to *hadith*, *tafsir* and *sira* – can be stifling. Of course, one cannot speak of medieval religious writing without recognizing the fact that its architects were overwhelmingly men, and that they deliberately and systematically excluded women and differently gendered people from participating in shaping medieval religious communities.[13] How could we 'rebalance' power and representation in this book? This was done in two ways: (a) attempting equal gender distribution throughout the book; (b) reorganizing the sequence in which chapter contributions appear, to prioritize non-traditional, non-patriarchal, heterodox communities. In other words, communities accentuating the importance of experience and gender were fronted, while communities built on largely textual or patriarchal foundations appear later (see table of contents).

---

[12] For an insightful analogy to this point, see generally, Gench, *Faithful Disagreement*.

[13] For more on this, see Hidayatullah, *Feminist Edges of the Qur'an*, pp. 40–50, 164–6.

Third, and finally, is the challenge of juxtaposing starkly different communities in one book (and one room) while faithfully allowing each community to speak freely, through its own voice. For example, when we planned the Communities of the Qur'an conference, we had prepared for a lively, perhaps even heated, theological exchange. This did not happen, and although the exchange became passionate at times, it was not theology but rather gender that caused the greatest tension. This was a teaching moment for the conference directors and current book editors. Patriarchal readings of the Qur'an, and modern patriarchal norms and conventions, were indeed the greatest hurdle in organizing both the conference and the book. From a distance it may appear that theology or salvation history is the fundamental break between each community; but up close, gender was a far more defining boundary. Is identity itself the driving force behind crafting theology? This is another question beyond us now, but about which there is ample literature.[14]

The chapters of this volume demonstrate how both contemporary and historical communities engage with the Qur'an in different ways, and often at odds with one another. The fundamental principles of justice and human dignity loom large in the discussions of the contributors. Aminah Beverly Al-Deen discusses the deep tensions between African-American Muslim communities and immigrant Muslim communities who consider themselves as representing a normative Islam. Her chapter also shows one expression of the dialectical relationship of African-American communities with the Qur'an through the reconfiguration and use of domestic space. Lien Fina and Ahmad Rafiq show us how an interpreter of the Qur'an, *Cak* Nun – one who does not claim the authority of an imam – guides the Ma'iyah community of Indonesia. Their chapter also demonstrates, in a quite different cultural context from the one Al-Deen discusses, the importance of direct connection between the Qur'an and daily life. Amina Wadud demonstrates how Islamic feminism gives voice to the lived experience of women as a theological principle that can help achieve gender equality and true justice. Similarly, Scott Kugle's chapter foregrounds the principles of justice and equality, while allowing us to listen to the

---

[14] See further, Baker, *One Islam, Many Muslim Worlds*, pp. 70–3, 90–113.

unfiltered voices of queer Muslims. Chapters by Ali Asani and Sajjad Rizvi focus on two different Shia communities. On one hand, Asani's chapter shows us how the Khoja Ismaili community engages with the Qur'an through the mediation of the living imam, and how having a living, authoritative interpreter of the Qur'an facilitates engagement with and adaptation to changing conditions in the contemporary world. Rizvi, on the other hand, explores classical Twelver Shia exegetical traditions which continue to develop without immediate access to an imam in the world, and which are key elements in shaping Shia identity. Ingrid Mattson shows how cohesion in the diverse Sunni community can be continually reconstituted through direct engagement with the Qur'an, and founded upon the ideals of justice and human dignity, rather than the historical principle of consensus. Todd Lawson's chapter shows how the Baha'i community was constituted through, among other things, its direct engagement with the Qur'an, while maintaining a distinct identity that is not Muslim. Finally, Ahmed Subhy Mansour and Mujeeb Ur Rahman provide direct access for our readers to statements of faith and exegetical principles of the Qur'anist movement and the Ahmadi community.

The following précis of the chapters provide snapshots of the contributor's key arguments.

Aminah Beverly Al-Deen: **African-American Communities of the Qur'an**

Approaches to the Quran across the African-American community are widely varied. During the first decades of the twentieth century, the earliest communities to engage with Islam depended upon the Holy Qur'an, as translated by Maulana Muhammad Ali of the Ahmadiyya Movement in Islam (India). It has been reported that many early Muslims kept both a Qur'an and a Bible in the home for reading and study. The Qur'an began to be read by many in fragments, with emphasis on marriage, duties, etc., rather than as a coherent text. Though many Muslims of this generation were college educated, Muslims from outside America asserted the Qur'an as a text that could not be read by ordinary people who had not mastered Arabic. This debate continues, as does the alienation from the text.

Ali Asani: **Nizari Ismaili Engagements with the Qur'an: the Ismaili Khojas of South Asia**

These verses portray the imam as the locus of knowledge and divine authority and reinforce the authoritative nature of the living imam's pronouncements and guidance. The imam's pronouncements, called *farman*s, are regarded by the community as the *ta'lim* (instruction) and *ta'wil* (esoteric interpretation) of the Qur'an as opposed to *tafsir* (commentary). In his public addresses, the current Ismaili imam, Prince Karim Aga Khan, speaks to the challenges of interpreting the faith of Islam in the contemporary world, particularly with respect to diversity, the inseparability of faith and world, and the interplay of faith and intellect.

Lien Iffah Naf'atu Fina and Ahmad Rafiq: **The Reception of the Qur'an in Popular Sufism in Indonesia: *tadabbur* among the *Ma'iyah* Community**

The Qur'an has been the backbone of the [*Ma'iyah*] community since the beginning. The concept of the *Padhangmbulan* gathering was *pengajian tafsir* – a religious gathering that discusses the meaning of the Qur'an – delivered by the [teachers of the community] *Cak* Nun and *Cak* Fuad. *Cak* Fuad provides 'textual *tafsir*'; he reads certain verses and their translation, explains the meaning of key words, delivers an interpretation by referring to hadith literature and commentaries of the Qur'an, before offering his own interpretation. On the other hand, *Cak* Nun delivers a 'contextual *tafsir*.' He links the verses with contemporary political, social, cultural and religious situations, using the former as the perspective to analyze the latter. This becomes the pattern of other Ma'iyah gatherings.

Amina Wadud: *Musawah*: **Gender Equity through Qur'anic Discourse**

The most distinguishing feature of Islamic feminism is a construction of Islamic knowledge based on a dynamic interaction with the

Qur'an as it relates to cultural attitudes, personal praxis and public policy. Indeed, this initiative – led by Muslim women on behalf of their own perceptions and experiences of Islam – involves an active relationship with the Qur'an as a tool for women's full agency, spirituality, interrelationships and empowerment. How do Muslim reformists wrestle equality out of the Qur'an? While there are ample examples of Qur'anic privilege to men and the male gaze, this chapter focuses on the methodologies used to advocate for gender neutrality as fundamental to the Qur'an. It discusses how Islamic feminism relates to text and context to achieve gender reform today.

Scott Kugle: The Reception of the Qur'an in the LGBTQ Muslim Community

Queer Muslims form an interpretive community to voice their own experiences – speaking in private, announcing in public, writings, life stories, engaging journalistic discussions, and expressing through the arts – and to take this voice into the arena of debate with the Islamic theological traditions. From the Qur'an, queer Muslims extract the ideal principles of justice, equality, deep diversity in God's creation, compassion and care, love and intimacy, and entrusting God alone to judge. Some queer Muslims do this intuitively, based on their own experience, while others are talking about scholarly and reformist writings.

Sajjad Rizvi: The Speaking Qur'an and the Praise of the Imam: the Memory and Practice of the Qur'an in the Twelver Shia Tradition

It is commonplace to hear Shia believers hold that the Qur'an is a long poem in praise of the family of the Prophet and the imams in particular. In one sense, this is an expression of the famous narration of the 'two weighty things' (al-thaqalayn) popular in Shia sources for an early period; in another it complements another early hadith corpus on traditions on how the intimacy of the Qur'an and the imam is such that the former is silent unless the latter makes it enunciate for believers. Both the scripture of the Qur'an and the person of the imam are acts of the self-revelation of God.

Todd Lawson: **The Qur'an and the Baha'i Faith**

According to the Baha'i teachings, the Qur'an is a sacred and absolutely authentic repository of the word of God. The earliest major Baha'i works, which are also considered divine revelation, whether from the Babi phase or the later Baha'i phase, are in fact works of Qur'anic exegesis. The Qur'an is the central focus of contemplation and explication by both the Bab and Baha'ullah. In addition, each author frequently comments on various sacred traditions (*hadith*). Perhaps it is more accurate to ask how the Baha'i faith embodies and spreads these Qur'anic verities to what might otherwise be thought rather unlikely quarters, instills great love for Islam and the Prophet Muhammad (whom Baha'ullah refers to as the 'Seal of the Prophets'), and identifies itself as an independent religion.

Ingrid Mattson: **How the Qur'an Shapes the Sunni Community**

Debate, dialogue, discussion and explanation – the Sunni community is, above all else, a discursive space that can be initiated at any point with a word of the Qur'an. The recognition of a core set of diverse, equally authentic interpretive methods and schools within Sunni Islam is an (aspirationally irenic) solution to the rejection of the imamate on the one hand, and the need to establish parameters of orthodoxy – or the appearance thereof – on the other. The embrace of an ethical pluralism that does not descend into relativism or anarchism is ideally the result of the Sunni approach to the Qur'an.

Mujeeb Ur Rahman: **The Qur'an and the Ahmadiyya Community: an Overview**

The Qur'an speaks of a living God who guides humans through continued revelation. The Qur'an is the living word of God, just as the universe is His living act, both unfolding their verities according to the needs of time. The Qur'an has no conflict with science, nor with rationality. It teaches freedom of conscience and rejects all forms of compulsion. Ahmadiyya tradition rejects the prevailing concept of armed jihad, which is a negation of Qur'anic teachings.

Ahmed Subhy Mansour: Why the Qur'anists are the Solution: a Declaration

In our belief, the Prophet Muhammad is the first Qur'anist, as he was ordered to uphold the holy Qur'an alone (Q 43:43). We also believe in the holy Qur'an as the only hadith (Q 7:185; 45:6; 77:50). We understand the Qur'an according to its unique Arabic terminology, in order to disentangle the true, abandoned Islam and its great values of peace, tolerance, freedom and justice. Instead of the so-called Sharia law, we want to convince the Muslim world to accept the Universal Declaration of Human Rights as Islamic laws, according to the real core of Islam.

Despite the diversity found within these communities, there is a discernable divide between communities of text and communities of experience. The former includes traditional forms of religion (Islamic sects and Baha'i faith, in this case) founded upon deep, literary and often patriarchal engagement with the Qur'an text, whereas the latter represent non-textual, culturally informed reimagination of what the Qur'an is and how it shapes a community. These communities include African-American communities, the Khojas of South Asia and LGBTQ communities, whose relationship with the Qur'an is imbued more by customs or subcultures than the text itself.

DOES THE QUR'AN HAVE MULTIPLE NATURES?

It would be fair to say that communities of the Qur'an disagree on its very nature. This diversity is rich and complicated. A number of provocative ideas came to light during both the panel and round-table discussions. Most striking is how some communities consider the Qur'an a foundational text, but one that is woven into the fabric of a broad, non-denominational salvation history. To say this differently, the Qur'an, New Testament, Hebrew Bible and the Avesta simply belong to all humankind. In this vein, Lawson evokes the writings of Baha'ullah (d. 1892). While Baha'i writings pay homage to the Arabic Qur'an and Muhammad the Prophet (as they do to other ancient religious texts and figures), it fashions out of their model a newer scripture altogether.[15] To put it plainly, it seems in this case that the Qur'an has been accepted and abrogated at the same time.

Similarly, when speaking through the lens of Islamic feminism, Wadud posits that the Qur'an text – namely its patriarchal language and ancient cultural background – represent a kind of transition in human salvation history. There will, in other words, come a time when the adherents of the Qur'an will no longer have recourse to the text, but rather its universal, egalitarian message to humanity.[16]

These views are in stark contrast to the unique, static and eternal nature of the Qur'an central to the Sunni tradition, despite its diversity and numbers. As Mattson suggests, the authenticity of the textual tradition (especially the Qur'an and hadith) is central to orthodoxy, and any criticism of or departure from it is highly suspect at best, or heresy at worst.[17]

The Imami Shia position demonstrated by Rizvi represents a sort of compromise between the text's eternal nature and the unfolding of salvation history in human terms. This is namely the doctrine of the Imam, of which there are two primordial, co-equal and co-eternal manifestations: (1) the silent Imam, i.e. the Qur'an; (2) the speaking Imam, i.e. the progeny of 'Ali.

Access to the speaking imam and his gnosis is granted, Asani argues, through the teachings of localized communities in South Asia. Centuries ago, trade with Persia brought Ismaili Shi'ism to the Khojas. As his chapter demonstrates, however, this complex and interwoven sectarian identity

---

[15] Cf. Baha'ullah, *Kitab-i-iqan* (*Book of Certitude*), p. 213.
[16] See in passing, Wadud, 'Interview.'
[17] Cf. Mattson, *Story of the Qur'an*, pp. 16–18.

of this one community had to be redefined in colonial times between Nizari Ismaili, Imami and Sunni.

This brief survey on the nature of the Qur'an does not do justice to its complexity, nor does it afford it the nuance it deserves. For that, readers will have to read the chapters themselves. However, even these summaries underscore the fact that the communities included herein have never agreed on a question as basic as 'What is the Qur'an?' Among historians it is natural for Muslim communities to disagree about the nature of the Qur'an, much as the Christian churches came to sharp disagreements with one another over the nature of Christ. As such, there has been a perpetual inability to achieve consensus through Christological controversies and Islamic civil wars. This is a sobering fact.

However, those bloody historical developments – controversies and civil wars – also had some positive repercussions; and they reinvigorated society after its fall. In this respect, it was the darkest days of the first Islamic civil war between the 'Alids, Umayyads and Kharijites (35–40 AH/656–61 CE) which pushed the people towards introspection and self-examination. At the turn of the seventh century they posed a basic question about human suffering: 'Where does evil come from?' From Basra to Baghdad, philosophical theology – Kalam – developed as the intellectual sparring ground of several competing communities of interpretation (including Jews, Christians, Manicheans and atheists) while attempting to answer that profound question. Islam had become an open rationalist discourse, and with far-reaching consequences. The ranks of the theologians grew, and they sparred with a new class of secular philosophers, as well as a burgeoning class of state judges and religious clerics. Kalam became the arena of cross-pollination with Jewish and Christian partners.[18] In the case of the former, a Jewish brand of Kalam gave rise to a rationalist Karaite Judaism, which flourished in conversation with Muslim interlocutors. And the Muslim theologians soon took up the Christological controversies, only in Islamic guise, they asked a different question: 'What is the nature of the Qur'an?'

The following centuries gave rise to the so-called Islamic 'golden age,' a time when the secular and religious sciences flourished in the Abbasid era

---

[18] Wolfson, *Philosophy of Kalam*, p. 79.

(750–1258 CE). So long as Islamic civilization produced knowledge for the world, it continued to debate scripture. At times when production declined, so too did the debate.[19] It would be fair to say that the 'intellectual freedom' enjoyed by early scholars to debate scripture has eroded dramatically over time. To be fair, however, bad governance plays a major role in the lack of freedom in many Muslim majority societies today. In those societies, critical academic study of the Qur'an is well-nigh heresy.[20] To say this differently, debating Islamic scripture – reclaiming an honest and critical understanding of the communities of the Qur'an – is essential to the 'health' of Islamic civilization as a whole.

CONFRONTING RELIGIOUS EXTREMISM

Rather than healthy debate, the Qur'an today is largely treated through polemics or apologetics. Western media and foreign policy frequently associate the Qur'an not with its respective communities, but rather with terrorism. Why? On the one hand, violent extremist terrorist groups are destroying Islam and Muslims – while committing murder in their names; but on the other, Western media interests and rising Islamophobia largely portray Islam itself as the problem. Forms of terrorism associated with Islamic extremism, fundamentalism and radicalism are given too much 'air time.' Must all public discussion on Islam pertain to bombings and wars in the Middle East? What about the 1.7 billion Muslims worldwide – or are they invisible? What about the hard-fought internal struggles within Islam? We decided our project, while giving voice to communities of the Qur'an, should offer sober reflection – rather than political or media bias – upon the problem of religious extremism especially.

As part of the conference, a moderated discussion between an imam and rabbi examining 'Faith and Extremism' was hosted by the World Affairs Council of Greater Houston; and it was covered on local television.

---

[19] Kristó-Nagy, 'Denouncing the Damned Zindiq!', p. 65.
[20] For more on this phenomenon, see El-Badawi, 'Intellectual Freedom and the Study of the Qur'an.'

They explored the use of religion, especially through violence, focusing primarily, but not exclusively, on Islam and Judaism. Rabbi Dr. Reuven Firestone and Imam Feisal Abdul Rauf – two seasoned interfaith speakers, authors and esteemed leaders of their respective communities – expressed their views on a number of pressing issues, including religious law, holy war, the challenge of the so-called Islamic State (IS, ISIS, ISIL) and the various conflicts in the Middle East. On this latter question, Firestone argues that, for Judaism, warfare based on religious goals was in decline until the first Arab–Israeli war of 1948, when it re-emerged.[21]

In the spirit of diversity and tolerance central to this project, Abdul Rauf equates 'democratic values' (especially human rights) with the 'objectives (maqasid) of Shariah.'[22] An increasing number of Islamic leaders worldwide are taking up this position – not without some debate of course – and in the case of Malaysia the government is making it law. Since modern nation states are the seat of legitimacy today, both secular as well as Islamic, he sees groups like ISIS as a 'rogue anomaly ... far from Islamic.'[23] The expertise of both Abdul Rauf and Firestone afforded some much-needed sobriety and perspective to otherwise politicized, misunderstood, hot-button issues.

Still, some may disagree with distancing ISIS from Islamic history and even the Qur'an. As Graeme Wood's controversial article makes clear: 'Muslims ... cannot condemn slavery or crucifixion outright without contradicting the Koran and the example of the Prophet,' adding that jihadist groups 'assiduously follow' the Qur'an's medieval penal laws and rules of retaliation.[24] Does this make ISIS its own dark and twisted community of the Qur'an? Most Muslims would say no. However, the last word on this debate has yet to be spoken.

---

[21] Firestone, *Holy War in Judaism*, p. 107.

[22] Abdul Rauf, *Defining Islamic Statehood*, pp. 116, 145–9.

[23] Ibid., p. 268.

[24] See Graeme Wood, 'What ISIS Really Wants,' *The Atlantic*, March 2015, which became the most widely read article in that magazine's history. For a more recent and systematic discussion on the warfare practiced by ISIS as an aberration to the rules of warfare within classical Sunni Islam, see Khalil, *Jihad, Radicalism, and the New Atheism*, pp. 78–94.

DIVERSITY OR CONSENSUS? TOWARDS
A NEW THEORY OF COMMUNITY

This introduction began with reference to an important Shia tradition ascribed to Imam 'Ali, and now concludes with reference to an equally famous Sunni legal tradition ascribed to the Prophet Muhammad. The mantra goes: 'Indeed God will not make my community (*umma*) agree upon error.'[25] What is the purpose behind promoting consensus on such a global scale? Power – in a word. The idea of a single, global community founded upon consensus is incredibly empowering to its leader and its adherents. It is also incredibly dangerous and humanly impossible. It also contradicts the teachings of the Qur'an (see earlier). Like the speaking imam, the idea of the consensus of the community has existed in Sunni legal and exegetical thought for over a millennium. Wahhabism, a brand of Sunni fundamentalism which could only eke out an existence in the desert, was given limitless political, economic and military power on the world stage with the founding of the Kingdom of Saudi Arabia in 1932. Similarly, by founding the Islamic Republic of Iran in 1979, the top Imami Shia Mujtahids (Ayatollahs) channeled the powers of a modern nation state through the newly crafted legal institution, 'governance of the jurist' (*velayet-i-faqih*). Since the 9/11 attacks in 2001, the US invasion of Iraq in 2003 and the so-called Arab Spring of 2010/2011, the global Muslim community(ies) has been subjected to unprecedented warfare, sectarianism and Islamophobia. Much of the Arab world in particular descended into civil war, religious sectarianism and political unrest. While the reasons for such phenomena are complex, the idea of consensus has always been fundamentally political. This is demonstrated throughout history, from the days of the first ecumenical council in 325 CE under emperor Constantine (d. 337), to the piously named 'year of consensus' ('*am al-jama'ah*; 661 CE), to the founding of the Umayyads under caliph Mu'awiyah (d. 60/680), to the founding of the Organization of Islamic Cooperation (OIC; 1969). It has been centralized political power that has pushed for consensus building. All this was done with ample reason, and with ample bloodshed.

---

[25] Tirmidhi 4:2167.

The story does not end here, however. Standing against the prophetic tradition glorifying the consensus of community is another stating: 'the disagreement of my community is mercy.'[26] The fact that diametrically opposed traditions exist side by side demonstrates that alternate readings, receptions and interpretations of scripture are not only possible, but also desirable. Believers, students and scholars exercise their intellect, skepticism and judgment, not because they are heretics or cynics, but rather because they are committed to understanding the Qur'an. The Qur'an commands as much (Q 4:82; 47:24). But we must go beyond our predecessors, whether in the realm of faith traditions or academic institutions. In the age of globalization, social media and open borders, transcending certain norms of classical tradition – notably consensus – is inevitable. This age, including the so-called 'rise of populism', comes with a myriad of new challenges for communities worldwide.

Diversity, nonetheless, can refer to the practice of smaller local communities, villages, groups and subcultures, or to large, new movements. Diversity refers to the natural order of things. This is why the classical Islamic ethics of disagreement on the one hand and the universal declaration of human rights on the other, are central. It is little surprise, therefore, that many communities of the Qur'an around the world participate in concomitant discourse between classical Islam and human rights. The Qur'an's communities of interpretation typically represent the diversity and tolerance of smaller or newer communities, not the grandiose, political power of a centralized government – whether secular or religious. This project teaches us much about the nuances of polyvalent Muslim and non-Muslim reception of the Islamic scripture, which is worthy in and of itself. However, it also teaches that the *umma* is caught between the push of diversity and the pull of consensus. Not even on the nature of the Qur'an – a text shared by all parties – do they agree. History teaches that true consensus is impossible. Our hope is that coexistence is not.

---

[26] Al-Tabari, *Ikhtilaf al-fuqaha'*, p. 6.

BIBLIOGRAPHY

Abdul Rauf, Imam Feisal. *Defining Islamic Statehood: Measuring and Indexing Contemporary Muslim States*. (London: Palgrave Macmillan, 2015)

Afsaruddin, Asma. *Striving in the Path of God: Jihad and Martyrdom in Islamic Thought*. (Oxford and New York: Oxford University Press, 2013)

Alalwani, Taha. *Adab al-ikhtilaaf fi al-islam [The Ethics of Disagreement in Islam]*. (London and Washington, DC: International Institute of Islamic Thought, 1993)

Baha'ullah, *Kitab-i-iqan [Book of Certitude]*. (Wilmete, IL: US-Baha'i Publishing Trust, 2003)

Baker, Raymond. *One Islam, Many Muslim Worlds: Spirituality, Identity, and Resistance across Islamic Lands*. (Oxford and New York: Oxford University Press, 2015)

Daftary, Farhad. 'Diversity in Islam: Communities of Interpretation.' In *The Muslim Almanac*. Ed. A Nanji, 161–73. (Detroit: Gale Research Inc, 1996)

'The Disputation Between a Monk of Bet Hale and an Arab Notable.' In *Christian-Muslim Relations: A Bibliographical History, vol. 1 (600–1500)*. Ed. David Thomas and John Chesworth, 268–73. (Leiden: Brill, 2009)

El-Badawi, Emran. 'Intellectual Freedom and the Study of the Qur'an.' *Oasis: Christians and Muslims in the Global World* 26 (2018): 42–50

El-Badawi, Emran. *The Qur'an and the Aramaic Gospel Traditions*. (London and New York: Routledge Press, 2013)

Firestone, Reuven. *Holy War in Judaism: The Fall and Rise of a Controversial Idea*. (Oxford and New York: Oxford University Press, 2012)

Fish, Stanley. *Is There a Text in this Class?: The Authority of Interpretive Communities*. (Cambridge, MA and London: Harvard University Press, 1980)

Gench, Frances. *Faithful Disagreement: Wrestling with Scripture in the Midst of Church Conflict*. (Louisville, KY: John Knox Press, 2009)

Hidayatullah, Aysha. *Feminist Edges of the Qur'an*. (Oxford and New York: Oxford University Press, 2014)

Khalil, Mohammad. *Jihad, Radicalism, and the New Atheism*. (Cambridge: Cambridge University Press, 2018)

Kristó-Nagy, István. 'Denouncing the Damned *zindiq*! Struggle and Interaction between Monotheism and Dualism.' In *Accusations of Unbelief in Islam: A Diachronic Perspective on Takfir*. Ed. Camilla Adang, Hassan Ansari, Maribel Fierro et al., 56–81. (Leiden and Boston: Brill, 2015)

Mattson, Ingrid. *The Story of the Qur'an: Its History and Place in Muslim Life*. (Oxford: Wiley Blackwell, 2013)

Muhammad b. Babawayh al-Qummi (al-Shaykh al-Saduq). *Risalat al-i'tiqadat*. Trans. Asaf Fyzee as *A Shi'i te Creed*. (London: Oxford University Press, 1942)

Shahrur, Muhammad. *The Qur'an, Morality and Critical Reason*. (Leiden and Boston: Brill, 2009)

Siddiq, Yusuf. *Hal qara'na al-qur'an, am 'ala qulub aqfaluha?* (Tunis: Dar al-Alif, 1989)

al-Tabari. *Ikhtilaf al-fuqaha'*. Ed. Friedrich Kern. (Beirut: Dar Al-Kutub Al-'Ilmiyya, 1999)

Wadud, Amina. *Inside the Gender Jihad: Women's Reform in Islam*. (Oxford: Oneworld, 2006)

Wadud, Amina. 'Interview,' *Frontline / WGBH Educational Foundation*, March, 2002

Wolfson, Harry. *The Philosophy of Kalam*. (Cambridge, MA and London: Harvard University Press, 1976)

Part I

Communities of Culture and Experience

Chapter 1

African-American Communities of the Qur'an

Aminah Beverly Al-Deen, DePaul University

A frican-American communities of the Qur'an are one of the newer communities to have embraced its worldview, with reservations forged out of religious coercion, distrust and victimization. While some of these communities have been researched for scholarly and popular writing, it has always been as if they are bereft of the one thing that binds individual members through at least five generations – the Qur'an. These communities have been regarded as marginal to the 'real' Islam that immigrants brought to the United States and that exists in many cultural forms in the world. While it is true that immigrant individuals and their cultural interpretations of Islam have made significant contributions to African-American Islamic understandings, these communities have made the Qur'an their own, just as have other historical communities.

The pivotal stories invoked by almost all communities begin with the Prophet of Islam's persecution in Mecca, estrangement from family, and later move to Yathrib. In many accounts of the history of the Arabian peninsula, Islam is established by a very small group of individuals who trust that the messages that Muhammad ibn Abdullah receives are true because of his trustworthiness. In the religiously plural town of Mecca, there was know-ledge of those who worshiped one God, such as Jews and Monophysite Christians. These communities were considered minorities, and the Arabs considered that the God worshiped by them belonged to them. This is interpreted as a story of moving to escape persecution, as well as a story about how Muslims leaving families to pursue Islam is justifiable, if neces-sary. African-American Muslims feel justified in their choice of Islam from among many other possible choices.

The story goes that the Prophet Muhammad was invited to come and bring order to a contentious society in Yathrib, quelling the conflict. In return he was given the office of leadership over the society as a trust to his honesty, fairness, and in recognition of his prophecy. Simultaneously, Muslims in Mecca needed to emigrate from the oppression of the Meccans. They were willing to leave, and also forced to leave family and property behind to commit themselves to Allah's message.

What is important in practical terms here is that the Prophet of Islam had to leave his family and much of his tribe as a result of their refusal to embrace Islam. Transitioning to Islam is more often than not a disengagement from family and friends. That the Prophet put Allah before family, friends, and all that was familiar, suffered persecution along with followers, and then lived in a contentious plural society, very much mimicked life for African Americans in the United States.

This short chapter does not intend to cover the full depth or breadth of uses of the Qur'an within African-American Muslim communities. Rather, it selects popular approaches to the Qur'an that many imams use in Jum'ah (Friday prayer) or other congregational settings, along with examples from life. Uses of the Qur'an have changed over the more than one-hundred-year history of African Americans within Islam. This time period saw the rise, shift and transition of Islamically affiliated communities. There is also a need to address Qur'anic literacies related to English translations and reading the text in Arabic. Imams, as leaders in the community, are central figures in the transitions, history and literacies of the text. This chapter provides some examples of how the text is read and used as guidance. Lastly, the *shahada* (testimony of faith) has a role beyond its initial role in the transition to the Islamic faith.

HISTORICAL SHIFTS AND TRANSITIONS

Before 1950 there were two Qur'ans available in English in the United States – that of Edward Lane and that of Maulana Muhammad Ali. African-American communities had access to only the Ali translation.[1] The name of the translator or commentator meant little to this audience, and the history of the Ahmadiyya movement and its place within Indian Islam were also not that significant.[2] The Ahmadiyya movement in Islam had not yet been banned. The fact that there was an English translation at all was what mattered, and this translation gave its new African-American audience access to an otherwise unapproachable, but important, scripture.

The translation by the Ahmadi community, along with its commentary, served as guidance to the reading of the text. This introduction to the Qur'an gave teachers and readers a superficial though thorough mastery of its history, organization and major themes. Though what lay behind much of Ahmadi commentary highlighted their thoughts on reformation of Islamic thought in India, African-American Muslims still had to reinterpret the commentary according to their own circumstances.

Many of the people who transitioned to Islam before 1950 (and even after) came from either intensely black Christian communities or were estranged from religion altogether. Few had the luxury of formal study of religion in academic settings, as the educational opportunities for black people were limited. Multiple black denominations of Christianity shaped their lives. They embraced literal interpretations of the Bible, more austere traditions such as Catholicism, and almost every variant in between, just as in other religious communities. In communities, the reasons for transition are typically pragmatic: people need a faith to feel comfortable in, or they feel a sense of belonging to the faith of ancestors, or they just need a faith which is not a bystander to the 'real' Christianity which was white altogether, and had a white god.

---

[1] Lane, *Selections from the Kur'an*; Muhammad Ali, *The Holy Qur-án*. The Muhammad Ali translation was adopted by the Nation of Islam under both Elijah Muhammad and Louis Farrakhan.
[2] On the Ahmadiyya movement, see Valentine, *Islam and the Ahmadiyya Jama'at*; Friedmann, *Prophecy Continuous*. See also Chapter 9 in this volume.

What did the Qur'an offer? It offered a non-derogatory place for black people, a place in the world, and a clean upright existence through continual reformation of the self. The Ahmadi commentary stressed faith in the uprightness of all the prophets (e.g. Q 6:83–6). This offered those transitioning to Islam an explanation of the familiarity and non-exclusivity of Islam regarding prophecy. Additionally, the scripture taught that women were the spiritual equals of men and had property rights, along with a heightened status (e.g. Q 4:1, 32). This realization came about in Jim Crow America, a nation where black women were raped and considered property, rather than citizens with rights.[3]

Members of various Islam-related groups – Ahmadi, Moorish Science Temple, Nation of Islam and Sunni – felt spiritually uplifted through the Qur'anic mandates against drinking, consumption of pork products, gambling, sex outside marriage, cleanliness, respect for parents, recognition of the faith of others, and a connection to others in the world. Prayer, three to five times daily, punctuated the lifestyles of all, as did *zakat*, fasting during Ramadan (and for the Nation of Islam, fasting during the month of December) and the hope of a journey to Mecca. Some changed names, while others added a Muslim name to reflect a new sense of community and belonging.[4] Study of the Qur'an was paramount, with some memorizing portions in English and Arabic for prayers and meditation. Arabic language study was engaged with enthusiasm, with Arab tutors for classes, especially within the Nation of Islam.

Arabic language and Qur'anic studies also brought changes to home decor. Pictures of family members were put in albums or placed in parts of the home were believers did not pray. Instead, walls were adorned with Arabic calligraphy or pictures of the Kaaba. Racks or designated areas for shoes to be placed became commonplace as Muslims in the African-American community stopped the practice of wearing shoes in the home, and many people kept house shoes or socks near discarded shoes.

Muslims in the African-American community continued, when they could, to be present for major family events such as births, family reunions

---

[3] See, for example, Thompson-Miller and Picca, 'There Were Rapes!'
[4] See Thomas, 'Influence of Malcolm X and Islam.'

and funerals. In some families, the clean living of Muslim members was seen as saving them from a 'life in the streets.' In other families, Islam was seen as an affront to Christianity, and thus an abomination which had to be inveighed against.

For the new African-American Muslim communities, other Muslims gradually transformed into the new family and community. To put this differently, these new Muslims began to prefer Muslim over non-Muslim friends and acquaintances, with the exception of the nuclear family. New Muslim acquaintances reinforced the new way of life. These communities interacted with and often internally debated literacy and class differences, and sometimes even Islamic understanding. Soon, individual perceptions and stark differences emerged among African-American Muslim communities, many of which continue until today. Nevertheless, today members of the Moorish Science Temple attend events of the Nation of Islam and Sunni communities, and vice versa. Members of these different communities can also be in a single family, either by marriage or by blood.

The presence of Muslim communities was noted by observers of black life in the novels of black writers and in newspapers. African and Arabic names began to surface, as did Muslim greetings and dress. The larger communities adapted to the fact that the majority of those who claimed Islam and their children did not eat pork, females did not wear revealing clothing, nor were they to be verbally harassed.

Musicians including Yusuf Lateef, Ahmad Jamal, John Coltrane and McCoy Tyner popularized Islam among the jazz crowds of the 1960s–80s.[5] Muslim groups such as the Last Poets anchored jazz in popular music. Muslim sensibilities and a basic, but popular, knowledge of Islam spread throughout these African-American communities. Islam was not seen as a religious competitor but rather as a part of community life. Many of these artists belonged to various communities throughout their lives and fought immigrant stances about the purported evilness of black music.

Immigrant Muslims brought cultural interpretations of Islam that condemned everything black, including their family structure, music,

---

[5] See Bayoumi, 'East of the Sun (West of the Moon).'

language and other aesthetics, and the tensions intensified after a large influx of Muslims following the 1965 Immigration and Nationality Act.[6] That immigrant Muslims arrived at a place with a variety of established (African-American) Muslim practices did not change their assessments. Soon, scholars and researchers of Islam absorbed this discriminatory attitude, and they too began to essentialize the great diversity of African-American Islam into a monolith, focusing most of their attention on the Nation of Islam vis-á-vis immigrant Muslims.[7]

This is an important point to be highlighted. Researchers and scholars, beginning with C. Eric Lincoln, recognized the Nation of Islam and its self-help platform as a variant of the Islam they knew was espoused, though not necessarily practiced, in the Muslim world.[8] A calculated effort was made to de-Islamicize this group by relegating all of their efforts to the realm of black nationalism, with no spiritual/religious importance.[9] This group was viewed almost exclusively as a nationalist rather than religious group. Then, all other African-American Muslim communities were cast as offshoots of the Nation of Islam. Thus, when immigrants came in some numbers after 1965, their racist leanings from various colonial experiences merged with their newfound religious prestige, and formed the erroneous basis for scholarly works on who African-American Muslims were.[10] Even in this edited volume, the focus is on outliers rather than all. Those with only tangential attachments to Islam are housed with those who have moved away from Islam, and though the African-American Muslim community has hosted them all, it is put in the same boat.

---

[6] H.R. 2580; Pub.L. 89–236, 79 Stat. 911, enacted June 30, 1968. The Act abolished quotas based on national origin.

[7] Lincoln, *Black Muslims in America*; McCloud, *African American Islam*; Turner, *Islam in the African-American Experience*.

[8] See, for example, Lincoln, *The Black Muslims in America* (3rd edn), esp. pp. 166–9 and 210–27.

[9] On the importance of considering Islam among African-American communities as a religious and spiritual worldview, rather than solely through the lens of black nationalism, see McCloud, 'Islam in the African American Experience;' McCloud, 'African-American Muslim Intellectual Thought.'

[10] For a broad overview of African-American Muslim communities, see Ansari, 'Islam among African Americans.'

Nonetheless, by the 1970s Abdallah Yusuf Ali's translation of the Qur'an made its way to the United States.[11] With its English of the King James Bible, it was not as accessible as Maulana Muhammad Ali's, though the two were used interchangeably for a while. African-American Muslims were mostly interested in what they could read, and 'King James English' was difficult at best, even for the highly educated. It was not until late in the 1980s that many Muslims found out that Yusuf Ali wrote his translation as a palliative for the British, and made some errors in commentary as if it was direct translation. For example, he wrote about Eve as if she was explicitly named in the Qur'an, which she is not. He did this to ease British sensibilities about Muslim treatment of women.[12]

Changing these problematic attitudes, and especially those about women, motivated many college-educated African-American men and women. They came from various Muslim communities, and soon became budding playwrights, such as August Wilson, Islamic scholars like Ihsan Bagby, Sherman Jackson, Amina Wadud and Aminah McCloud, sports figures such as Muhammad Ali, Kareem Abdul Jabar, Eddie Mustapha Muhammad and Hasim Rahman, to name but a few. Members with college and postgraduate educations determined a great deal of the content for the internal structure and community outreach programs. They became leaders of communities for a time. Internally, in many of these communities, imams were elected and regularly tested for their knowledge of the Qur'an.

On a practical level, several *masajid* in Washington, DC, such as the Islamic Party, provided breakfast programs, newsletters with health, educational and after-school programs for kids, and literacy programs for adults.[13] These particular *masajid* were open to people of all faiths, and relationships with churches and Christian family members were common. Family members came to many events in the *masjid* without it being labeled interfaith. The *masjid* was a part of the community, not a house of worship that had to be integrated into the community. The rise of African-American

---

[11] Yusuf Ali, *The Holy Qur'an*. Ali (1872–1953) was an Indian civil servant. The first edition of his translation was published in Lahore in 1934, and has been reprinted numerous times.

[12] See Iqbal, 'Abdullah Yusuf 'Ali and Muhammad Asad'; Khan, 'English Translations of the Holy Qur'an,' esp. pp. 95–7.

[13] McCloud, *African American Islam*, pp. 64–9.

Muslim communities not welcoming outsiders was down to those modeled on less tolerant Sunni immigrant communities.

Given the Qur'anic exhortations and the example of Prophet Muhammad as trustworthy, some imams found themselves as arbiters of issues in the larger community. Many sat on city councils or worked in the offices of aldermen or mayors, especially in major eastern cities like Philadelphia, Washington, DC and New York. Islam and the Muslim presence became part of the religious and social landscape. In most urban spaces they were there, but unassociated with the malicious forces that birthed jihad-based terrorism.

As some in the community sought to enhance their secular learning with Islamic learning, travel oversees became common. Having a US college education with some foreign language study enabled them to undertake the study of Islam as an extension of their academic programs. Many had majored in religious studies, Middle Eastern studies or Near Eastern studies in some of the best schools in America, and gained a firm grasp of Islamic tradition. Upon their return, some devoted weekend time to teaching Islamic sciences to their community. As religious literacy improved, so too did the recognition that various medieval commentaries (*tafasir*) were written for a time and place far removed from twentieth-century America.

Some communities had always kept a focus on the Islamic experience in black America. Many others focused on Islam as a worldview reflecting Arab or South Asian cultural interpretations of the Qur'an. This difference in focus caused tension, but did not significantly impede their continued socialization in the larger black community.

GAINING QUR'ANIC LITERACY

African-American Muslim communities have apportioned their time differently on matters of concern to their existence as African Americans. For some, establishing their spiritual and religious identity in opposition to the racism of whites and others, along with preserving African-American history from erasure, have had the highest priority. Some communities have also joined hands with other groups to protest disparities in employment, housing and education. Other communities have placed their focus on Islamic literacy as a priority, but not forsaken the ongoing struggles of people of color and the middle and lower classes.

Since there are at least three generations of Muslims in some families, and as many as five in others, along with a constant stream of people transitioning to Islam, Qur'anic literacy as a priority eventually became a must. African Americans witnessed the racism of immigrant Muslims almost immediately. The insidious nature of this racism made the need to empower the community through Arabic literacy a priority. In the 1940s the Nation of Islam began to employ Arabic teachers in its schools, and by the 1970s other African-American communities followed suit. Furthermore, some community members in undergraduate or postgraduate training began to take Arabic. This does not mean that there was Arabic fluency, but that there was an increase in Qur'anic literacy. In the African-American community there is no need to speak Arabic.

The Qur'an as a living guide for relationships and self-enhancement, and handling it daily, are cornerstones of life. While there are shifts and transitions they have a purpose. When African-American Muslims read that they are supposed to kill the enemies of Islam wherever they find them (cf. Q 9:5), the frequent rejoinder is that they are forced to read this in its historical context. It is a given that an enemy of Islam may be their own mother or father or brother or sister, and they certainly are not going to kill them. The Prophet of Islam did not murder his family members, except perhaps in battle, and only then after efforts at peace were exhausted.

THE IMAM

There are at least three type of imam: (1) the authoritative, (2) the charismatic, and (3) the educated. The *authoritative imam* is one whose community is generally dependent on his claims of Qur'anic knowledge and interpretation of that knowledge to provide knowledge for them. This imam is always in charge and is the only authority. At best he may have several assistant imams whom he instructs directly; most questions make reference to something the authoritative imam has said or are deferred to a time when he is present. There is to be little challenge to his authority. This imam may indeed be informed and educated in the Qur'an, but he may or may not be charismatic.

The *charismatic imam* is strong in character, captivating, and a leader extraordinaire. He has his community take classes, which he supervises. He trusts that his community will always compare his assistants' charisma with his own. He may not have a great deal of Qur'anic literacy, but he is always studying to increase it, and befriends those with knowledge of the Qur'an.

Generally speaking, the *educated imam* is well educated – i.e. he has earned a college degree and done some postgraduate training. He may be self-taught regarding Arabic, or has studied overseas long enough or often enough to get what his community needs. This imam is generally an organizer who not only knows his community and its needs, but is also adept at making Qur'anic guidance a reference for them. He is often the educator of the community who invites outside educators to enrich the knowledge base of all.

As with all attempts to characterize, there exist hybrid imams possessing various traits of the three types listed earlier; readers may know of other types as well. It is important to know that African-American Muslims have become especially weary of those men who have studied for extended periods of time overseas, and who therefore have little knowledge of communities they wish to lead within the US. Many of these men have been relegated to the periphery of African-American Muslim communities, sometimes forming tributary organizations to push their particular understanding. These men are occasionally invited as guest imams to African-American *masajid*. Rarely do African-American Muslims invite immigrant imams to speak or to lecture on Fridays.

A HOLISTIC UNDERSTANDING OF OBEDIENCE TO ALLAH

The *charismatic* or *educated* imam typically chooses one or several points about which to speak to the community. For example, to reiterate the meaning of Islam he then provides the root of the word *s-l-m*, and where it can be found in several places in the Qur'an. Most African-American Muslims understand that the object of Islam as an ethical code of conduct requires obedience, rather than a literal reading of 'peace'. Peace is what comes after obedience to the principles of obeying Allah. It is worship as a vehicle influencing one's conduct, speech and so on, in the order Allah sets before humanity. This holistic understanding of obedience achieves peace, not as the absence of aggression or violence, but as a way of living.

BIBLIOGRAPHY

Ali, Abdullah Yusuf (trans.) *The Holy Qur'an: Text, Translation and Commentary* (Lahore: Shaikh Muhammad Ashraf, 1938)

Ali, Maulvi Muhammad (trans.) *The Holy Qur-án, Containing the Arabic Text with English Translation and Commentary*. (Woking, Surrey, England, 1917 (1st edn), and many subsequent reprinting). Available open access online at http://ahmadiyya.org/m-ali/quran-1917.htm

Ansari, Zafar Ishaq. 'Islam among African Americans: An Overview.' In *Muslims' Place in the American Public Square: Hope, Fears, and Aspirations*. Ed. Zahid H. Bukhari et al., 222–67. (Walnut Creek: AltaMira Press, 2004)

Bayoumi, Moustafa. 'East of the Sun (West of the Moon): Islam, the Ahmadis, and African America.' *Journal of Asian American Studies* 4:3 (October 2001): 251–63

Friedmann, Yohanan. *Prophecy Continuous: Aspects of Ahmadi Religious Thought and its Medieval Background*. (Berkeley: University of California Press, 1989; second printing with new preface, New Delhi, 2003)

Iqbal, Muzaffar. 'Abdullah Yusuf 'Ali and Muhammad Asad: Two Approaches to the English Translation of the Qur'an.' *Journal of Qur'anic Studies* 2:1 (2000): 107–23

Khan, Mofakhar Hussain. 'English Translations of the Holy Qur'an: A Bio-Bibliographic Study.' *Islamic Quarterly* 30:2 (1986): 82–108

Lane, Edward William. *Selections from the Kur'an*. Ed. Stanley Lane-Poole. (London: Trubner & Co., 1879)

Lincoln, C. Eric. *The Black Muslims in America*, 3rd edn, with epilogue by Aminah Beverly McCloud. (Grand Rapids: Wm. B. Eerdmans Publishing Co., 1994; 1st edn, 1961; 2nd edn, 1973)

McCloud, Aminah Beverly. *African American Islam*. (New York and London: Routledge, 1995)

— 'African-American Muslim Intellectual Thought.' In *Souls* 9:2 (2007): 171–81

— 'Islam in the African American Experience.' In *Voices of Islam*. Ed. Vincent J. Cornell and Omid Safi, vol. 5, 69–83. (Westport, CT: Praeger, 2007)

Thomas, Griselda. 'The Influence of Malcolm X and Islam on Black Identity and Naming Pratices in American Culture.' In *Muslims and American Popular Culture*. Ed. Anne R. Richards and Iraj Omidvar, vol. 2, 35–55. (Santa Barbara, CA: Praeger, 2014)

Thompson-Miller, Ruth and Leslie H. Picca. '"There Were Rapes!": Sexual Assaults of African American Women and Children in Jim Crow.' *Violence Against Women* 23:8 (2016): 934–50

Turner, Richard Brent. *Islam in the African-American Experience*. (Bloomington: Indiana University Press, 1997)

Valentine, Simon Ross. *Islam and the Ahmadiyya Jama'at: History, Belief, Practice*. (New York: Columbia University Press, 2008)

Chapter 2

Nizari Ismaili Engagements with the Qur'an: the Khojas of South Asia

Ali Asani, Harvard University

BACKGROUND: WHO ARE THE NIZARI ISMAILIS?

As Shia Muslims, the Nizari Ismailis believe that after the death of the Prophet Muhammad, his authority over his followers, as well as the esoteric knowledge he possessed, were inherited by his designated heir, Ali ibn abi Talib, his cousin and the husband of his daughter Fatima.[1] They assert that this authority and knowledge, manifest in the office of the imam ('leader' or 'guide'), is to continue on a hereditary basis among Ali and Fatima's direct descendants with each imam declaring his successor through explicit divine designation, or *nass*. In this regard, the imams are divinely designated temporal and spiritual heirs of the Prophet, as well as guardians and teachers over the esoteric meaning of the Qur'an. The history of the Shia is characterized by disputes over the issue of succession to the office of imam, leading to several schisms. The most significant of these took place in 765 CE, after the death of the Imam Ja'far as-Sadiq.

---

[1] The author would like to gratefully acknowledge Khalil Andani for his assistance with this chapter.

One group, which upheld the claims of his elder son Ismail, came to be known as Ismailis, while those who supported the younger son Musa al-Kazim eventually became identified as Ithna 'Ashari or Twelvers. They are named such since their twelfth imam, Muhammad al-Mahdi, went into occultation and is yet to return. Perceived as significant threats to the authority and legitimacy of Umayyad and Abbasid caliphs – both of whom were Sunni – the imams of both Shia groups, and their supporters, have been intensely persecuted. Notwithstanding this oppression, the imams of the Ismailis successfully managed to establish the Fatimid Empire (named after their matron, Fatima) with a new capital city, al-Qahira or 'The Victorious,' known today as Cairo. At its peak in the eleventh century, the Fatimid Empire, extended over North Africa, much of the Mediterranean and the Levant; and it posed a serious challenge to the Abbasid dynasty. Indeed, in 1058, the Fatimids managed for a short while to capture and rule over Baghdad, the capital of their Abbasid rivals. In 1094, on the death of the Fatimid Caliph-Imam al-Mustansir b-Illah, the Ismailis split again over the issue of succession to the imamate, resulting in two further subgroups: (1) those who supported his eldest son Nizar, and came to be known as Nizari Ismailis; (2) those who upheld the claims of the younger son al-Musta'li and his descendants, who came to be known as Tayyibi Ismailis, and who are popularly referred to as Bohras in South Asia.

The Nizari Ismailis today, the focus of this chapter, recognize Karim al-Husayni, Aga Khan IV, as their imam. He is forty-ninth in descent from the Prophet Muhammad in the line of Ali and Fatima. In this regard, they are the only contemporary Shia community which claims direct descent from the Prophet Muhammad as their imam; the imams of the other communities (Twelvers and Tayyibis) are believed by their followers to be in occultation. Today, some ten million Nizari Ismailis live in communities scattered over some twenty-five countries in East Africa, South and Central Asia, parts of the Middle East, and in Europe and North America. They are governed by the Aga Khan through a network of institutions that oversees their religious, social, educational and economic needs. The Aga Khan also presides over the Aga Khan Development Network (AKDN), one of the world's largest networks of private development agencies, which operates primarily in thirty countries of Asia and Africa, focusing on health, education, culture, rural development, institution building and the promotion of economic development. While the AKDN agencies are non-denominational in terms of the beneficiaries they serve, the ethical and moral framework underlying their activities is described as 'the endeavor of the Ismaili Imamat to realize the social conscience of Islam.'[2]

ISMAILI CONCEPTIONS OF REVELATION

Ismaili conceptions of revelation are distinctive in two ways. According to early Ismaili thought, God's transcendent Word is revealed, by means of divine inspiration, through certain humans, such as prophets. However, this divine inspiration is not in the form of actual words and phrases. Rather, it is in the form of spiritual, luminous knowledge (referred to as the *ruh al-qudus* or 'Holy Spirit' in the Qur'an) which prophets then 'translate' or 'encode' into symbolic human language to guide their followers.[3] Thus, the Qur'an represents the Prophet Muhammad's expression of divinely inspired knowledge into the Arabic language in its most eloquent form. Another distinctive aspect of Ismaili thought is the belief that the Divine or the Truth (*haqiqa*) can only be accessed by penetrating the esoteric (*batin*) dimension concealed by the physical or exoteric (*zahir*) realm. As a result of their emphasis on the esoteric, the Ismailis have been referred to as the people of the *batin* (*batiniyya*). In this regard, they perceive their imams to be holders of authoritative knowledge (*'ilm*) of: both the exoteric and esoteric truth found in the Qur'an, *sharia* and legal rulings, occult knowledge, and gnosis (*ma'rifa*). The imams provide authoritative instruction (*ta'lim*) and the esoteric interpretation (*ta'wil*) of divine revelation by decoding the revelatory discourse (*tanzil*) brought by the prophets. They receive this knowledge through inspiration (*ta'yid*) from God's creative Word or Command. In this sense, they are informed by the same transcendent spiritual source of the Qur'an. Their knowledge remains independent of the Qur'anic text insofar as it exists in the form of Arabic words

---

[2] See The Aga Khan Development Network (AKDN), 'Ethical Framework.'
[3] For a discussion of Ismaili concepts of revelation, see Andani, 'The Merits of the Batiniyya.'

and phrases. Thus for the Ismailis, the imam and the Qur'an are parallel manifestations of the transcendent Word of God. The imam, like the Qur'anic text, serves as a locus of manifestation (*mazhar*) of this reality. In the Ismaili view, the text of the Qur'an is conjoined to the imam and proper understanding of it is not possible without the instruction of the imam and teachers appointed by him. Since the imam is also a recipient of inspiration (*ta'yid*) from the Qur'an's transcendent archetype, the Word of God, he is sometimes called the Speaking Qur'an or the Speaking Book of God, while the written text is referred to as the Silent Qur'an.[4] The relationship between the imam and the Qur'anic text is one where the imam is the active agent and the Qur'an is the passive recipient – such as in the case of a carpenter and his raw materials, a potter and his clay, or form and matter.[5] That such ideas continue to underpin contemporary expressions of the Nizari Ismaili imamate's relationship with the Qur'an are evident in the preamble of the constitution ordained by Aga Khan IV in 1986 to govern Ismaili institutions worldwide. Articles A and B of the preamble state:

(A) The Shia Imami Ismaili Muslims affirm the *Shahadat la ilaha illa-llah, Muhammadur rasulu-llah,* the *Tawhid* therein and that the Holy Prophet Muhammad is the last and final Prophet of Allah. Islam, as revealed in the Holy Qur'an, is the final message of Allah to mankind, and is universal and eternal. The Holy Prophet through the divine revelation from Allah prescribed rules governing spiritual and temporal matters.

(B) In accordance with Shia doctrine, tradition, and interpretation of history, the Holy Prophet designated and appointed his cousin and son-in-law Hazrat Mawlana Ali *Amiru-l-Mu'minin,* to be the first imam to continue the *Ta'wil* and *Ta'lim* of Allah's final message and to guide the murids [disciples] and proclaim that the Imamat should continue by heredity through Hazrat Mawlana Ali and his daughter Hazrat Bibi Fatimat-az-Zahra, *Khatun-i-Jannat.*

---

[4] Ayoub, 'The Speaking Qur'an and the Silent Qur'an.'
[5] Poonawala, 'Ismaili ta'wil,' p. 206.

Article F states:

> Historically and in accordance with Ismaili tradition, the imam of
> the time is concerned with spiritual advancement as well as improve-
> ment of the quality of life of his murids. The imam's *ta'lim* lights the
> murid's path to spiritual enlightenment and vision. In temporal
> matters, the imam guides the murids, and motivates them to develop
> their potential.[6]

Contemporary Nizari Ismaili communities engage with the imam's authoritative *ta'lim* and *ta'wil* through *farman*s (directives) through which they
receive counsel and guidance on a wide range of religious and secular issues,
such as the regular practice of faith, spirituality, ethics and morality, education, healthcare, and economic well-being. For them, the *farman*s embody
the ongoing and infallible guidance of the imams, providing a road map to
guide one along the journey of physical and spiritual life. Hence, obedience
to them is obligatory. In the last century or so, with the advent of print
media, these *farman*s have been compiled into books and translated into
various local languages so that they are accessible to communities around
the world. They have become a *bona fide* genre of Ismaili religious literature, representing the word of the imam. Regularly read out during Ismaili
religious services, the *farman*s are the principal source for the normative
understanding of faith for Nizari Ismailis today.[7]

ENGAGING WITH REVELATION IN DIVERSE
CULTURAL AND HISTORICAL CONTEXTS

Paul Walker, a historian of Ismaili thought, has remarked that in the course
of its development the Ismaili tradition has demonstrated 'a surprising
intellectual flexibility and leeway.'[8] Some scholars have regarded this

---

[6] *Constitution of the Shia Imami Ismaili Muslims*, p. 6.
[7] Asani, 'From Satpanthi to Ismaili Muslim,' p. 111.
[8] Walker, 'Abu Ya'qub al-Sijistani,' p. 8.

flexibility as a strategic part of *taqiyya*, the Shia doctrine that permits the faithful to dissimulate or hide their true beliefs to avoid persecution and possible death from one's enemies. However, I would argue that much more is involved in this embrace of diversity. Ismaili emphasis on the esoteric, the *batin*, and the belief that a single existential reality underlies what appears as a plurality on the exoteric or material plane, has meant that Ismaili thinkers have engaged with diverse theological and philosophical systems with remarkable confidence. Characteristically, Nasir-i Khusraw, the eleventh-century Ismaili poet-philosopher, writes:

> All the Books of God are the Qur'an without any difference. Whatever the ignorant know to be differences within the Torah, the Gospel, and the Qur'an are not differences with respect to meaning, but they are different only with respect to the exoteric aspect (*zahir*), the expressions (*lafz*), the similitudes (*mithal*) and symbols. Thus, the Gospel is with the Romans, the Torah is with the Russians, and the Scrolls of Abraham are with the Indians.[9]

Not surprisingly, such an ecumenical outlook resulted in Ismaili thinkers being comfortable in expressing key concepts related to revelation within a wide range of contexts. Thus, for example, in the late tenth and eleventh centuries, some Fatimid thinkers and preachers (*da'is*), who claimed to receive mediated inspiration (*ta'yid*) from the imam, elucidated Ismaili concepts by creating a philosophical synthesis of Neoplatonic and Gnostic ideas. Others, such as renowned jurist Qadi al-Nu'man (d. 974), adopted a legalistic framework that would resonate with Sunni counterparts. Thinkers like Hamid al-Din al-Kirmani (d. after 1021) drew upon Jewish scripture. In the Iranian context, we discern within Ismaili discourses a synthesis of Manichean and Zoroastrian elements. With regard to this ecumenical outlook, Azim Nanji has remarked that the motivation to integrate, reformulate and acculturate to different environments is part of the Ismaili legacy.[10] One of the consequences of this legacy is that premodern

---

[9] Nasir-i Khusraw, *Wajh-i din*, p. 68.
[10] Nanji, *Nizari Ismaili Tradition*, p. 132.

Ismaili communities often exhibited ambiguous and less well-defined identities.

THE KHOJAS OF SOUTH ASIA

We can observe a similar embrace of religious and cultural diversity in South Asia among the Khojas of Gujarat and Sind, whose beliefs were historically rooted in a tradition known as *Sat Panth* – 'the true path.' Ismaili Khojas consider *Sat Panth* an expression of Ismaili *da'wa* (preaching) in the region. They assert that between the thirteenth to fifteenth centuries CE, Ismaili imams in Persia sent various *pir*s or teacher-guides to the subcontinent. Khoja traditions also assert that they belonged originally to trading castes – the Lohanas and Bhatias. When they became disciples of one of the most prominent of these *pir*s, the fifteenth-century CE Pir Sadr al-Din, he gave them the title 'khwajah' (a Persian term of which Khoja is a derivation) to replace the original Lohana 'thakkur', both meaning 'lord' or 'master.'[11] Tradition also credits Pir Sadr ad-Din with the establishment of *jama'at khana*s (houses of congregation and community) as well as the invention of *khojki*, a script peculiar to the Khojas.[12] The teachings of these *pir*s are embodied in hymns called *ginan*s which are still sung as part of the daily prayers in the *jama'at khana*. Believed to number about a thousand, the *ginan*s are composed in several languages and dialects prevalent in western India and southern Pakistan, and recited in various *raga*s (melodies) indigenous to the region. Since Khojas consider the *pir*s to have been spiritually guided and authorized by the imams in what they preached, the *ginan*s have acquired a special sanctity.

In the *ginan*s, the *pir*s utilize a variety of frameworks to formulate two core teachings of *Sat Panth*. First, the role of the imams and *pir*s as

---

[11] Ivanow, 'Khodja,' p. 256. Some scholars, such as Mumtaz Ali Tajdin and, more recently, Iqbal Akhtar, have challenged this derivation which commonly appears in Khoja narratives by arguing that the word 'Khoja' is derived from the Sindhi verb *khojanu*, meaning 'to seek.' Without providing historical or ethnographical evidence for this derivation and usage, Iqbal Akhtar argues that Khojas meant those who 'seek economic security and perfected form of spiritual being.' Akhtar, *Khoja*, pp. 33–4.

[12] For more on the Khojki script, see Asani, 'Khojki Script.'

preceptors on the path to spiritual enlightenment, the goal of which was to experience or 'see' the Divine Light or *nur*, an idea resonating with the Qur'anic notion of 'seeing the face of God' (Q 2:115). In representing the experience of enlightenment as an inward journey, *ginans* are used not only in language and expressions associated with the Sufi tradition (*murshid*, *dhikr*, *didar*, etc.), but also in vocabulary drawn from contemporaneous Indian traditions of spirituality, particularly the *sant* movement. A group of lower-caste poet-saints, the *sants* represented a powerful anti-caste movement that challenged the efficacy of ritualism and rote learning as paths to salvation. Instead, the *ginans* exhort listeners to seek liberation from the transitory material world through constant contemplation of the Divine Name, a blessing bestowed upon those who are on the true path (*Sat Panth*) by the True Guide (*Sat Guru*) identified ambiguously as the *pir* or imam. The second core teaching is related to the relationship between the imam, the manifestation of Divine Light, and his disciples. In accordance with the Ismaili doctrine of *walaya*, this relationship is one of love and devotion. In portraying this relationship, the *ginans* drew upon the powerful traditions of *bhakti* or devotion that were prevalent across north India. In particular, they used the symbol of the *virahini*, the woman longing for her beloved, best exemplified by Radha's longing for Krishna. In the *ginans*, however, the imam becomes the longed for bridegroom.

To 'translate' the notion of the imam in terms that would make sense to audiences from differing contexts, the *pirs* embraced a variety of traditions, resulting in a formulation that was multilayered. Within a Vaisnavite framework, the imam, designated as Ali, was presented as *nakalanki* 'the one without blemish' (cf. Arabic *mutahhar*). This term was a *Sat Panth* reframing of the name of Kalki, the long-awaited tenth *avatara* of the Hindu deity Vishnu who would bestow wisdom and salvation upon his devotees by rescuing them from the forces of evil. Within the framework of the *sant* tradition, the imam was represented as the *Sat Guru*, the true guide to truth and enlightenment. Within the traditions of *bhakti* or devotion, he was the beloved utter devotion from whom would emanate salvation. In a Sufi framework, he was the *murshid*, the keeper of the mysteries of the *batin*, whose representatives – the *pirs* – would guide disciples upon the path. Regardless of the way the imam was represented, the goal was to orient followers to the ultimate spiritual experience – *didar* – the 'vision of the divine.'

Through these multiple discourses, the *ginan*s recreate and cross-pollinate within an Indic milieu key themes that have been integral to the Ismaili tradition. In this regard, it is noteworthy that the *ginan*s also understand the Qur'an and the broader conception of Islamic revelation within indigenous Indic frameworks. Of significance here is the fact that the term *ginan* is derived from *gyan*, the Sanskrit word for 'knowledge' – in the sense of 'esoteric truth' – corresponding to the term *haqa'iq* used in the Arabo-Persian Ismaili traditions to refer to the true or real knowledge at the level of the *batin*. In this sense, the *ginan*s may be understood as hymns that contain and lead to esoteric wisdom. The knowledge that they embody, like that of the Qur'an, is primarily emotive and experienced through the aesthetics of *raga*s (melodies) in which they are sung. In keeping with traditions of north Indian classical music, each *raga* is intended to evoke within the listener specific moods or emotions (*rasa*). Indeed, Khoja traditions record several accounts of individuals being overwhelmed and transformed by hearing and singing *ginan*s. The most commonly cited example was that of Ismail Gangji (d. 1883), who was so overcome by a *ginan* recitation that he tearfully sought forgiveness for his past misbehavior and turned over a new leaf.[13] Some ginanic verses acknowledge their transformative effect on both the reciter and the listener. For example, a verse in popular *ginan* instructs the believer: 'recite the *ginan*s which are filled with light; boundless will be the joy in your heart.'[14]

The use of the symbol of light appropriately points to the role that the esoteric wisdom embodied in the *ginan*s can play in bringing about an inner transformation within the reciter. Such notions resonate with the well-known impact of the aesthetics of the recited Qur'an on its listeners as they commune through sacred sound with the Divine. The unparalleled aesthetic quality of the Qur'an came to be seen as a sign of its divine origin.[15] In this regard, the Russian scholar Ivanow has expounded upon

---

[13] H.S.H. Prince Aly S. Khan Colony Religious Night School, *Great Ismaili Heroes*, pp. 98–9.
[14] *Mahan Ismaili sant pir Sadardin racit ginan no na sangrah*, p. 61 (translation mine).
[15] Kermani, *God is Beautiful*.

the impact of the 'strange fascination, the majestic pathos and beauty' of the *ginans* as they are being recited to the 'mystical appeal of the Qur'an on Arabic-speaking peoples.'[16]

Beyond the similarity of their aesthetic impact on listeners, several *ginans* explicitly relate their teachings to the esoteric truths (*haqa'iq*) symbolized in the Arabic Qur'an which they often associate with the *Athar Veda*, the scripture of the current age. In this regard, these *ginans* are considered secondary scriptures that mediate between the community of the faithful and the Qur'an. Thus, a composition titled *Moman Chetamani* ('A Warning to the Believers') depicts the Qur'an as the source of *Sat Panth*, stating:

> *Sat Panth* began from Ali and the Prophet [Muhammad]; follow it most discreetly. This *Sat Panth* is according to *Athar Veda* (the last Veda) and you can find its proof in the Quran. [162][17]

The association of the teachings of the *ginans* with the esoteric truths symbolized in the Qur'an is also found in several verses attributed to Pir Shams, stating:

> The True Guide says: Pir Shams has preached the Qur'an and preached the four Vedas. Sitting among the Gat Jamat (congregation) he has narrated the true signs.[18]

Pir Shams narrates the knowledge of the Qur'an. A believer is one who knows the divine knowledge.[19] Another verse attributed to Pir Shams, who composed a series of twenty-eight *ginans* in the form of a *garbi* – traditional Gujarati dance – explicitly identifies what he is singing with the spiritual essence of the Qur'an: the spiritual guide dances the *garbi* and sings the Qur'an.[20]

---

[16] Ivanow, 'Sect of Imam-Shah,' p. 68.
[17] Muhammad and Kamaluddin, *Qur'an and Ginan*, p. xv.
[18] Ibid., p. xiv.
[19] Ibid.
[20] Ibid.

In addition to the association of the Qur'an as the source of *Sat Panth*, several *ginans* also elaborate various themes from the Qur'an in vernacular idioms. A renowned example is the *ginan Allah ek khasam sabuka*, which outlines in verse form the story of Adam's creation and Azazil's refusal to obey God's command to prostrate before Adam. Another interesting example is the *ginan Ruhani Visal* (Spiritual Union) attributed to Pir Hasan Kabir ad-Din, which describes the return of the soul to the Divine Beloved in fulfillment of a primordial covenant – namely the covenant on the day of *alastu* (Q 7:171). The *pir* explains this concept by invoking the pan-Indian literary symbol of the *virahini* – the yearning woman's soul – longing for her marriage or union (*suhag*) with her Beloved.[21]

REARTICULATING KHOJA ENGAGEMENT WITH THE QUR'AN IN COLONIAL AND POSTCOLONIAL SPACES

In the nineteenth and twentieth centuries, Khojas experienced a fundamental shift in the articulation of their identity and religious practices.[22] The convergence of two sets of factors made it difficult, if not impossible, to sustain the polyvalent formulations through which they had understood the *Sat Panth* tradition for centuries. The first related to the establishment and nature of British colonial rule over most of South Asia. The British viewed their Indian subjects through post-Enlightenment European lenses, specifically the notion that religions are ideologies of identity. As a result, the idiom of British colonial rule became communalist, systematically institutionalizing India into a nation of communities defined along religious lines through various bureaucratic practices.[23] Religious identity markers were strongly emphasized over others, forcing people to categorize themselves and others primarily in religious terms. As a result, communities that shared common cultural heritage, language and ethnicity came to be divided

---

[21] For a commentary and translation of this *ginan*, see Asani, *Ecstasy and Enlightenment*, pp. 54–70.

[22] For a detailed discussion of the rearticulation of Khoja identity in this period, see Asani, 'From Satpanthi to Ismaili Muslim.'

[23] Hardy, *Muslims of British India*, p. 116.

from each other on religious lines. Muslims, regardless of their sectarian, ethnic, linguistic and other differences, came to be 'imagined' as one community united by a single faith. Adherents of various strands of indigenous Indian sectarian, devotional, philosophical beliefs were lumped together and categorized as 'Hindus' following a religion called 'Hinduism.'

A second set of factors related to the move in 1845 of the Ismaili imam, Hassan Ali Shah, Aga Khan I, to India, as result of political unrest in Iran. He eventually set up his headquarters in Bombay, the nucleus of a large Khoja community. Prior to this, the Khojas had venerated their imam from afar, and the affairs of the community and its property were in the hands of elites. Now the imam's move to India, and his attempt to consolidate direct authority over the affairs of the community, upset the traditional power structures in the Khoja hierarchy. As a result, dissensions and schisms, often led by wealthier Khojas, split the community, with the Aga Khan's authority over the Khojas being challenged in the British courts. An initial group of dissenters claimed that the Aga Khan had no authority as the Khojas were originally Sunni. Later dissenters challenged his authority by claiming that the Khojas were in fact Ithna 'Ashari (Twelver) Shia. The colonial courts eventually ruled in the Aga Khan's favor, declaring the Khojas to be Ismailis. As a result, the Khojas were now divided along sectarian lines – Sunni, Twelver Shia and Nizari Ismaili. Nizari Ismaili Khojas differentiated their identity from that of Sunni and Ithna 'Ashari Khojas, through their allegiance to the Ismaili imam whom they now understood as being rooted in the Islamic tradition. Centuries-old formulations of the imam in terms of the Vaisnavite frame of reference were discontinued. Terms and concepts that could be interpreted as 'Hinduistic' were dropped or replaced by a new historiography of the Ismaili imamate tracing the descent of the current imam to Ali ibn Abi Talib and Fatima, the daughter of the Prophet Muhammad. Increasingly, Nizari Ismaili Khojas articulated their identity in terms of the fundamental and more universal concepts of the larger Muslim community. Fundamental to the new articulation was a greater emphasis on the Qur'an and Arabo-Persian culture and a de-emphasis of the vernacular, the local and the Indic.

Under the direction of Aga Khan III (d. 1957) and Aga Khan IV, a new daily ritual prayer in Arabic was introduced, replacing the previous vernacular one in Gujarati. Different in form from the Sunni or Shia *salat*, it is called the *Du'a*.[24] In keeping with the Quranic injunction to 'establish worship at the two ends of the day' (Q 11:16), it is recited thrice daily: early in the morning at dawn, at sunset and after sunset. It maintains a distinctive Ismaili character through the reaffirmation of the authority of the present Ismaili imam in each of its six parts. It also includes specific verses that Shia communities evoke as proof-texts for the authority of the *Imamat*:

Part 1: *Surat al-Fatihah* (Q 1), whose main theme is '*ibada* (worship) of God.

Part 2: *Surat al-Nisa* (Q 4:59 – 'O you who believe, obey God, and obey the Messenger and the holders of authority amongst you') and *Surat Yasin* (Q 36:12 – 'And We have encompassed all things in a manifest Imam') whose main themes are obedience (*ta'a*) to God's representatives.

Part 3: *Surat al-Ma'idah* (Q 5:67 – 'O Messenger, proclaim that which has been revealed to you by your Lord . . .') whose main theme is the declaration (*tabligh*) of the Imamat.

Part 4: *Surat al-Fath* (Q 48:10 – 'Verily, those who give their *bay'a* unto you (Muhammad), they give their *bay'a* unto God Himself . . .') whose main theme is the *bay'a* or *mithaq* (covenant) with the Imam.

Part 5: *Surat al-Anfal* (Q 8:27 – 'O you who believe, do not betray God and His Messenger and do not betray your trusts (*amanat*) while you know') whose main theme is trust (*amana*).

Part 6: *Surat al-Ikhlas* (Q 112 – 'Say: He is God, the Unique. God is Independent. He does not beget nor is He begotten. And there is none like unto Him') whose main theme is the recognition (*ma'rifa*) of *tawhid*.

---

[24] For more on the Ismaili *Du'a*, see Kassam, 'Daily Prayer.'

Through these verses, the prayer reinforces the notion of the imam as the locus of knowledge and divine authority. In Part 6, to emphasize the continuity of the institution of the imamat, the names of all the imams are invoked, starting from the first imam, Ali ibn abi Talib, to the present forty-ninth imam, Shah Karim Al-Husayni. The *Du'a* also reaffirms the authoritative nature of the present imam's guidance and pronouncements – *farmans*. The *farmans* are regarded by the community as the *ta'lim* (instruction) and *ta'wil* (esoteric interpretation) of divine revelation, as opposed to Qur'anic *tafsir* (commentary). Since the Arabic *Du'a* is recited as a common prayer by Nizari Ismailis living in different cultural contexts, it has served to cultivate among Khojas a sense of belonging to a transnational worldwide community, united in their allegiance to the Ismaili imam.

Accompanying the change in the fundamental prayer ritual were changes in the religious education curriculum and textbooks, centrally produced at the Institute of Ismaili Studies in London, and disseminated worldwide in several languages. The curriculum approaches the study of Islam in general, and the Shia Ismaili tradition specifically, from humanistic and civilizational perspectives, engaging with Qur'anic texts through Ismaili viewpoints. In this regard, the Institute has a special unit dedicated to Qur'anic Studies with a view to promoting scholarship on the plurality of traditions inspired by the Qur'an and developed throughout Muslim history, up to the present time. It conducts research on the plurality of interpretations that have been produced by Muslims throughout history, as well as the ways in which various contexts, and types of methodology, have shaped those interpretations.[25] The importance of Qur'anic discourse within the community became particularly pronounced during the celebrations of the current imam's twenty-fifth, fiftieth and sixtieth jubilees. Each jubilee was associated with a particular Qur'anic verse selected by the imam and intended to emphasize the key message for that jubilee.[26] The verse was also calligraphed on official logos commemorating the jubilee and recited in the imam's presence whenever he visited his followers to perform religious ceremonies.

---

[25] https://iis.ac.uk/research/quranic-studies (accessed March 25, 2018).
[26] See Q 3:103 for the Silver Jubilee, 4:1 for the Golden Jubilee, and 49:13 for the Diamond Jubilee.

With the increased focus on the Arabic Qur'an among the Khojas, the need to clarify the relationship of the *ginans* – the devotional hymns that have been so central to the Khoja tradition – to the Islamic scripture also became urgent. Within the new context, the *ginans* came to be increasingly perceived as constituting a kind of commentary on the Qur'an. Aga Khan III clarified this relationship in several of his pronouncements (*farmans*):

> The *ginans* composed and presented before you by Pir Sadardin are from commentaries on the Qur'an.[27]

He adds:

> If there were amongst you individuals who had read the Qur'an and were well-versed with the *ginans*, I would be able to point out to you each verse of the *ginans* from the Qur'an.[28]

Not surprisingly, several publications within the community match Qur'an verses with ginanic ones to demonstrate that the *pirs* have successfully delivered the message and gist of the Qur'an in the language and idiom of the *ginans*. Such clarifications serve to legitimize the Islamic character of the literature, staving off criticisms that their Indic character makes them Hinduistic:[29]

> We [Nizari Ismaili Khojas] should be proud to possess such a literary divine corpus [*ginans*] and proclaim that we are the true followers of the Holy Qur'an and all the parables, stories, metaphors, allegories which appear in our Holy Ginans are nothing but the true message of the religion of Islam.[30]

---

[27] Bhoga, *Bahare rahemat yane rahematno dariyo*, p. 17.

[28] Ibid., p. 13.

[29] Aziz Ahmad, for example, judges the 'literary personality' of the ginans to be 'unIslamic.' See *Intellectual History of Islam in India*, p. 20.

[30] 'Suggestive Guide,' p. 11.

CONCLUSION

This chapter has focused on the Nizari Ismailis, a Muslim minority with a unique engagement with the Qur'an. Doctrinally, this community's understanding of the Qur'an has been shaped by, and dependent on, its relationship to the institution of the Ismaili imamate. The imam as the Speaking Qur'an decodes and provides access to the exoteric and esoteric truths in the Silent Qur'an. We also looked at a manifestation of the Ismaili tradition within South Asia as *Sat Panth*, and how its polyvalent understandings of the imam, as well as the quest for spiritual enlightenment, was understood within the idioms and contexts of premodern India. With the rise of monolithic notions of religion in South Asia, and their instrumentalization by colonial and nationalist ideologies, local and indigenous understandings were replaced by ones with greater resonance with global or transnational understandings of Islam based on Qur'an. The increased engagement with the Qur'an among the Nizari Ismailis does not, however, overshadow the authority of the imam, who continues to provide *ta'lim* (instruction) and *ta'wil* (esoteric interpretation) of revelation according to the times.

The current Nizari Ismaili imam, Karim Aga Khan IV, who has been in the office of imamate for sixty years, has been recognized by Muslims and non-Muslims alike as an eloquent spokesperson for Islam, and for his commitment to uplift the quality of life for all peoples, irrespective of faith. Ismailis see their imam as deploying *ta'lim* when he speaks about the ways we can resolve many challenges we face with regard to diversity, rampant materialism, the role of the intellect, issues of social justice, health, education and the obligations towards the sick, the needy, and the elderly. Imam's *ta'lim* is also manifested through the work of the institutions of the Ismaili imamate, including the Aga Khan Development Network (AKDN), whose 'ethical framework' is heavily informed by reference to the Qur'anic ethos of social justice and human dignity.

As a concluding example of the imam's *ta'lim* in a public setting, we can cite his speech to the Canadian parliament:

I am most grateful to the Prime Minister and to you who have given me this opportunity to share – from a faith perspective – some of the issues that preoccupy me when looking ahead. I hope I have explained why I am convinced about the global validity of our partnership for human development. Let me end with a personal thought. As you build your lives, for yourselves and others, you will come to rest upon certain principles. Central to my life has been a verse in the Holy Qur'an which addresses itself to the whole of humanity. It says: 'Oh Mankind, fear your Lord, who created you of a single soul, and from it created its mate, and from the pair of them scattered abroad many men and women' [Q 4:1]. I know of no more beautiful expression about the unity of our human race – born indeed from a single soul.[31]

BIBLIOGRAPHY

'A Suggestive Guide to the "Islamic" Interpretation and Refutation of the "Hindu" Elements in our Holy Ginans.' Unpublished paper presented at the Islamic Association International Conference, Nairobi, 1979.

Aga Khan IV. (2014, 27 February) 'Address to both Houses of the Parliament of Canada in the House of Commons Chamber.' Ottawa, Canada. (http://www.akdn.org/speech/his-highness-aga-khan/address-both-houses-parliament-canada-house-commons-chamber) (accessed March 26, 2018)

Aga Khan Development Network. (2000) 'The Aga Khan Development Network (AKDN): An Ethical Framework.' [Online] (http://www.akdn.org/sites/akdn/files/media/documents/various_pdf_documents/akdn_ethical_framework.pdf). (Accessed March 19, 2018)

Ahmad, Aziz. An Intellectual History of Islam in India. (Edinburgh: Edinburgh University Press, 1969)

Akhtar, Iqbal. The Khoja of Tanzania. (Leiden: Brill, 2015)

Andani, Khalil. 'The Merits of the Batiniyya: al-Ghazali's Appropriation of Isma'ili Cosmology.' Journal of Islamic Studies 29:2 (2018): 181–229

Asani, Ali. Ecstasy and Enlightenment: The Ismaili Devotional Literatures of South Asia. (London: I.B. Tauris, 2002)

— 'From Satpanthi to Ismaili Muslim: The Articulation of Khoja Ismaili Identity in South Asia.' In A Modern History of the Ismailis: Continuity and Change in Modern Muslim Community. Ed. Farhad Daftary, 95–128. (London: I.B. Tauris, 2011)

— 'The Khojki Script: The Legacy of Ismaili Islam on the Indian Subcontinent.' Journal of the American Oriental Society 107 (1989): 439–49

Ayoub, Mahmoud. 'The Speaking Qur'an and the Silent Qur'an: A Study of the Principles and Development of Imami Tafsir.' In Approaches to the History of the Interpretation of the Qur'an. Ed. Andrew Rippin, 177–98. (Oxford: Clarendon Press, 1988)

---

[31] http://www.akdn.org/speech/his-highness-aga-khan/address-both-houses-parliament-canada-house-commons-chamber (accessed March 26, 2018).

Bhoga, Hasham (comp.) *Bahare rahemat yane rahematno daria*. (Bombay: Lalji Bhai Davaraj, Khoja Sindhi Printing Press, 1911)

The Constitution of the Shia Imami Ismaili Muslims. 1986

H.S.H. Prince Aly S. Khan Colony Religious Night School. *The Great Ismaili Heroes: Contains the Life Sketches and the Works of Thirty Great Ismaili Figures*. (Karachi: H.S.H. Prince Aly S. Khan Colony Religious Night School, 1973)

Hardy, Peter. *The Muslims of British India*. (Cambridge, UK: Cambridge University Press, 1972)

Ivanow, Wladimir. 'Khodja.' In *Shorter Encyclopedia of Islam*. Ed. H.A.R. Gibb and J. H. Kramers, 256–7. (Leiden: Brill, 1953)

— 'The Sect of Imam-Shah in Gujarat.' *Journal of the Bombay Branch of the Royal Asiatic Society*, New Series, 12 (1936): 19–70

Kassam, Tazim R. 'The Daily Prayer (*Du'a*) of the Shi'a Isma'ili Muslims.' In *The Columbia Sourcebook of Muslims in the United States*. Ed. Edward E. Curtis IV, 358–68. (New York: Columbia University Press, 2008)

Kermani, Navid. *God is Beautiful: The Aesthetic Experience of the Quran*. (Cambridge, UK: Polity Press, 2015)

Mahan Ismaili sant pir Sadardin racit ginan no na sangrah (Collection of Ginans composed by the Great Ismaili Pir Sadr ad-Din). (Bombay, 1952)

Muhammad, Kamaluddin Ali and Zarina Kamaluddin. *Qur'an and Ginan: Quranic Teachings in the Ginan*. (Karachi: Z.A. Printer, 2014)

Nanji, Azim. *The Nizari Ismaili Tradition in the Indo-Pakistan Subcontinent*. (Delmar, NY: Caravan Books, 1978)

Nasir-i Khusraw. *Wajh-i din*. Ed. Ghulam Reza Avani, trans. Khalil Andani. (Teheran: Anjuman-i Shahanshahi-i Falsafah-i Iran, 1977)

Poonawala, Ismail. K. 'Ismaili ta'wil of the Qur'an.' In *Approaches to the History of the Interpretation of the Qur'an*. Ed. Andrew Rippin, 199–222. (Oxford: Clarendon Press, 1988)

Walker, Paul E. 'Abu Ya'qub al-Sijistani and the Development of Ismaili Neoplatonism.' (PhD. thesis, University of Chicago, 1974)

Chapter 3

The Reception of the Qur'an in Popular Sufism in Indonesia: *tadabbur* among the *Ma'iyah* Community

Lien Iffah Naf'atu Fina and Ahmad Rafiq, Sunan Kalijaga State Islamic University, Yogyakarta, Indonesia

T his chapter concerns the reception of the Qur'an[1] in a popular Sufi community in Indonesia – Ma'iyah. Its reception of the Qur'an manifests in their activity called *tadabbur*.[2] In principle, *tadabbur* is learning from the Qur'an, not learning the Qur'an – the latter is an act of *tafsir*. In addition, *tadabbur* emphasizes the spiritual consciousness mani- fested in daily life (affective), not pure knowledge (cognitive), resulting from interaction with the Qur'an. The goal of *tadabbur* is that one becomes a better person and closer to God. *Tadabbur* is also a counter-discourse to a popular perception that grasping the meaning of the Qur'an is limited to scholars who are formally trained in Qur'anic sciences. Thus, it also aims to make the Qur'an meaningful for, and accessible by, everyone.

Ma'iyah, founded in 1993, attracts thousands to its events. Since its founding, the Qur'an has been an intimate part of the gatherings. The Qur'an provides a way to address Ma'iyah's main concerns – secularism

---

[1] On the theory of reception of the Qur'an, see Eagleton, *Literary Theory*, 64, and Rafiq, 'Reception of the Qur'an in Indonesia', pp. 144–56.

[2] It literally means 'reflection, meditation, thinking about, consideration, contemplation.' See Wehr, *Arabic–English Dictionary*, p. 271.

and materialism – which eventually lead to narrow-mindedness in religious thinking. Ma'iyah actively addresses and criticizes political and social situations in Indonesia, in which leaders and non-leaders alike are seen as detached from intimate connection with God.

Here we describe Ma'iyah as a Sufi community,[3] how *tadabbur* is used as an approach to interpret the Qur'an, and how it is practiced by Emha Ainun Nadjib, known as *Cak* Nun,[4] the main teacher in the Ma'iyah community[5] and thus the mediator between the Qur'an and the community.[6] We shed light on how Ma'iyah, as a Sufi religious and social

---

[3] Note that the Ma'iyah community never calls itself a Sufi community. This attitude is not unique to the Ma'iyah context, but is rather part of the character of Sufi communities. See Sands, *Sufi Commentaries*, p. 4. In fact, Ma'iyah consistently avoids any form of strict labeling. However, in an interview with Nadjib on December 29, 2016, he did not disagree with our opinion that Ma'iyah is, in a way, a Sufi community: elements of Sufism permeate its principles and rituals. Another primary character of Ma'iyah is that, unlike several Sufi communities, its goal is not spiritual ecstasy but social action and service. See Daniels, *Islamic Spectrum*, p. 143; Knauth, 'Performing Islam,' p. 151.

[4] *Cak* is a Javanese term meaning 'older brother,' and it implies a sense of respect and friendliness. In academic work, he is referred to as Nadjib; in other contexts, including daily life, he is referred to as *Cak* Nun. Nadjib was born on 27 May 1953, in Jombang, East Java. He started his career as a poet and cultural expert in the 1970s. He obtained religious education from Pondok Pesantran (*madrasa* in the Indonesian setting). It is difficult to define his role. He himself refuses any categorical definition, but he is known as a poet, playwright, essayist, composer, singer, religious leader, political critic and visionary, all at the same time. He has published eighty-two books, which are anthologies of his essays, poems and scripts. See Betts, *Jalan Sunyi Emha*, p. 25; Rasmussen, *Women*, p. 34; and Knauth, 'Performing Islam,' p. 152. Nadjib is known as *kyai mbeling* ('the naughty cleric') and an out-of-the-box thinker. See Rasmussen, 'Performing Religious Politics,' p. 170.

[5] Ma'iyah has three teachers, who are called *marja'* (meaning 'reference'). They are Nadjib himself; Ahmad Fuad Effendy (known as *Cak* Fuad), Nadjib's older brother and a professor of Arabic literature; and Muhammad Nursamad Kamba, a professor of Sufism. Nadjib is highly influenced by these two figures. (Interview with an editor of www.caknun.com, January 30, 2017.)

[6] The sources used here were gathered from observation (participating in Ma'iyah gatherings), interviewing key people, and documentation. We thank Ma'iyah management for providing us with videos and voice recordings of the gatherings across Java. Nadjib's essays, mainly published on Ma'iyah's official site (www.caknun.com) are also important sources. Since February 2016, Nadjib had written two series of essays (called Daur – 'cycle') published daily on his official website, which heavily relate to the topic of the Qur'an. Daur-I was published on the website from February 3–December 7, 2016 (309 essays); Daur-II was started from January 1, 2017– March 3, 2018 (319 essays). The subtitle of Daur-II is *Membaca Iqra'* (meaning 'reading Iqra'). *Iqra'* is believed to be the first passage of the Qur'an revealed by God to Muhammad, which shows Nadjib's attempt to invite the reader to reflect on Qur'anic instruction to read not only

movement, tackles the challenges of the twenty-first century. We also focus on how Nadjib proposes a unique approach to understanding the Qur'an to tackle narrow-mindedness in religious thinking, which leads to intolerance, violence and sectarianism[7] in the name of Islam. The study of tadabbur provides a method to make the Qur'an down to earth and practical for Muslims everywhere in the twenty-first century.

MA'IYAH: A COMMUNITY WITHOUT A BOUNDARY

Ma'iyah covers various religio-cultural gatherings in different regions in Indonesia, particularly Java. The embryo of Ma'iyah was a monthly gathering called Padhangmbulan (literally, 'full moon'), founded in 1993 in Nadjib's hometown, Jombang, East Java. Ma'iyah is open to all people, regardless of gender, socioeconomic status, education, ethnicity, or piety, and without any requirement to convert or adhere to new beliefs.[8] Ma'iyah even has a loyal audience of non-Muslims. The idea of openness inspires people from all walks of life to participate in the events arranged by the Jamaah Ma'iyah[9] because they feel at home and welcomed. As an expression of Nadjib's concern about – not to mention protest against – the Indonesian New Order regime's social problems, injustice and pragmatism, this movement sought broader changes in Indonesian society. Adopting a socio-religious approach and an existentialist theme – a door to Sufism – and creatively combining Sufism/mysticism and politics, the movement attracted people in East Java, and soon expanded its influence throughout Indonesia.[10]

---

the Qur'an, but also the universe and daily phenomena. Daur's nature remains reflective and intellectual, sometimes sarcastic and satirical. In 2017, the first Daur series was published in four edited volumes by Bentang Pustaka (Yogyakarta, Indonesia).

[7] We intentionally avoid using common terms here like conservatism, fundamentalism, radicalism, and extremism to refer to rigid and violent Islamic understanding and practices, just as Nadjib and the Ma'iyah community deliberately avoid labeling and generalization.

[8] See Rasmussen, 'Performing Religious Politics,' p. 156.

[9] From the Arabic jama'a, meaning group or community. See Wehr, Arabic–English Dictionary, p. 160.

[10] This approach was expected because Nadjib's concern for justice and spirituality, and his advocacy for the lower classes, had developed early in his career in the 1970s and 1980s, as reflected in his literature. See Daniels, Islamic Spectrum, p. 134.

Ma'iyah gatherings are conducted monthly in at least five cities on the island of Java, and each has its respective name (Padhangmbulan in Jombang (since 1993), Mocopat Syafaat in Yogyakarta (1999), Gambang Syafaat in Semarang (2001), Kenduri Cinta in Jakarta (2001) and Bangbang Wetan in Subaraya (2008). Besides the monthly gatherings, Nadjib and his group, KiaiKanjeng,[11] are also invited to hold gatherings in different cities across Indonesia.[12] He was disappointed with the direction of the Reformation Era, the period after the fall of the Soeharto regime in 1998. Instead of working together for a better Indonesia, religious figures fought for political positions and created friction. Nadjib decided to walk the 'silent road',[13] detaching himself from any religious or political groups. As a result, Ma'iyah is not attached to any existing religious or Sufi group; in fact, it has intentionally avoided an attachment as well as a formalized structure.[14] The Ma'iyah community is self-consciously a Muslim community, but its very character is inclusive, beyond the boundaries of traditional–modern, rural–urban, younger–older, male–female, and intellectual–layperson, even though it attracts mainly young adults. Consequently, its community is very fluid, and its members are not bound by an oath of allegiance (bay'a). Nonetheless, loyal audiences attend Ma'iyah in neighboring areas. By February 10, 2018, there had been 3,882 Ma'iyah gatherings throughout Indonesia and beyond.[15]

Ma'iyah gatherings have several elements. First, there is the ritual

---

[11] KiaiKanjeng was founded in the 1990s, but the musicians involved in this group had accompanied Nadjib's theatrical performances since the 1980s. In fact, the name KiaiKanjeng was from one of his plays, Pak Kanjeng (Mr. Respected), which talks about political tyranny and a figure who protested against it. See Knauth, 'Performing Islam,' pp. 148–60. Nadjib and his group is known as CNKK (Cak Nun and KiaiKanjeng).

[12] Nadjib and KiaiKanjeng have also been invited to European countries, and to South Korea, Malaysia and Australia. See Betts, Jalan Sunyi Emha; Daniels, Islamic Spectrum, pp. 134–9. The community is aware of the need to cope with the digital era, so they actively post materials via their official website, YouTube channel, Facebook page, Twitter account, and Instagram account, so that Jamaah Ma'iyah who are not able to physically attend the gatherings can keep up. This expands the significance of Ma'iyah to virtual audiences.

[13] See Betts, Jalan Sunyi Emha.

[14] Daniels, Islamic Spectrum, p. 154.

[15] Interview with the editor of www.caknun.com (May 12, 2017).

– conducted together by Nadjib, as the leader, and the audience – of Qur'anic recitation and prayers, followed by the recitation of praise for the Prophet (*salawat al-nabi*) and remembrance of or praise for God (*dhikr*). Music played by KiaiKanjeng on *gamelan* (a Javanese set of musical instruments) and modern musical instruments accompanies the singing and chanting, creating a moving state of mutual love and togetherness. Second, there is dialogue or discussion on a variety of topics, including politics, religion and spirituality, delivered with a great amount of humor, that often invites the audience into sustained laughter. The jokes create intimacy and a sense of community. The exegetical delivery of the Qur'an takes place randomly, either to respond to contemporary problems or to seek answers to foundational questions. The structural presentation of these elements is random. Nadjib decides the flow of the gathering on the basis of his observation of its atmosphere and audience.

The name Ma'iyah as a reference to the gatherings began in July 2001. The word is from the Arabic *ma'a*, meaning 'together with', 'in the company of', 'accompanied by', 'connected' and 'along with'.[16] The name is inspired by Moses' prayer (Q 26:62), *qala inna ma'iya rabbi sayahdin*,[17] and Muhammad's purported words of consolation to Abu Bakr during the *hijra* (migration from Mecca to Medina), *la tahzan inna-llah ma'ana* (Q 9:40).[18] This term evokes a sense of connectedness, togetherness and communion between human beings and with God and His messenger. Thus, there is a triangular dimension: God–Muhammad–human beings.[19] Furthermore, Nadjib or the teachers of Ma'iyah are not the only source of 'truth'. The truth is sought together.[20] Scholars and important figures are invited to the stage, low by design, which symbolizes that everyone involved in Ma'iyah gatherings is equal, and the audience is welcome to ask questions or make comments.

---

[16] Wehr, *Arabic–English Dictionary*, p. 1073.

[17] 'No, my Lord is with me: He will guide me.' See Abdel Haleem, *The Qur'an*, p. 234.

[18] 'Do not worry, God is with us.' See ibid., p. 120.

[19] On the Qur'anic concept of Ma'iyah, see Ahmad Fuad Effendy, *Ma'iyah dalam al-Qur'an*, published in 2009 by Progess (Nadjib and KiaiKanjeng's management team) for internal circulation among the Ma'iyah community.

[20] Thus, other names for Ma'iyah gatherings are *Sinau Bareng* and *Ngaji Bareng*, Javanese phrases that literally mean 'learning together'. *Ngaji* also means 'reciting the Qur'an'.

Before presenting an argument, usually one that is Qur'an-related, Nadjib starts by saying that what he is going to deliver is only his opinion and that the audience is encouraged to actively and independently seek their own understanding. For example, in a Suluk Maleman gathering,[21] just before he explained his *tadabbur* of Q 24:35, Nadjib stated: 'This is my opinion. You do not need to use it as guidance. I am not your teacher, your *murshid* (spiritual leader), nor your prophet. Your position and mine are the same [meaning that both are seekers of truth].'[22] In an interview, he also emphasized that acknowledging ignorance, and constantly seeking God's guidance as the beholder of the absolute truth, is a necessity.[23]

TADABBUR AS AN APPROACH TO THE QUR'AN

The Qur'an has been the backbone of the community since the beginning. The concept of Padhangmbulan gathering is a *pengajian tafsir* (a religious gathering that discusses the meaning of the Qur'an) led by both Nadjib and Effendy. The latter provides 'textual *tafsir*'; he reads certain verses and their translation, explains the meaning of key words, delivers an interpretation by referring to hadith literature and commentaries of the Qur'an, and then offers his own interpretation. Nadjib, in contrast, delivers a 'contextual *tafsir*.' He links the verses with contemporary political, social, cultural and religious situations, using the Qur'an as the perspective from which to analyze them.[24] This has become the pattern of other Ma'iyah gatherings.

The Ma'iyah views the Qur'an as the ultimate source of guidance. Because humans are far from grasping truth, God kindly sent a perfect human being to follow (Muhammad) and the book from which to seek guidance (the Qur'an).[25] In the Ma'iyah community, there is no

---

[21] A monthly Ma'iyah gathering in Pati, a town in Central Java. Nadjib attends the gathering only once in a while.

[22] Suluk Maleman, July 20, 2013.

[23] 'Cak Nun: "Kun!" Maka Berlangsunglah Islam' (video).

[24] Mustofa, 'Al-Qur'an, Pengajian *Maiyah*, dan Masyarakat (1)' and 'Mbok Dimaafkan Jangan Dendam Terus.'

[25] Nadjib, 'Min Adab-idDunya ilaa Fuad-ilJannah.'

intercession: God and Muhammad are the direct teachers, and the Qur'an is a means to communicate with them. Muhammad is an important figure in Ma'iyah, and love for him is manifested in the *salawat* chanting during the rituals. Nadjib affectionately wrote about the Qur'an and Muhammad:

> I am learning *iqra'.* As we live in a separate time from the revelation of the Qur'an, that I cannot ask and express my love to him (Muhammad), the Qur'an becomes the main interlocutor that I can feel and touch him. Every time I look at the *mushaf*, I imagine his face. Every time I read its letters, I imagine that I listen to him reciting.[26]

He continues: 'I am reading the Qur'an while embracing my longing for Muhammad.'[27]

Nadjib believes that the Qur'an is the solution to all questions and problems. Because the Qur'an comes from God, it is the only source of guidance about which humans can be completely sure of its truth and absoluteness. Nadjib once said that 'we are swimming in the pool of untruthfulness' and illusions.[28] Other sources might be *mutanajjis* ('impure') because they come from humans, but the Qur'an is the only *mutahhar* ('pure') source.

TADABBUR

Even though the discussion of the Qur'an has been the foundational element of Ma'iyah, the term *tadabbur* was popularized only in 2016. The word, from the root *d-b-r*, means 'reflection, meditation, thinking, consideration, contemplation, and deliberation.'[29] *Tadabbur* is Nadjib's strategic term to make the Qur'an meaningful for wider audiences. There are at least two aspects that can explain his preference for the term. First, the term

---

[26] Nadjib, 'Membayangkan Wajahnya,' Daur-II.087.
[27] Nadjib, 'Al-Qur'an Sembarang Orang,' Daur-II.088.
[28] Kenduri Cinta, January 9, 2015.
[29] Wehr, *Arabic–English Dictionary*, p. 313.

tafsir is an elite one; to qualify as a *mufassir* (meaning 'an interpreter of the Qur'an'), one has to master the Qur'anic sciences. Second, the Qur'an itself uses the term *tadabbur* instead of *tafsir* as an approach to interact with it (Q 4:82; 47:24; 38:29). *Tadabbur*'s ultimate goal is spiritual consciousness manifested in daily life – namely, to be closer to God and to be a good human being – rather than pure knowledge.

The aim of *tadabbur* to make the Qur'an meaningful and accessible to everyone is completely in line with Nadjib's concern and advocacy for the neglected, as well as with his continuous effort 'to encourage individual pride and agency'.[30] Nadjib avers that the Qur'an belongs to those who believe in it, not just to those who are traditionally trained to interpret it. If the Qur'an is untouchable by lay Muslims, then it is as if they do not have the right to be true Muslims.[31] He is against the idea that to grasp the meaning of the Qur'an one has to study with *'ulama'* (Islamic clerics) instead of studying the Qur'an itself.[32] He advocates for the right of Muslims, even those who are seen as the most vulnerable religiously, to directly interact with the Qur'an:

> You have the right to recite, perform and enjoy *bism-llah al-rahman al-rahim* (in the name of God, the Lord of Mercy, the Giver of Mercy), *hasbuna-llah wa ni'm al-wakil, ni'm al-mawla wa ni'm al-nasir* (God is enough for us: He is the best protector, an excellent protector and an excellent helper),[33] the whole of alFatiha (the first chapter of the Qur'an), any verse in any chapter, without the need to know the occasion of the revelation, the etymology of the words, hadiths and the wisdom of *'ulama.'* The parameter is what comes out from the *dubur* of your life . . . You, pedicab drivers and traditional market coolies, do not know Arabic . . . the occasion of revelation of a certain verse, Meccan and Medinan suras, any Qur'anic commentaries that provide the interpretation of that verse, have never seen and heard what is written

---

[30] Rasmussen, 'Performing Religious Politics,' p. 161.
[31] Nadjib, 'Qarunumania,' Daur-II.133; Nadjib, 'Tabi'it Tabi'in Pangkat Seribu,' Daur-II.113.
[32] Nadjib, 'Al-Qur'an Hak Para Ulama,' Daur-II.091.
[33] These are Qur'anic passages often recited in Ma'iyah gatherings as a form of *dhikr*. The first part is Q 3:173, and the second Q 8:40 and 22:78.

and spoken by the *mufassirs*. But God's revelation is for all of you, not only for the Prophet and the *'ulama'*, the heirs of the Prophet . . . [The Qur'an] must be able to be utilized in the details of your life in the workplace, home, street, sentry post . . . anywhere.[34]

Many times he also speaks about whether it is possible for him, who is not an *'alim* (the singular form of *'ulama'*) or *mufassir*, to directly interact with the Qur'an.[35]

Nadjib's encouragement for the people to independently conduct *tadabbur* also bolsters the idea that all people have the responsibility to educate themselves. The people are encouraged not to follow, especially not blindly, an *'alim*, but instead to interact with the Qur'an on the basis of the capacity and knowledge they acquire. Such a personal approach of *ijtihad* (independent reasoning, interpretation, judgment) is also encouraged in the Sufi tradition. Sam D. Gail describes this typical Sufi approach to the Qur'an as performative, in which the meaning of the text is referring not solely to its linguistic structure but also to personal reflection by the reader.[36]

To religiously legitimize his concept of *tadabbur*, in addition to the Qur'anic instruction to conduct *tadabbur* mentioned earlier, Nadjib also challenges the use of a popular hadith narrated by Ibn 'Abbas – 'He who says (something) concerning the Qur'an without knowledge (*bi ra'yihi*), he has taken his seat of fire' – to discourage the role of *'aql* ('intellect or reason') in reading the Qur'an. He argues that *ra'y* in this hadith means baseless personal opinion mingled with carnal desire, and that it is clearly not to be confused with *'aql*.[37] In Nadjib's epistemology, *'aql* occupies a sacred place. It is the sparkle of God's light, the tip of God's finger that touches and transfers His love to human beings; thus, it has divine potential.[38] Owing to its sacred source and its distinguishing potential between humans and

---

[34] Nadjib, 'Tadabbur, Dubur, Knalpot Akhlaq,' Daur-I.61.
[35] Nadjib, 'Eksplorasi Manfaat,' Daur-II.111.
[36] Gail, 'Nonliterate Traditions.'
[37] Nadjib, 'Tafsir Bebas Nafsu,' Daur-II.090, May 1, 2017.
[38] Hadi, *Semesta Emha Ainun Nadjib*, 37, and Ma'iyah gathering in Petrokimia Gresik, May 20, 2016.

other creatures, 'aql is indeed the primary tool for reading the Qur'an. However, the common misunderstanding of the role of logic in understanding the Qur'an results from an imprecise understanding of the hadith mentioned earlier. This hadith is meant only to eliminate carelessness in grasping the meaning of the Qur'an, because it is human nature to err.[39]

Apart from the wise use of 'aql, creativity in discovering the possibilities of the Qur'an's meaning is made possible by spiritual qualities: gratitude to God, and love of the Prophet and the Qur'an.[40] Pure intention is ultimately significant in the process. Nadjib says, 'When you learn *from* the Qur'an, empty yourselves from the world. Close your eyes, and open the Qur'an. Each dot in the Qur'an is the center.'[41]

Nadjib discusses the importance of spiritual purification in his *tadabbur* of Q 56:77–80.[42] The group of verses is commonly understood to mean that people are required to perform ablutions prior to touching the Qur'an. However, to him it means that humans can touch the truth of Qur'anic information, or grasp its meaning and wisdom, only if the soul, heart, 'aql, and life are purified (*mutahharun*) by God.[43] A state of being purified is required for *iqra*' (reading), or grasping the meaning of the Qur'an. Otherwise, its meaning, let alone its wisdom, will not be understood. To Nadjib, purification of the outward and, mainly, inward are both achieved and granted; purification is a matter of perfect cooperation between humans and God (Q 13:11). Thus, this verse encourages people to actively seek spiritual purification. However, God decides to whom He grants his guidance (Q 5:17).[44] In sum, both 'aql and spiritual purification are requirements of *tadabbur*. Thus, *tadabbur* is not a lightly undertaken reading of the Qur'an. Even though Nadjib does not offer a detailed procedure for conducting *tadabbur*, he asserts these principles, which might be perfectly called 'aql sahih wa qalb salim ('truthful intellect and sound heart').[45]

---

[39] Nadjib, 'Menakut-nakuti Tafsir,' Daur-II.100.

[40] Nadjib, 'Logika Mencenderungi Kesucian,' Daur-II.099.

[41] Padhangmbulan, November 27, 2015.

[42] 'That this is truly a noble Qur'an, in a protected Record . . . that only the purified can touch, sent down from the Lord of all being.' See Abdel Haleem, *The Qur'an*, p. 357.

[43] Nadjib, 'Berdetak dan Mengalir,' Daur-II.085.

[44] Nadjib, 'Menyentuh dan Disentuh,' Daur-II.086.

[45] Nadjib, 'TKI-1,' Daur-I.69; Nadjib, 'Al-Qur'an Sembarang Orang,' Daur-II.088.

After all, the most important aspect of *tadabbur* is an outcome (*dubur*) in which spiritual consciousness is manifested in daily life. Here, method is less important than outcome. Any understanding is correct as long as the outcome is the increase of goodness and *iman* ('belief' or 'faith'); a closer relationship with God; love of God, the Prophet, and friends of God (*awliya'*); and being a better person socially.[46] Interaction with the Qur'an might not even need to be intellectual. Nadjib once outlined an extreme example: if only by looking at the Qur'an, a person is already inspired to be closer to God and be a better person, that is already a form of *tadabbur*.[47] There is no judge besides God and the individual; each person has an ability to honestly judge whether his or her religious attempt leads to what it should be.[48]

THE PRACTICE OF *TADABBUR*

Nadjib does not claim to be a traditional expert when it comes to interpreting the Qur'an.[49] Although he speaks about the Qur'an, he never regards himself as a *mufassir* of it.[50] He knows he is not a *mufassir*, but his love for the Qur'an cannot keep him from wondering what it means for him to approach the Qur'an authentically. He posits a rhetorical question:

> Can I interact with the Qur'an authentically? Because the Qur'an is not only words, but [also] meaning, is there any possibility that I grasp its meaning? In order to grasp its meaning, I need to understand it. May I do so? Because in order to understand it, I need to interpret it. Am I allowed to do so? ... It is said that only certain people have the right to interpret the Qur'an ... while I do not belong to these people. Do I still have the right to interpret it?[51]

---

[46] Nadjib, Daur-I.60–2.
[47] Ma'iyah gathering in Magelang, Central Java, April 28, 2016.
[48] Kenduri Cinta, March 22, 2016.
[49] On the conditions of a *mufassir*, see al-Suyuti, *al-Itqan fi 'Ulum al-Qur'an*, pp. 763–82.
[50] Nadjib, 'Wewenang Ahli Tafsir,' Daur-II.004.
[51] Nadjib, 'Al-Qur'an Sembarang Orang,' Daur-II.088.

Nadjib does not have formal rigorous training in the Qur'anic sciences, but he is not unfamiliar with Arabic and Islamic tradition. If to be regarded as a *mufassir* one needs to master the details of Qur'anic sciences, which is a traditional standard, then his understanding of the Qur'an belongs to what Andreas Görke calls 'lay exegesis', an interpretation by those who do not traditionally meet the requirements of a *mufassir*.[52]

Unlike Effendy, Nadjib never outlines his method of *tadabbur*, apart from basic principles mentioned here earlier. However, there are at least several characteristics apparent in his reading of the Qur'an. Nadjib proposes to read the Qur'an as *methodology*, by finding its wisdom for the current context (learning *from* the Qur'an, not learning the Qur'an). He pays attention to the basic meaning of the words and to the structure of a verse, a group of verses, or a chapter (*Sura*), and afterward, he appropriates the Qur'an to the current situation – not the current situation to the Qur'an. Speaking about this aspect, Nadjib does not require himself to find the historical context of the Qur'an. His *tadabbur* of the Qur'an is taken straight from its basic meaning to the contemporary context. Finally, his *tadabbur* is delivered in a way that is contextual to the audience and easy to relate to.

In the following section, we present his *tadabbur* of several passages in the Qur'an, particularly on the topic of living in a pluralistic society. In previous sections, we stated that he sees a fundamental crisis in humans' way of life and thinking, which can be summed up as the problems of secularism, materialism and narrow-mindedness, which endanger pluralism as *sunnatu-llah* ('God's law of nature'). The strategic and foundational solution is to go back to the very root of humanity, which brings one to the spiritual approach of Ma'iyah. Here, the Qur'an becomes the ultimate source of wisdom and guidance.

---

[52] Görke, 'Redefining the Borders of *Tafsir*,' p. 365.

LIVING IN A PLURALISTIC WORLD

Nadjib's view is that what endangers good social interaction with others – mainly with those who have differing outlooks – is religious narrow-mindedness. This rigidity is characterized by a claim to truth and by anti-plurality. Conversely, he sees plurality or diversity as part of *sunnatu-lLah*, which allows peaceful engagement. In 2002, Nadjib wrote these Ma'iyah greetings:

> The country-wise language of the Ma'iyah is nationalism. The international language of Ma'iyah is universalism. The civil language of Ma'iyah is pluralism. The cultural language of Ma'iyah is heterogeneity, or diversity that is allowed, understood, and managed. The method or administrative management is called democracy.[53]

Nadjib highly values the plurality and diversity of Indonesia, and the Ma'iyah community is actively and consistently promoting peace and harmonious society. They conduct this mission in different ways. Ma'iyah welcomes and invites people from different faith backgrounds to sit on the stage. Inclusivity is also encouraged through music and cultural jokes. For example, Nadjib and KiaiKanjeng (known together as CNKK) engage in *salawat al-nabi* using the melody of the Christian song 'O Holy Night'. Predictably, this invites religious debates. Indeed, in Ma'iyah, the audience is encouraged to distinguish between form and matter. The content of *salawat al-nabi* is the essence, and music is only a vehicle for it. This principle also works in attempts to understand religious expressions.

CNKK's reputation for promoting peace is known beyond Indonesia. They have performed in non-Muslim majority countries and in other religions' places of worship. For example, just after the movie *Fitna* became popular in 2008, CNKK was invited by Protestantse Kerk in the Netherlands to foster mutual understanding among religious groups and to help combat Islamophobia.[54] CNKK also performed at the Vatican

---

[53] Nadjib, 'Salam Maiyah,' in Daniels, *Islamic Spectrum*, p. 144.
[54] See Betts, *Jalan Sunyi Emha*.

only a few days after the death of Pope John Paul II in 2005. Nadjib himself is an advocate for intrareligious and interreligious pluralism. He stands on the side of persecuted communities, like the Shias and the Ahmadis. Also, Nadjib's practice of not representing any religious group makes it easy for him to engage in dialogue with groups considered exclusive, such as the Islamic Defenders Front (FPI) and the Hizb ut-Tahrir Indonesia (HTI), and figures like Abu Bakar Ba'asyir.[55]

In the gatherings, Nadjib offers Qur'anic readings that creatively challenge narrow-mindedness, and he invites the audience to rethink popular belief. First, he proposes to reread verses on several key Islamic concepts, such as *din* (religion), *islam, jihad* (striving in the path of God), *al-amr bi l-ma'ruf wa lnahy 'an almunkar* ('commanding good and forbidding evil'), *takfir* ('declaring another Muslim an unbeliever'), and *da'wa* ('the essence and strategy of disseminating Islamic faith'). These terms are frequently used in the daily life, and their meanings are understood to be fixed. An attempt to be *radical* by going back to the original meaning of certain terms is apparent in Nadjib's method, which is a deconstruction of the concepts usually attached to the terms.

For example, since 2016 Nadjib has repeatedly discussed the terms and concepts of *islam* (Q 3:19, 83). Just like *din*, he asserts that *islam* is not an institution or a social identity,[56] even though its adherents may form institutions, groups and schools, which is inevitable to manifest *islam* for the need of a certain context. *Islam* is submission to God, which is a 'salvific program' allowing humans and the universe to be able to return to God (*ilayhi raji'un*).[57] Recently, Nadjib has popularized the idea that *islam* did not begin in the time of Muhammad. The Qur'an itself calls previous prophets Muslims (Q 2:130–3; 3:52, 67). *Islam*, in his theory, has existed

---

[55] The spokesman of Hizb ut-Tahrir, Ismail Yusanto, showed his appreciation of Nadjib by stating that '[Nadjib] speaks of politics but without politicizing; of the dilapidated bureaucracy, but not as a bureaucrat; of deceitful business, but neither is he a businessman, of Islam and caring, yet he is not an Ulama.' See Widiyanto, 'Religious Pluralism,' p. 171. Since the fall of the Soeharto regime and the allowance of freedom of speech, Indonesia has witnessed the growth of the so-called radical Muslim groups. See ibid., pp. 162–3.

[56] Nadjib, 'Fithri Seribu Tahun Lagi,' Daur-II.069.

[57] Nadjib, 'Tak Kunjung Lulus Iqra,' Daur-II.055, p. 55; 'Cak Nun: "Kun!" Maka Berlangsunglah Islam' (video).

since God said, 'Kun, fayakun' (Q 36:82) during the process of creation.[58] Islam literally means 'total submission and surrender'. In Nadjib's mind, it is impossible that all creation is not essentially in total submission to God (that is, to God's law of nature). In short, islam in his concept was born at the time of creation. The universalization of the term islam encourages one to go beyond identity to universal values.[59]

Nadjib also discusses the Qur'anic terms iman and kafir. He observes that Muslims mainly interpret the Qur'anic passage ya ayyuha l-ladhina amanu ('Oh you who believe', or 'believers') as referring only to Muslims. In fact, Nadjib believes that we should ask whether God means here all people believing in Him, or only Muslims. Kafir refers not to a religious identity but rather to a nonbeliever in a generic sense – one who denies God's decree, or law of nature, and anyone may hold this attitude regardless of his or her religious identity.[60] He also explains a popular verse on how to treat a kafir (Q 5:54).[61] The common understanding of this verse is to be gentle to the Muslims and to be harsh (a'izza) to a kafir. Nadjib explains, however, that he has a different understanding of this term. He links a'izza to a term God uses to denote Muhammad's character towards his community, 'azizun 'alayhi ma 'anittum (Q 9:128).[62] Thus, he prefers to define the term a'izza as distress or worry about kafirs, creating a sense of caring and mercy (in Indonesian: tidak tega; in Javanese: mesakne) instead of harshness. This becomes a basis for living harmoniously with others.[63]

---

[58] 'Cak Nun: "Kun!" Maka Berlangsunglah Islam' (video); Nadjib, 'Islam Belum Lahir Padanya', Daur-I.299, and Ma'iyah gathering in Pondok Pesantran al-Huda Boyolali, August 20, 2016. The whole verse reads, 'When He wills something to be, His way is to say, "Be" – and it is!' See Abdel Haleem, The Qur'an, p. 284.

[59] Ma'iyah gathering in Semarang City Hall, April 25, 2017.

[60] 'Cak Nun: "Kun!" Maka Berlangsunglah Islam' (video).

[61] 'You who believe, if any of you go back on your faith, God will soon replace you with people He loves and who love Him, people who are humble towards the believers, hard on the disbelievers, and who strive in God's way without fearing anyone's reproach. Such is God's favour. He grants it to whoever He will. God has endless bounty and knowledge.' See Abdel Haleem, The Qur'an, p. 73.

[62] 'A Messenger has come to you from among yourselves. Your suffering distresses him: He is deeply concerned for you and full of kindness and mercy towards the believers.' See Abdel Haleem, The Qur'an, p. 127.

[63] Nadjib, 'Berat Hati dan Tidak Tegaan,' June 3, 2017.

Similarly, Nadjib suggests that the term *murtadd* (Q 5:54), which is typically understood as referring to apostates, should instead be interpreted as 'one who does not apply the principles that should be applied.' *Din*, commonly translated as 'religion', is 'consciousness and loyalty in the service [Javanese: *bebektii*] of God.'[64] Nadjib proceeds to the next passage of the verse, which says that 'God will soon replace you (the *murtadd*) with people He loves and who love Him.' When he reads this passage, he imagines an Indonesian context, where, in general, people have essentially become *murtadd*. He highlights God's promise that He will replace them with a better generation. He states that the young generation – including, but not limited to, those who are the most loyal audience of Ma'iyah gatherings – mirror the character of the people mentioned in the passage, thus giving hope to this generation regarding the future of Indonesia.[65]

Deconstructing a concept's original meaning in the Qur'an, rather than just accepting its conventional meaning, not only brings clarity but also fosters humility. Nadjib emphasizes that even though he and his audience are Muslims, that does not mean they are automatically excluded from groups the Qur'an criticizes: 'Let alone declaring another person as a *kafir* or deviant, we might not be qualified to call ourselves Muslims.'[66] He always invites audience members to reflect upon themselves – to be humble – before pointing a finger at others. Problems among Indonesian Muslims and other groups in the world arise when people force their opinions on others and claim that they are the only possessors of truth.

In addition to offering an essential reading of key terms, Nadjib also conducts *tadabbur* of Qur'anic verses that support pluralism. He points out that the ultimate outcome of every religion is noble character (*akhlaq*). Thus, people do not have to be Muslims for their good deeds to be accepted by God.[67] In fact, in some Indonesian Muslim contexts or beyond, a key idea is that possessing a true creed (*'aqidah*) – in a limited sense of belonging to a religion called Islam – is the requirement for a person's deeds to be accepted and counted by God. He bases his argument

---

[64] Ibid.
[65] Ibid, and Ma'iyah gathering in Malang, East Java, June 2, 2017.
[66] Kenduri Cinta, March 22, 2017.
[67] Ma'iyah gathering in Solo, Central Java, July 26, 2016.

on two verses in the Qur'an. The first is Qur'an 3:110,[68] in which the words 'believing in God' are placed in the third row after 'ordering what is right and forbid what is wrong', showing that good deeds are not a prerequisite for believing in God. Deeds are counted, not one's identity. The second is Qur'an 2:62.[69] The injunction in this verse is clear: rewards (*ajr*) are granted to the doers of good deeds, no matter what religion they belong to.

Nadjib also explains religious tolerance and the plurality of religions with analogies to ease understanding. His teaching about the ultimate goal of religion, particularly in relation to living with others, is best illustrated in an analogy involving a kitchen. The ultimate goal of each religion is noble character (*akhlaq*). Noble character is analogous to food ready for serving; rituals and doctrinal beliefs are the cooking process, which belongs to the kitchen. In the Javanese tradition, the kitchen is situated in the back of the home, hidden, just as rituals are not to be shown in public. What is to be displayed is the food – a noble character.

In addition, Nadjib uses an analogy from marriage to promote religious tolerance. He explains that one's own religion is like one's wife. A husband would regard his wife as the best, the most beautiful of all women. But to see her in that manner, the husband does not need to proclaim that another man's wife is ugly.

Furthermore, he uses an analogy about the growth of coconuts to explain the development of Qur'anic religions: the Torah corresponds to a *bluluk* (a seed). The Zabur represents a *cengkir* (the seed that has grown a leaf, such as a coconut sprout). The Gospels represent a *degan* (a young coconut). The Qur'an represents the last stage of development – the coconut itself. Nadjib asserts that many people are mistaken by regarding the four as four separate things when they are essentially one.[70]

---

[68] '[Believers], you are the best community singled out for people: you order what is right, forbid what is wrong, and believe in God. If the People of the Book had also believed, it would have been better for them. For although some of them do believe, most of them are lawbreakers.' See Abdel Haleem, *The Qur'an*, p. 42.

[69] 'The [Muslim] believers, the Jews, the Christians, and the Sabians – all those who believe in God and the Last Day and do good will have their rewards with their Lord. No fear for them, nor will they grieve.' See Abdel Haleem, *The Qur'an*, p. 9.

[70] Nadjib, 'Agama Bluluk,' Daur-II.127; Nadjib, 'Rasa Agama Nusantara.'

Finally, Nadjib explains the plurality of religions by using an analogy involving cassavas. Different religions are just like the variety of food or snacks made of cassavas. (In Javanese, they are called *gethuk, thiwul, gatot, cimplung*, etc.) The difference lies in form and appearance, but in essence, they are cassavas. The different religions are essentially from one substance. Cassava plantations are common in Indonesia, which makes it easy for people to relate to the analogy.

In sum, Nadjib regards the plurality of religions as part of God's design; that God creates different paths to belief in Him is purely His prerogative.[71] He believes that all religions possess truth, even though he views Islam as the perfected version of truth, as seen in the coconut analogy.[72] His approach is to strengthen people's pride in tradition while teaching them to be humble in the midst of plurality, because to God, the perfect expression of humans' love is to love all His creatures.

CONCLUSION

Tadabbur as a process of grasping the meaning of the Qur'an exemplifies an actual practice of a popular Sufi group in Indonesia dealing with contemporary issues. Studying how the Qur'an is perceived in a community sheds light on how that community copes with the challenges of the twenty-first century. *Ma'iyah* tackles the issues of intolerance, violence and sectarianism in the name of Islam and widely embraces the pluralistic nature of all of God's people. The community highly values Indonesia's pluralism, and it actively and consistently promotes peace and a harmonious society through interpreting the Qur'an's teachings.

Muslims interact with the Qur'an in at least three modes of reception: exegetical, aesthetic and functional. The activities of exegetical reception are usually conducted within a community. It is transferred orally by the teacher as the mediator between the Qur'an and the community. Despite

---

[71] 'Cak Nun: "Kun!" Maka Berlangsunglah Islam' (video).

[72] Widiyanto distinguishes between religious pluralism as a theological concept and as a civic-political concept. See Widiyanto, 'Religious Pluralism,' pp. 165–6.

its widespread use, 'oral exegesis' and its 'regional particularities' still need more attention in the field of Qur'anic studies.[73] Most works on Qur'anic exegesis are dedicated to the written *tafsirs*, mainly from the older centers of the Muslim world, rather than from the far-reaching regions, including Indonesia. The study of Qur'anic exegesis beyond its written works, and beyond that produced in the older Muslim world, is necessary to untangle how the Qur'an is understood and approached by Muslims in wider Muslim regions. The description in this chapter of practices in a Javanese Sufi community is an attempt to fill this gap.

BIBLIOGRAPHY

Ma'iyah and Daur

Daur-I essays are available both online and in print form. Daur-II essays are currently available only online. Daur essays have both a title and a number. We give both in the bibliography, along with the date provided on the website. Daur-I essays were also published in print in 2017: Emha Ainun Nadjib, *Daur*. vol. 1: Anak Asuh Bernama Indonesia; vol. 2: Iblis Tidak Butuh Pengikut; vol. 3: Mencari Buah Simalakama; vol. 4: Kapal Nuh Abad 21. (Yogyakarta: Bentang, 2017).

'Cak Nun: "Kun!" Maka Berlangsunglah Islam.' (April 6, 2017) [Online] (https://www.youtube.com/watch?v=yKWZCMGWJoI&t=6s). (Accessed May 5, 2017)

Effendy, Ahmad Fuad. 'Antara Tafsir dan Tadabbur', April 8, 2016 [Online] (www.bangbang-wetan.org/antara-tafsir-dan-tadabbur/). (Accessed March 2, 2017)

— *Ma'iyah dalam al-Qur'an*. (Jakarta: Progress, 2009)

'Fiqih Tanpa Aqidah, Bumi Tanpa Langit.' Report of Kenduri Cinta, March 22, 2016 [Online] (https://www.caknun.com/2016/fiqih-tanpa-aqidah-bumi-tanpa-langit/). (Accessed May 5, 2017)

Mustofa, Helmi. 'Al-Qur'an, Pengajian Ma'iyah, dan Masyarakat (1)', April 10, 2017 [Online] (https://www.caknun.com/2017/). (Accessed May 10, 2017)

— 'Al-Qur'an, Pengajian Ma'iyah, dan Masyarakat (2)', April 11, 2017 [Online] (https://www.caknun.com/2017/). (Accessed May 4, 2017)

— 'Mbok Dimaafkan Jangan Dendam Terus.' Report of Padhangmbulan November 27, 2015, December 9, 2015 [Online] (https://www.caknun.com/2015/mbok-dimaafkan-jangan-dendam-terus/). (Accessed May 4, 2017)

Nadjib, Emha Ainun, 'Agama Bluluk.' Daur-II.127, June 7, 2017 [Online] (https://www.caknun.com/2017/agama-bluluk/). (Accessed June 7, 2017)

— 'Al-Qur'an Hak Para Ulama.' Daur-II.091, May 2017 2, [Online] (https://www.caknun.com/2017/al-quran-hak-para-ulama/). (Accessed May 12, 2017)

— 'Al-Qur'an Sembarang Orang.' Daur-II.088, April 2017 9, [Online] (https://www.caknun.com/2017/al-quran-sembarang-orang/). (Accessed May 9, 2017)

---

[73] Görke, 'Redefining the borders of *Tafsir*.'

— 'Belajar Manusia kepada Sastra.' July 26, 2016 [Online] (https://www.caknun.com/2016/belajar-manusia-kepada-sastra/). (Accessed December 11, 2018)

— 'Berakhirnya Era Kemanusiaan.' June 14, 2017 [Online] (https://www.caknun.com/2017/berakhirnya-era-kemanusiaan/). (Accessed June, 14 2017)

— 'Berat Hati dan Tidak Tegaan.' June 3, 2017 [Online] (https://www.caknun.com/2017/berat-hati-dan-tidak-tegaan/). (Accessed May 9, 2017)

— 'Berdetak dan Mengalir.' Daur-II.085, April 26, 2017 [Online] (https://www.caknun.com/2017/berdetak-dan-mengalir/). (Accessed May 9, 2017)

— 'Dakwah Pelit.' Daur-II.117, May 28, 2017 [Online] (https://www.caknun.com/2017/dakwah-pelit/). (Accessed May 13, 2017)

— 'Ditimpa dan Musibah.' Daur-II.021, February 21, 2017 [Online] (https://www.caknun.com/2017/ditimpa-dan-musibah/). (Accessed May 12, 2017)

— 'Eksplorasi Manfaat.' Daur-II.111, May 22, 2017 [Online] (https://www.caknun.com/2017/eksplorasi-manfaat/). (Accessed May 23, 2017)

— 'Engkau dan Ibumu.' Daur-II.051, March 23, 2017 [Online] (https://www.caknun.com/2017/engkau-dan-ibumu/). (Accessed May 12, 2017)

— 'Fithri Seribu Tahun Lagi.' Daur-II.069, April 10, 2017 [Online] (https://www.caknun.com/2017/fithri-seribu-tahun-lagi/). (Accessed May 5, 2017)

— 'Gagah dan Ikhlas Berhijrah.' Daur-II.012, February 12, 2017 [Online] (https://www.caknun.com/2017/gagah-dan-ikhlas-berhijrah/). (Accessed May 3, 2017)

— 'Islam Belum Lahir Padanya.' Daur 299, November 29, 2016 [Online] (https://www.caknun.com/2016/islam-belum-lahir-padanya/). (Accessed May 5, 2017)

— 'Kilabunnar.' Daur-II.029, March 1, 2017 [Online] (https://www.caknun.com/2017/kilabunnar/). (Accessed May 5, 2017)

— 'Larangan Berpendapat.' Daur-II.089, April 30, 2017 [Online] (https://www.caknun.com/2017/larangan-berpendapat/). (Accessed May 12, 2017)

— 'Logika Mencenderungi Kesucian.' Daur-II.099, May 10, 2017 [Online] (https://www.caknun.com/2017/logika-mencenderungi-kesucian/). (Accessed May 12, 2017)

— 'Markesot Ahli Dubur.' Daur 60, April 2, 2017 [Online] (https://www.caknun.com/2016/markesot-ahli-dubur/). (Accessed May 7, 2017)

— 'Membayangkan Wajahnya.' Daur-II.087, April 28, 2017 [Online] (https://www.caknun.com/2017/membayangkan-wajahnya/). (Accessed May 9, 2017)

— 'Membersihkan Tanpa Ikut Mengotori.' Daur-II.011, February 11, 2017 [Online] (https://www.caknun.com/2017/membersihkan-tanpa-ikut-mengotori/). (Accessed May 3, 2017)

— 'Menakut-nakuti Tafsir.' Daur-II.100, May 11, 2017 [Online] (https://www.caknun.com/2017/menakut-nakuti-tafsir/). (Accessed May 12, 2017)

— 'Menyentuh dan Disentuh.' Daur-II.086, April 27, 2017 [Online] (https://www.caknun.com/2017/menyentuh-dan-disentuh/). (Accessed May 9, 2017)

— 'Meranjau Diri Sendiri.' Daur-II.009, February 9, 2017 [Online] (https://www.caknun.com/2017/meranjau-diri-sendiri/). (Accessed May 2, 2017)

— 'Min Adab-idDunya ilaa Fuad-ilJannah.' November 21, 2012 [Online] (https://www.caknun.com/2012/min-adab-iddunya-ilaa-fuad-iljannah/). (Accessed May 3, 2017)

— 'Pemimpin yang Takabur.' June 6, 2017 [Online] (https://www.caknun.com/2017/pemimpin-yang-takabur/). (Accessed May 12, 2017)

— 'Qarunumania.' Daur-II.133, June 16, 2017 [Online] (https://www.caknun.com/2017/qorunumania/). (Accessed June 16, 2017)

— 'Rasa Agama Nusantara.' June 16, 2017 [Online] (https://www.caknun.com/2017/

rasa-agama-nusantara/). (Accessed June 16, 2017)

— 'Revolusi Tlethong.' Daur-I.62, April 4, 2017 [Online] (https://www.caknun.com/2016/revolusi-tlethong/). (Accessed May 7, 2017)

— 'Rumus Kehinaan.' Daur-II.123, June 3, 2017 [Online] (https://www.caknun.com/2017/rumus-kehinaan/). (Accessed June 3, 2017)

— 'Sembilan Lelaki Perusak.' Daur-II.010, February 10, 2017 [Online] (https://www.caknun.com/2017/sembilan-lelaki-perusak/). (Accessed May 2, 2017)

— 'Sombong, Kejam dan Menyakiti.' Daur-II.013, February 13, 2017 [Online] (https://www.caknun.com/2017/sombong-kejam-dan-menyakiti/). (Accessed May 3, 2017)

— 'Tabi'it Tabi'in Pangkat Seribu.' Daur-II.113, May 25, 2017 [Online] (https://www.caknun.com/2017/tabiit-tabiin-pangkat-seribu/). (Accessed May 14, 2017)

— 'Tadabbur, Dubur, Knalpot Akhlaq.' Daur-I.61, April 3, 2017 [Online] (https://www.caknun.com/2016/tadabbur-dubur-knalpot-akhlaq/). (Accessed May 3, 2017)

— 'Tafsir Bebas Nafsu.' Daur-II.090, May 1, 2017 [Online] (https://www.caknun.com/2017/tafsir-bebas-nafsu/). (Accessed May 12, 2017)

— 'Tafsir Logika Semata.' Daur-II.096, May 7, 2017 [Online] (https://www.caknun.com/2017/tafsir-logika-semata/). (Accessed May 12, 2017)

— 'Tak Kunjung Lulus Iqra.' Daur-II.055, March 27, 2017 [Online] (https://www.caknun.com/2017/tak-kunjung-lulus-iqra/). (Accessed December 18, 2018),

— 'TKI-1.' Daur-I.69, April 11, 2016 [Online] (https://www.caknun.com/2016/tki-1/). (Accessed May 2, 2017)

— 'Wewenang Ahli Tafsir.' Daur-II.004, February 4, 2017 [Online] (https://www.caknun.com/2017/wewenang-ahli-tafsir/). (Accessed May 12, 2017)

Secondary sources

Abdel Haleem, M.A.S. The Qur'an. (Oxford, UK: Oxford University Press, 2005)

Betts, Ian L. Jalan Sunyi Emha. (Jakarta: Kompas, 2006)

Daniels, Timothy. Islamic Spectrum in Java. (Burlington, VT: Ashgate, 2009)

Eagleton, Terry. Literary Theory: An Introduction. (Malden, Oxford and Carlton: Blackwell Publishing, 2005)

Gail, Sam D. 'Nonliterate Traditions and Holy Books: Toward a New Model.' In The Holy Book in Comparative Perspective. Ed. Frederick M. Denny and Rodney L. Taylor, 224–39. (Columbia, SC: University of South Carolina Press, 1985)

Görke, Andreas. 'Redefining the Borders of Tafsir: Oral Exegesis, Lay Exegesis and Regional Particularties.' In Tafsir and Islamic Intellectual History: Exploring the Boundaries of a Genre. Ed. Andreas Görke and Johanna Pink, 361–78. (Oxford, UK: Oxford University Press, 2014)

Graham, William. Beyond the Written Word: Oral Aspects of Scripture in the History of Religion. (Cambridge, UK: Cambridge University Press, 1987)

Hadi, Sumasno. Semesta Emha Ainun Nadjib. (Bandung: Mizan, 2017)

Knauth, Dorcinda. 'Performing Islam Through Indonesian Popular Music, 2002–2007.' (PhD diss., University of Pittsburgh, 2014)

Ong, Walter J. Orality and Literacy: The Technologizing of the Word. (London and New York: Routledge, 1982)

Rafiq, Ahmad. 'The Reception of the Qur'an in Indonesia: A Case Study of the Place of the Qur'an in a Non-Arabic Speaking Community.' (PhD diss., Temple University, 2014)

Rasmussen, Anne. 'Performing Religious Politics: Islamic Musical Arts in Indonesia.' In Music *and Conflict*. Ed. John Morgan O'Connel and Salwa el-Shawan Castelo-Branco, 155–74. (Urbana, Chicago and Springfield: University of Illinois Press, 2010)

— *Women, the Recited Qur'an and Islamic Music in Indonesia*. (Los Angeles: University of California Press, 2010)

Sands, Kristin Zahra. *Sufi Commentaries on the Qur'an in Classical Islam*. (New York: Routledge, 2006)

al-Suyuti, Jalal al-Din. *Al-Itqan fi 'Ulum al-Qur'an*. (Beirut: Resalah Publishers, 2008)

Wehr, Hans and J. Milton Cowan. *Arabic–English Dictionary: The Hans Wehr Dictionary of Modern Written Arabic*. (Ithaca: Spoken Language Services, 1976)

Widiyanto, Asfa. 'Religious Pluralism and Contested Religious Authority in Contemporary Indonesian Islam: A. Mustofa Bisri and Emha Ainun Nadjib.' In *Islam in Indonesia: Contrasting Images and Interpretations*. Ed. Jajat Burhanuddin and Kees van Dijk, 161–72. (Amsterdam: Amsterdam University Press, 2013)

Meetings

Kenduri Cinta, January 9, 2015, EAN library private documentation

Kenduri Cinta, March 22, 2016

Kenduri Cinta, March 22, 2017Ma'iyah gathering in Magelang, Central Java, April 28, 2016, EAN library private documentation

Ma'iyah gathering in Malang, East Java, June 2, 2017

Ma'iyah gathering in Petrokimia Gresik, May 20, 2016

Ma'iyah gathering in Politeknik College Malang, June 2, 2017

Ma'iyah gathering in Pondok Pesantran al-Huda Boyolali, August 20, 2016

Ma'iyah gathering in Solo, Central Java, July 26, 2016

Ma'iyah gathering in Sunan Ampel State Islamic University, Surabaya, East Java, December 30, 2015

Ma'iyah gathering in the Semarang City Hall, April 25, 2017

Mocopat Syafaat, September 17, 1999

Mocopat Syafaat, September 17, 2001

Mocopat Syafaat, August 17, 2012

Mocopat Syafaat, May 17, 2017

Padhangmbulan, November 27, 2015

Suluk Maleman, July 20, 2013

Part II

Between Gender and Community

Chapter 4

Musawah: Gender Equity through Qur'anic Discourse

Amina Wadud, Virginia Commonwealth University

At the dawn of the new millennium, a critical mass of Muslim women began directing the conversation about what it means to be Muslim and female today. At no other time in history has there been a duplication of what we're seeing today. Even at the advent of Islam, when women were especially beneficiaries of a mandate for social justice, they were not themselves the agents of this movement. Today, Muslim women are involved at every level, in every context, and on every aspect of the experience of being Muslim and female. Still, they do not all go about it in the same way. Three distinctive responses of Muslim women arose and were put in conversation with each over how best to achieve dignity and honor for Muslim women: secular feminism, Islamism, and Islamic feminism.

This chapter highlights the strategic relationship between sacred texts and gender reform as articulated in a global movement called *Musawah*, a community of interpretation founded upon gender neutrality as fundamental to the Qur'an.[1] I situate the emergence of *Musawah* in the history global discourses about human rights, women's rights, and Islam, showing

---

[1] http://www.musawah.org/ (Accessed June 8, 2018). See also Mir-Hosseini, *Men in Charge?*

how Muslim women constructed diverse responses to asymmetrical gender relations. One of the major distinctions between these diverse responses and methodologies centers on the significance of sacred Islamic texts to achieve equality and justice. A unique part of the creation of Islamic feminism is developing an inclusive dialogue between Islamic sources, national constitutions, international human rights instruments and the lived realities of Muslim women.

HUMAN RIGHTS AND IDEAS OF THE HUMAN

Whether embedded in secular human rights discourse or classical *fiqh* (jurisprudence), twentieth-century human rights discourses and ideas of the human are founded upon patriarchal assumptions. In the middle part of the twentieth century the United Nations was formed, beginning a postcolonial global discourse over the idea of universal human rights. In the UN, that idea was built upon a notion of the human being constructed primarily by male thinkers, policymakers and government representatives from the global north. These were the same primary architects and beneficiaries of colonialism, which was still prevalent while UN debates about human rights were going on. Several quarters launched opposition to the UN configurations of universal human rights in the modern global discourses. The oppositions were based upon competing and intersecting characteristics of real human beings in real-life global circumstances. Muslims, who were among those who deconstructed the UN definitions, came up with their own declarations of human rights.[2] The architects of these declarations were also overwhelmingly male, and they re-inscribed both new and old patriarchal ideas in their definitions of the human being. Their configurations would leave women in a secondary status, if not deviant, and these configurations would not shift until women themselves became agents as well as stakeholders in these declarations of human rights, and uncovered the constructed limits on human-ness that informed traditional human rights discussions.

---

[2] http://hrlibrary.umn.edu/instree/islamic_declaration_HR.html

The notion of who constitutes a human being, in classical Islamic *fiqh*, was built upon several competing value systems which would come to characterize the main schools of Islamic thought. The primary architects of classical *fiqh* were male scholars. While diligent and earnest in their efforts, they did not interrogate gender as a category of thought when constructing the principles and practices of Islamic jurisprudence. As such, patriarchal privileges prevailed, and inequality in gender relations became encoded in traditional *fiqh*. Furthermore, centuries of these same jurisprudential constructions would lead to ideas within Islamic communities over time that authority rested squarely upon patriarchal privilege within the notion of the human being.

These ideas, and the diverse jurisprudential practices associated with them, would be transformed in critical ways when they encountered and were incorporated into the modern nation-state system. The project of political Islam, which undertook to think through the relationship of Islamic intellectual traditions in relation to the nation state, absorbed the gendered assumptions of classical *fiqh*. The definition of rights that emerged in modern states uses gendered understandings of constitution and citizenship. The state may grant certain rights as fundamental to all citizens, and simultaneously deny them to female citizens using 'Islam' as the basis for exemptions or exceptions. The resurgence of a state model of Islamic law after liberation from colonial powers led to further implementation of family law codes that had been consolidated during colonialism. In them, male dominance was crystallized and made sacred. Patriarchal privilege, interpretation and cultural practice is so entrenched that every challenge to gender inequality is accused of going against the Qur'an, or going against Islam – even going against Allah.

CONSTRUCTING A GENDER-NEUTRAL IDEA OF THE HUMAN THROUGH QUR'ANIC DISCOURSE

Islamic feminism, which emerged at the turn of the current millennium, worked to create new policies and to promote new practices and cultural attitudes, starting with a radically inclusive notion of the human being.

This notion of the human being was built using Islamic primary sources, most notably the Qur'an. However, it was not premised upon gender asymmetry.

For Islamic feminism, this equitable construction of the idea of the human is founded upon Qur'anic discourses over cosmology, teleology and eschatology. By cosmology, I mean here both theories that explain the origin of the universe and those that explain the relative positions of human beings in the universe in relation to God and to one another. Traditional Islamic cosmology is patriarchal. At the top of the hierarchy is Allah, then humans over all other creations, and men above women. Ayesha Chaudhry describes this schema as a 'patriarchal idealized cosmology,' that is, a cosmology that idealizes normative asymmetrical constructions of gender and their manifestation in conventional social relations. However, direct engagement with the Qur'an that is not filtered through the history of male-dominated exegesis allows for the construction of an egalitarian idealized cosmology, one in which men and women are equal in their human value before God, and in which every individual has an independent and unmediated relationship with the divine.

The teleology or purpose of human creation is to be a *khalifa* – a moral agent. The Qur'an shares the story of a primordial conversation between Allah, as Creator, and angels, as transcendent, non-corporeal created beings in which is said, 'Indeed I will create on the earth a *khalifa*' (Q 2:30). Since this precedes the actual creation of human beings, or the original parent Adam, it is a statement of purpose. It indicates two significant aspects: humans are meant to be **on** the earth and they are meant to be *khalifa*. This *khilafa*, or moral agency, is not conditioned by other characteristics of actual human beings; there are no limits or degrees relative to gender, sexuality, nationality, religion, class, race, ethnicity, disability, or any other personal or cultural constructs. All are human, and all share in this destiny on the earth.

The Qur'an's eschatological scheme gives *taqwa* – consciousness of God – the highest value in its ethical evaluation of human beings. 'Verily we have created you from a male and female. (We have) made you into nations and tribes that you might come to know one another. Indeed, the most noble of you in the sight of Allah is the one with the most *taqwa*' (Q 49:13).

Since *taqwa* refers to both inner consciousness and outward ethical actions towards all of creation, it cannot be determined except by Allah as the Ultimate Judge with the individual. In this eschatology, humans will not face their ultimate measure until we arrive all together on the day of reckoning. Thus, although *taqwa* has certain manifest behaviors, it is ultimately part of a divine scheme. As such, it cannot be instituted, legislated or enforced.

These cosmological, teleological and eschatological Qur'anic discourses allow an unequivocal and ungendered definition of what it means to be 'human.' That applies to every social, political and religious duty; to the benefits of all rights and privileges; and to access to resources to fulfill those duties and receive these benefits. Most importantly, promoting an agenda that would insure that these are shared equally is the objective of Islamic feminism. There is no exceptionalism between one human being and another, for any reason. So, for example, while there are obvious biological differences in sexual reproduction, creating different experiences regarding childbirth – with women granted the exclusive role of childbearing and wet-nursing – no other distinction is implied or warranted. Reproductive capabilities are not evaluated to determine actual degrees of basic human-ness. Thus, while women and men have different reproductive capabilities, nothing in relation to child-rearing is so determined, except by social construction. A woman is neither more nor less than a man in human-ness, despite her centrality with biological reproduction. To extend this biology to private and public social roles has long been a false assertion of the privilege of patriarchy. Modern Muslim *fiqh* interpretations erroneously equate reproduction with the domestic realm, and even chores within that space.

DISCOURSES ABOUT HUMAN RIGHTS AND RELIGION

The World Conference on Women, at which Muslim women formed a noticeable presence and where implementation of the Convention on the Elimination of All Forms of Discrimination Against Women (CEDAW) was tabled, demonstrates the different methodological and strategic distinctions, particularly regarding the use of Islamic primary sources, in the struggles for gender reform, that dominated at Beijing. These two dominant discourses are Islamism and secular (including liberal) feminism.

SECULAR FEMINISM

Secular feminism decries Islam (or any religion) as an aspect of modern gender reform and human rights. It makes a case for its goals primarily based upon the ideas of human rights as a modern phenomenon following the UN designation of universal human rights, no matter who the architects or even primary audience. Muslim liberal feminism borrows somewhat randomly from the strategies of secular feminism, and occasionally from Islamic intellectual thought. Liberal feminism is the place where personal belief finds its home, while simultaneously promoting the Universal Declaration of Human Rights and a democratic constitutional nation state. Because it does not have a significant and distinctive methodology distinguishing it from secular feminism, it should be noted that liberal feminism is the place where most Muslim feminists meet, and where they form a primary interpretive community. Secular feminists, however, say you cannot have both human rights and Islam. They give up Islam in preference to human rights and align their strategies with UN instruments.

ISLAMISM

Islamism maintains that Islam is the only legitimate foundation for community. For Islamists, Islam is its patriarchal interpretation with the additional assertion of patriarchal privilege to its notion of authority. These authoritative and patriarchal interpretations constitute 'real Islam.' Anyone who disagrees with their methods, interpretive conclusions and practical implementation is dubbed anti-Islamic, pro-Western or disbeliever. Furthermore, Islamists maintain that, considering the reality of the nation state, all states should implement modern Islamist interpretations of *sharia* to consolidate their authority and legitimacy. Islamist women also assert that you cannot have both Islam and human rights.

All gender reform movements have varying degrees of public advocacy for ideological and political change. Islamist women, for example, take an active public role in promoting the sanctity of the family as constructed in classical Islamic thought. Their focus on ritual and liturgy is only an extension of the way these were constructed and handed down to them by male thinkers and policymakers. Islamist women promote privacy and modesty for the Muslim woman, like the right to choose to wear *hijab* or *niqab* (head and face covering), but they do so in a very public way.

Islamist women defer to an ideal Islam which is wholly contrived in modernity: it maintains strict male privilege, and the instrument of implementation is the nation state. There is little reconciliation between notions of international campaigns for universal human rights, constitutional equality and the primacy of the fabricated, quasi-nostalgic notion of an ideal Islam. In fact, to interrogate too vigorously upon the constituent parts of this ideal Islam is tantamount to disbelief. There can be nothing superior or equivalent to this Islam because supremacy belongs only to Allah the Creator. That Allah does not construct religion or religious responses to the divine order is largely inconceivable. At best, the architects of classical Islamic thought – all of them male – are the exclusive authorities on how Islam is meant to be understood, practiced, and believed in.

During the Beijing meetings, when the large number of Muslim women attendees tried to consolidate their efforts, they were unsuccessful. Nightly meetings turned into shouting matches between these secular Muslim feminists and Islamists. Because they agreed you cannot have both Islam and human rights, a third group on the fringes would grow to became more coherent in the following decade. This third group was the origin of Islamic feminism. Islamic feminism contests the formula that says you cannot have both Islam and human rights by constructing its own definitions of human rights and its own definitions of Islam. While definitions of human rights were already prominent by postcolonial thinkers and activists, including Muslims, no one had contended with the problematic constructions of 'Islam' to the full extent that it would become necessary and integral to Islamic feminism.

READING FOR GENDER IN THE QUR'AN: ISLAMIC FEMINISM'S KNOWLEDGE-BUILDING PROJECT

Keeping in mind that all these women's reform movements have effected positive change in the well-being of Muslim women, the distinctions I draw here are not meant as a critique of the potential all movements have shown. However, since both secular Muslim feminists and Islamists agree that Islam and human rights are mutually exclusive, a new framework in which Islam and human rights can inform one another is needed. Islamic feminism provides that framework, unmediated by the history of male-dominated assumptions and interpretations, through gender-inclusive analysis of the Qur'an. This direct engagement with the Qur'an, and the creation of new traditions of interpretation founded on egalitarian principles, is what I call Islamic feminism's knowledge-building project.

Islamic feminism's knowledge-building project aligns with other feminisms in maintaining the radical idea that women are human beings. It then develops its own ideas about the meaning of the human being by rigorous interrogation of how Islam is constructed. By looking through an egalitarian lens at Islamic thought, the basis of the Islamic feminist project is a definition of the human being premised upon fundamental equality and reciprocity. These premises are derived from Islamic primary sources – especially the Qur'an – in tandem with the lived realties of Muslim women across the globe.

As a knowledge-building project, Islamic feminism takes full agency in defining all principles, precepts, values and realities in accordance with the strength of those principles and values to enhance the quality of life and integrated human well-being. The definitions espoused by Islamic feminism may be the same as, distinct from, or interrelated with definitions proposed over time and place for any number of knowledge-building projects. There is no single line of agreement or disagreement between Islamic feminism and classical Islamic intellectualism. There is the principal assertion that every generation of Muslims, and every location of Islamic peoples, must construct its own definitions and indicate the rationale ('illa) for their definitions, providing a coherent analysis of the relationship found between these constructions and the Islamic primary sources of the Qur'an, *ahadith* (sing. hadith), Sunna and *fiqh*. For Islamic feminism, the use of Islamic primary sources is foundational to the knowledge-building project, with the caveat that critical reading for gender as a category of thought is fundamental to how we interpret those sources.

One of the most exciting components to the construction of knowledge in Islamic feminism is respecting that, like the word 'human', the word 'Islam' is used in diverse ways and with multiple meanings. In fact, the word 'Islam' becomes meaningless without understanding the basis of the definitions. All Muslim reform movements seek legitimacy in their claims by referring back to the Qur'an. This is no different with today's reform. In the case of Islamic feminism, a part of reform Islam, reading for gender in the Qur'an heralded a new hermeneutical framework in Qur'anic exegesis. It could be said that *Qur'an and Woman: Re-reading the Sacred Text from a Woman's Perspective* was pivotal at the start of the Islamic feminist movement. Before that publication, using the Qur'an and its interpretation as the foundation to gender equality was largely unknown.

What does it mean to read for gender in the Qur'an? It does not mean to only read what the Qur'an says about women – although clearly, that is important. Rather, it means to read before the text, behind the text as well as **through** the text to determine rhetorical devices of hegemony and their power assertions along gender lines. It means to deconstruct gender binaries wherever they occur, and to construct a rubric of understanding for *musawah* (horizontal reciprocity). Reading for musawah means that every passage is read for its potential to address both men and women, interchangeably. This kind of reading takes into consideration the integrity of the sentence structurally, rhetorically and spiritually, to avoid creating and maintaining gender biases for either males or females. It is based on a syllogism that says woman is to man as man is to woman. If the logic of the linguistic construct fails, then possibilities of unequal treatment prevail. However, the question of ontological merit may not be usurped because the basic notion of a human being who is *khalifa* – a moral agent – is inclusive.

Islamic feminist knowledge construction builds a critical re-reading of sacred texts, their exegesis, and their implementation in policy and jurisprudence, and then applies these to the lived realities, especially of Muslim women. In contrast to atomistic approaches to Qur'anic exegesis (*tafsir*) – that is, the interpretation of individual words, short phrases, or single sentences in isolation from the whole text, and without regard to historical context – gender reading of the Qur'an builds modes of understanding and application based upon the guiding principles and values of the Qur'an in conversation, sometimes over and above the literal utterances.

The most significant concept for analysis in a gender-informed exegesis is justice. However, the definition of justice is drawn from a direct interrogation of the Qur'an read through the lived realties of women. Thus it circumvents centuries of defining justice for women as some kind of benevolence on the part of men. Justice cannot be owed from another person; it is fundamentally from God, and to God it will be returned for judgment. Given the idea of equality between all human beings, Islamic feminism – unlike both secular feminism and Islamism – does not see Islam and human rights as irreconcilable, and so it can promote the full principles of the UN Convention on the Elimination of All Forms of Discrimination Against Women (CEDAW).

For Islamic feminism to be effective in the context of the nation state, it must align with the mechanisms for effecting reforms within the state. The state – a member of the United Nations – becomes the primary channel for advocating for reforms. All states are also simultaneously in conversation with international bodies, like the UN, and are invited to become signatory to all UN conventions. The state is the primary means for achieving the goals laid out in those conventions. Although almost all Muslim majority nation states have signed CEDAW, they also propose certain reservations against some of the articles, asserting that these would go against 'Islam.' Showing how all definitions of Islam are constructed, Islamic feminists contest the reservations as merely extensions of the patriarchal privilege, and not divine.

TAWHID (THE UNICITY OF ALLAH) AS A PARADIGM FOR GENDER EQUALITY AND SOCIAL JUSTICE

Musawah (horizontal reciprocity) is built upon a direct analysis of *tawhid* (the unicity of Allah, i.e. monotheism) in the Qur'an. The tawhidic paradigm is fundamental to the work of Islamic feminism. Starting with the Quranic conversations about cosmology and eschatology to show all humans were created equal and will equally be held accountable on the Day of Judgment, we then bring together the idea of one God to issues of social justice, including gender equality.

Tawhid is the umbrella term which encompasses the world, the place where we really live. As the notion of *tawhid* has complete consensus, it is in its application to social communities that we get the most currency. St. Augustine said, 'imagine . . . that God is a circle. The centre of which is everywhere, the circumference of which is nowhere.' The world is not two-dimensional, so imagine the circles as a sphere. God is everywhere and nowhere, all at the same time. In Eastern traditions when they talk about the yin and the yang they are talking about the relationship between two forces. This is a harmonious relationship, including the fact that there's a bit of each in each other. Furthermore, it is dynamic, not static.

With *tawhid* we build upon the idea that Allah is one – *qul huwa allahu ahad* ('Say: He is Allah the One,' or 'Say: Allah is One;' Q 112:1), that Allah is united – *la ilah ill-allah* ('There is no god but God'), and that Allah is unique – *laysa ka mithlihi shay'* ('There is nothing like Him;' Q 42:11) to demonstrate how Allah unites. Coincidentally, *min kulli shay'in khalaqna zawjayn* means 'from all things we created pairs' (Q 51:49). As I explain in *Men in Charge*:

> It is thus impossible for Allah to have gender. He is not male. She is not female. Gender is a social construct often ascribed to the biological sex of animals, plants and women and men. In uniqueness, Allah, the Creator, cannot be subjected to any such created ascription . . . Thus female and male are part of the paired system in the created world while Allah, the Creator, is not subject to the conditions and limitations of creation and thus cannot have gender. (*Men in Charge*, p. 266)

In all of my research into Islamic sources, I noticed that the main corpus worked under an understanding of Allah as the highest focal point, metaphysically, with a single arrow directed from Allah to the male and then to the female. Sometimes this conversation is very aesthetic, including analogies with the pen and the tablet or with the heavens and the earth. The pen cannot write if it doesn't have the tablet. Whatever the heavens let down, the earth must pick up. Still there's a single direction from God to the male, or the active principle, like the yang; then from male to female, the receptive principle, like the yin. I found this problematic.

The most problematic part is that such a construction separates the female from a direct and unmitigated relationship to Allah. Such a conception contradicts the basic understanding confirmed throughout the Qur'an and corroborated by centuries of intellectual traditions that there is no intermediary between each created human being and her or his Creator. When I began to toy with this idea, I realized that the construct itself was not working and we needed a new construct. That is how I came up with the tawhidic paradigm, which allows for both the male and female to have a reciprocal relationship with God that is direct and unmediated. Because in this construct, we still consider Allah the highest focal point, as One and Unique but as a consequence of giving both the male and the female direct access to Allah, then there can be no relationship between the male and the female except on a line of horizontal reciprocity. That line of horizontal reciprocity is *musawah*: equality based on reciprocity, not complementarity and not subjectivity. Thus, *tawhid* becomes the basis for gender equality.

The next and most important step is how to implement musawah in practical terms, first by unpacking the many ways in which hegemonic relationships between women and men have been encoded in the law and promoted in Muslim cultures. The critical work of Musawah demonstrates how two terms have been built into an entire system undergirding all patriarchal practices and attitudes and requiring women to be protected and maintained by men. The terms express the interrelated ideas of male guardianship over female family members (*wilaya*) and of the husband's authority over, and financial responsibility towards, his wife (*qiwama*).

Omaima Abou Bakr gives the genealogy of *qiwama*, showing the path it took to be made into a construct. She asks the critical question that underlies the knowledge-building project of Musawah: 'How exactly did the Qur'anic sentence "*al-rijal qawwamun 'ala al-nisa' bima faddala allah ba'dahum 'ala ba'd wa bima anfaqu min amwalihim*" – which is part of the larger verse Q 4:34, in its turn part of a larger passage, and part of a larger structure of governing principles – become an independent and separate (transcontextual) patriarchal construct?'[3] The term *qiwama* does not appear in the Qur'an; it is derived from the Qur'anic term *qawwamun* – a descriptive term – which exegetes and jurists transformed into a prescriptive concept called *qiyam* and later *qiwama*. Once having created the prescriptive concept of *qiwama*, they treated it as if it were original to the Qur'an. But it was not. This emerging concept was then consolidated into a general precept with justifications as if it were a divinely ordained preference with authority. Eventually, scientific 'facts' drawn from other fields of knowledge (e.g. social sciences, medicine) were added to corroborate the existing ideas of the exegetes about gender difference.

Once we understand the way that the concept of *qiwama* was constructed over time by human beings, founded upon atomistic and highly tendentious readings of the Qur'an, we can choose to construct an interpretive tradition that is shaped by the tawhidic paradigm and founded upon the relationship of equality and reciprocity – *musawah* – that is also fundamentally present in the Quran (*wa ja'ala baynakum mawadda wa-rahma*): 'We made between you love and loving intimacy and mercy (or compassion)' (Q 30:21). But the jurists did not choose to build their notions of personal status law on that concept; they chose to build it on *qiwama*, and therefore they began to inflate the meaning of *qiwama* and then to fix it as if it was required and divine.

Tawhid is a rubric not only of an affirmation of belief in Allah, but also the integration of that belief into your relationships with other human beings on the planet. Not just your relationships with people who are like you; not just your relationships of men to men; not just your relationships of Muslim to Muslim – but relationships of each human being to each human being. We engage *tawhid* as a fail-safe test of whether or not the

---

[3] Omaima Abou-Bakr, 'The Interpretive Legacy of *Qiwamah* as an Exegetical Construct,' pp. 44–64.

value of the life of every *khalifa* is considered equal, and also to ask what that equality means in actual practice in terms of constructing political systems, family systems, and international relations. From this position we can now form a different concept of justice. Just as *qiwama* and *wilaya* were constructed over time and on the basis of particular assumptions and understandings bounded by time and place, so too is the concept of justice dynamic.

In the process of constructing our communities and belief systems – an ongoing process – we encoded fundamentally different notions of what it means to be a human being, notions in which some human beings are not fully equal, as in the case of slavery and its practice in Muslim hands, or in which women are considered to be under the dominion of men. The concept of justice developed in this context was one of benevolence, and certain people were extended this benevolence from those who were considered to be fully human agents – i.e. free male Muslims – to those who were not considered to be fully human agents – i.e. women, children, slaves, enemies.

The concept of justice that follows from the tawhidic paradigm is founded upon the direct relationship of every human being to their Creator, which means a concept of justice that assumes the basic equality of every human being. In this context, we must grapple with the real-life formations of actual families, actual communities, governments, and relationships at the international level in order to create a political system that will allow every individual to fulfill their *khalifa* – that is, the capacity to live within the cosmic order of the universe, and therefore be in surrender to Allah. And grappling with these real-life formations means that they must stand up to the fail-safe test by comparing whether or not *tawhid* manifests in the realities for Muslim women and the well-being of women. We do this by using life stories to show a disjuncture between the conventional representation of justice and reciprocal justice and well-being in women's lives.

WOMEN'S LIVED REALITIES AS A
PRINCIPLE FOR EXEGESIS

The implementation of Muslim personal status law in many Muslim communities – majority or minority – is irredeemably patriarchal. Musawah organizers understand that the representatives of different countries prioritize their most pressing needs, and we develop multiple strategies within a nation-state context. National constitutions and Muslim personal status laws are not aligned. Internationally we work with the United Nations through CEDAW, which most Muslim countries have signed, but which they have not fully embraced. Reservations to CEDAW by Muslim countries are based on static and yet diverse notions of Islam, but all of these notions are fundamentally patriarchal. We use CEDAW as an instrument to hold nations accountable with reports.

When we juxtapose these reports to women's lived reality, we can demonstrate that women are not actually experiencing the justice that everybody says is fundamental to Islam. We provide an evidentiary basis for saying there is something wrong, and then we use alternative interpretations grounded in the tawhidic paradigm to challenge when the government claims that a solution is not possible because that is not Islam.

It should be no surprise then that the interpretations of men, with long-standing patriarchal privilege, are soon aligned with 'Islam' and (even) Allah. If we do not interrogate the postulates of the patriarchal trajectory on what is Islam, what does the Qur'an say, and what does Allah mean, we might become complacent towards existing patriarchal standards, and eventually all 'authority' will be assigned to these dominant interpretations. Therefore we recommend a democratization of authority where the experience of believers comes into dialogue with policies and practices. We begin the process of democratizing authority by reading through the text with its own principles as guidance. One major marker of our capacity to read is *lived* reality.

Traditionally, women's lived realities had very little to do with the formulation of foundational canon, and worldview. However, Islamic feminism starts with the proposition that the experiences of women matter for how we read, understand and apply the Qur'an, for how we form families, and for how we adjudicate those families in Muslim personal status law, as well as for how we form societies or political systems and governments. Thus, women need to be present with their experiences to test whether or not those systems are inclusive of their well-being. We advocate that you can have both Islam and human rights as long as you step back and understand that defining them both belongs to all who will be impacted by those definitions.

Islamic feminism challenges the patriarchal status quo by insisting that there is no passive receiving of a fixed definition from someone if you have not also participated in the construction of that idea. The democratization of authority, which is grounded in the tawhidic paradigm, provides an alternative universal understanding of human rights from an Islamic perspective. So one of the primary features of Islamic feminism is the recognition that Islamic primary sources are still crucial to the articulation of justice and dignity for Muslim women, but that women did not participate equally in the construction of what we consider to be fundamental to Islam. We correct that lack of women's participation in the construction of conventional Islam, not only by engaging gender as a category of thought, as we discussed earlier, but by using the lived realities of women to test whether any specific law, policy, or cultural attitude achieves justice in women's lives.

The knowledge-building project of Musawah demonstrates how this method is used. The conclusion is overwhelming: statistical and anecdotal evidence ('illa) shows that Muslim women are **not** experiencing justice and well-being in their lives, despite adhering to what has heretofore been dubbed 'divine.' We highlight the wide disjuncture between proposed, that is theoretical models of ideal family, and the lived realities of women, by asking fundamental questions. How is it that the foundational jurists chose qiwama and wilaya to be the cornerstone of all relations between women and men? How did they inculcate the ideas of women's subservience to men and men's domination over women? Why is hierarchy as male authority assumed to be normative – even divinely sanctioned? Why did they not choose Qur'anic passages of equality and reciprocity to enshrine gender relations on a more egalitarian basis? Furthermore, can it be done now? If so, how?

In Musawah workshops we teach critical reading to activists as part of how we seek to empower them to read for themselves. Together we use an exegetical method that uses the lived realities of Muslim women in diverse circumstances globally to determine the full meaning and application of the text. The construction of an egalitarian perspective for Muslim society is built upon a dynamic relationship between text, context and pretext. Nasr Abu Zayd proposes a multidimensional worldview of the Qur'an, with cosmology,[4] human/divine relations, ethical, moral and societal issues, and punishment – all connected – to understand gender and gender relations. When cosmology and the ethical moral are inclusive and egalitarian, but the relations and societal location of gender is hegemonic, there is a disjunction that needs to be rectified towards the higher ideal found in the cosmology and ethics. We therefore contest the notion of a merciful and compassionate God/Allah as mandating unjust treatment and calling it Islam. Can there be justice if women do not experience it?

BIBLIOGRAPHY

Abou El Fadl, Khaled. *Speaking in God's Name: Islamic law, Authority and Women.* (Oxford: Oneworld, 2001)

Abou-Bakr, Omaima. 'The Interpretive Legacy of *Qiwamah* as an Exegetical Construct.' In *Men in Charge? Rethinking Authority in Muslim Legal Tradition.* Ed. Ziba Mir-Hosseini, Mulki Al-Sharmani and Jana Rumminger, 44–64. (London: Oneworld, 2015)

Abu Zayd, Nasr Hamid. 'Islamic Cosmology and Qur'anic Exegesis.' In *Religion Wandel der Kosmologien.* Ed. Dieter Zeller, 217–30. (Sonderdruck: Peter Lang, 1999)

Committee on the Elimination of All Forms of Discrimination against Women (CEDAW) [Online] (http://www.un.org/womenwatch/daw/cedaw/cedaw.htm). (Accessed December 11, 2018)

Mir-Hosseini, Ziba, Mulki Al-Sharmani and Jana Rumminger (eds). *Men in Charge? Rethinking Authority in Muslim Legal Tradition.* (London: Oneworld, 2015)

Wadud, Amina. 'The Ethics of *Tawhid* over the Ethics of *Qiwamah.'* In *Men in Charge? Rethinking Authority in Muslim Legal Tradition.* Ed. Ziba Mir-Hosseini, Mulki Al-Sharmani and Jana Rumminger, 256–74. (London: Oneworld, 2015)

— *Qur'an and Woman: Re-Reading the Sacred Text from a Woman's Perspective.* (New York: Oxford University Press, 1999)

---

[4] Abu Zayd, 'Islamic Cosmology and Qur'anic Exegesis.'

Chapter 5

The Reception of the Qur'an in the LGBTQ Muslim Community

Scott Siraj al-Haqq Kugle, Emory University

If you grasp the well-hidden fact that there is a community of lesbian, gay, bisexual and transgender Muslims, it may still surprise you that many in this community value the Qur'an enough to receive it, recite it, and struggle to interpret its meaning against the grain of hegemonic tradition. They often identify with the general label 'queer', a term of rebellious pride that they appropriated from its former use as a denunciation of anything diverging from 'normal'. Thus the label LGBTQ has come into being. This chapter presents a sketch of LGBTQ Muslim engagement with the Qur'an, highlighting their commonalities – despite the diversity in their gender or sexuality – documenting their emergence as a new Muslim community, and pointing to more scholarly resources about them.

The chapter contains interviews with five members of this community – of varied ethnicity, national origin, and doctrinal affiliation – who are linked through a global network. It uses the term 'queer Muslim' because many of those interviewed use this identifier, which is easier to say and read than LGBTQ. The interviews emphasize how a religion that does not focus on the lived experience of real people, especially those who struggle against marginalization and injustice, is not a religion of compassion. This insight conveys principles that Queer Muslims find essential to engaging the Qur'an: (a) realistic assessment of social life, (b) affirmation of deep diversity in creation (see definition below), (c) protection of human dignity, (d) adherence to justice, (e) and insistence on care and compassion as the foundation of Islam.

LGBTQ MUSLIMS: AN EMERGING COMMUNITY

Queer Muslims are an emerging community, not an established one. Queer Muslim is not an exclusive but rather an additive identity; they come from Shia, Ismaili, Sunni, Salafi and Sufi backgrounds. Not defined by dogma or ritual, Queer Muslims are defined by their disempowered position in patriarchal society. They form a community to resist oppression that is woven deep into the fabric of their lives, both in religious and secular environments. Their existence is precarious and their presence is perceived as a sin in families and religious communities. As Queer Muslims find ways to emerge from this suppression and speak in their own voices, they form a new community at once vulnerable and vibrant, sometimes organic and sometimes intentional, a community focused mainly on internal support, but sometimes expressing protest. I have argued elsewhere that theirs is 'deep diversity in a condition of dispersity unified by adversity while resisting the stigma of perversity.' Let us unpack this statement.

No single sketch can capture the 'deep diversity' of Queer Muslims – people defined by difference in sexual orientation and gender identity.[1] Interviews, life histories and clinical studies demonstrate that Queer people do not chose to be lesbian, gay, bisexual or transgender. Their sexual orientation and gender identity arise from beyond rational choice and control (much like that of 'straight people').[2] For this reason, the

---

[1] In contemporary social scientific and human rights literature, 'difference in sexual orientation and gender identity' is often labeled SOGI. These terms come from clinical psychiatry, sociology and human rights discourse – see Kugle, *Living Out Islam*, pp. 13–20 and Habib, *Female Homosexuality*, pp. 23–44.

[2] Diversity in sexual orientation and gender identity may arise from genetic imprint, prenatal hormonal exposure, infantile experience or childhood social environment, or a potent combination of these factors; many LGBTQ scholars argue that searching for causes – either biomedical or social – is misguided and fuels homophobia, the irrational fear of alternative sexualities and their spread.

contemporary diagnostic manual for psychiatrists and social workers does not list homosexuality or transgender behavior as a disease. People can try to control their behavior in society, but they cannot change their internal psychic disposition; attempting to 'control' behavior through repression often leads to severe consequences, such as self-loathing, destructive behavior, uncontrolled rage, depression, anxiety, despair and suicide. These psychic problems are caused by society's marginalization of people because of their orientation or identity, not by their orientation or identity itself.[3]

Queer Muslims are an invisible disempowered minority, whose existential condition is of 'dispersity.' They are a small minority that cannot rely on family resources, mainstream religious communities or local custom to protect them. They are 'different' in psyche, identity and behavior, rather than in body structure or phenotype; they are often isolated or grow up feeling that they are 'the only one' who cannot conform to the expectations of parents, pressure of peers, and preaching of religion. This isolation is the result of society's fear of LGBTQ persons and the constant potential that they will appear in families and communities. This fear is concretized in moral policing, perpetual stigma and violent rhetoric linked to family honor, national pride and religious rectitude. Yet Queer Muslims are increasingly uniting against this 'adversity.' They have always been part of Muslim communities and have deep roots in Islamic history, back to the Prophet's own household in Medina; armed with this knowledge, they resist the 'stigma of perversity' through which mainstream Muslim leaders marginalize them. Queer Muslims are not a Western import, even if they increasingly use clinical terms that originate in the West to describe themselves, terms which gain authority through globalization. Queer Muslims are not necessarily harmful to society or religion; in fact, they play important social roles as caretakers, healers, educators, advocates, artists and performers. They take refuge in human rights discourse, which is part of secular governance, as well as secular citizenship, national constitutions,

---

[3] For example, the Church of England's General Synod recently voted overwhelmingly to ban conversion therapy: https://www.churchofengland.org/more/media-centre/news/general-synod-backs-ban-conversion-therapy

and UN resolutions; but this does not mean that they reject religion, spirituality and faith.[4]

RELIGIOUS ORIENTATION OF LGBTQ MUSLIMS

Queer Muslims engage the Qur'an as 'an interpretive community.' Some suggest that interpretive communities are either 'textual' or 'experiential' in orientation. Leaders of the Sunni tradition, and its main opposition in the Twelver Shia tradition, both claim a venerable 'textual' tradition. Other communities that are based on oral tradition or personal experience are relegated to being 'experiential,' and dismissed altogether. This posited bifurcation between 'textual' and 'experiential' is misleading. In 'textual' traditions, the experiences of patriarchal, aristocratic, slave-owning men have been thoroughly textualized in the remote past.[5] Thus the experiential views of elite men, which are necessarily partial and partisan, are accepted as normal and natural, rather than being recognized as the experience of certain men with a will-to-power and access to the tools of domination.

Queer Muslims do not have a long-established textual tradition of the Qur'an interpretation to mediate between themselves and scripture. Queer Muslims are part of the Islamic feminist movement; even if they are not women, they adopt the methodology of feminist critical reflection.[6] Queer Muslims form an interpretive community to voice their own

---

[4] Hamzic, *Sexual and Gender Diversity*, pp. 18–33 documents how sexual orientation and gender identity concepts gain traction in international human rights discourse, and the conservative Islamic reaction to this.

[5] Ahmed, *Women and Gender in Islam*, pp. 79–101.

[6] Hidayatullah, *Feminist Edges of the Qur'an*, pp. 65–124 gives a good overview of Islamic feminist interpretation of the Qur'an. Shaikh, 'Islamic Feminism,' pp. 147–63 gives a clearer reading of the ideals and imperatives of Islamic feminism. Advocating justice and equality for women is the foundation for any lesbian, gay, bisexual or transgender claim to recognition and rights. Yet, Queer Muslims assert that social, economic and political equality for women require the very nature of sexuality and gender to be interrogated, and a simplistic binary must be abandoned if religion is to be based upon a realistic assessment of human nature and sociality. Amina Wadud advocates this approach for the Islamic feminist movement to make space for Queer Muslims; see Wadud, *Inside the Gender Jihad*, pp. 177–86.

experiences – speaking in private, announcing in public, writing life stories, engaging journalistic discussions, and expressing through the arts – and to take this voice into the arena of debate with the Islamic theological traditions.

Raising the Qur'an above other kinds of texts – above hadith reports and legal decisions of *fiqh* – is a basic strategy of reform.[7] From the Qur'an, Queer Muslims extract the ideal principles of justice, equality, deep diversity within God's creation, compassion and care, love and intimacy, and entrusting God alone to judge. Some Queer Muslims do this intuitively based on their own experience, while others do it textually referring to scholarly and reformist writings. Mainstream religious leaders often describe them as 'diseased' using metaphors of viral contagion, criminal conspiracy, or apocalyptic disaster.[8] Faced with condemnation, it is not surprising that Queer Muslims see themselves reflected in the Qur'an's invocation of 'the downtrodden' (*mustad'afun fi l-ard*), meaning those oppressed and driven underground (see Q 4:75, 127; 8:126; 28:5 and 34:31).[9]

DIVERSE LIVES OF LGBTQ MUSLIMS

Queer Muslims constitute an interpretive community despite highly varied life paths, where they have received religious education as children in different communities. The best way to show their engagement with the

---

[7] Many Queer Muslims sympathize with modernist Islamic reformers, like Fazlur Rahman or Ustad Mahmoud Taha, who articulate the difference between universal ideals and limited compromises in the Qur'an, arguing that the compromises must evolve and grow based upon the ideals as the social conditions of society change.

[8] Kugle and Hunt, 'Masculinity, Homosexuality and the Defense of Islam.' Such statements are made by Islamic leaders in Arab or Muslim-majority countries, and also made by members of 'respectable organizations' in the USA, such as the Islamic Society of North America. The organization's former president, Muzammil Siddiqi, has said: 'Homosexuality is a moral disorder. It is a moral disease, a sin and corruption. No person is born homosexual, just like no one is born a thief, a liar or murderer. People acquire these evil habits due to a lack of proper guidance and education.' Cited from MSNBC News Online: www.nbcnews.com/id/44993807/ns/us_ news-life/t/battling-gay-rights-allahs-name/ (accessed June 10, 2017).

[9] Kugle, *Homosexuality in Islam*, pp. 35–9; see also, Rahemtulla, *Qur'an of the Oppressed*, and Barlas, *Believing Women in Islam*.

Qur'an is through life stories. This chapter presents five interviews, conducted in 2016, with Queer Muslims from diverse backgrounds, though all interviewed come from Sunni backgrounds.[10] The chapter distills some insights and strategies that are common to those interviewed, reinforced by earlier interviews I conducted for my 2014 book, *Living Out Islam*. Some of those interviewed use pseudonyms to protect their security and their families.

Hanif

Hanif is a convert to Islam in his late twenties, now pursuing a PhD in Islamic Studies. He is ethnically 'white' and from the Midwest, in the USA. As a budding linguist, Hanif was attracted first to the power of Arabic language and then to the beauty of Qur'anic recitation. He recalls, 'The love of language came first, before adopting Islam.'[11] As he read the Qur'an in translation with a Muslim friend, he found his beliefs changing, for he was forming a new religious worldview:

> It was the Abraham story that really got me thinking. It says that the Christians insist that you become Christian to be guided and the Jews insist you must be Jewish, but then all the Prophet asked of you was to submit to this one God. Then there is the story of Abraham being the original monotheist and it uses the word *Hanif* there, to describe Abraham.[12] So that is the word I chose for my own name.

The Qur'an helped Hanif resolve theological questions that disturbed him. 'I was raised Christian in Greek Orthodoxy. I was very much in love with the ritual of the church but . . . I had doubts about Jesus being God – that was really a problem for me. I guess that is a typical problem for Christian converts!' he said, laughing at himself. Because he valued the spirituality

---

[10] A larger study would include interviews from people in Shia, Ismaili, Bohra, Ahmadi, the Nation of Islam and other communities. There is greater pressure on Queer Muslims from smaller communities to keep silent to protect their minority community from external criticism, as they are already under pressure from Sunni, Salafi and other more dominant groups.
[11] All quotations of Hanif are from a personal interview on November 26, 2016.
[12] Hanif refers to Q 2:135.

and ritual of the Orthodox Church, Hanif searched for a worship community with whom to pray.

He joined an Islamic Center, whose members were mainly from Saudi Arabia and dedicated their time to teach him proper recitation. When he asked the practical meaning of the Qur'an itself, their answers amounted to a stark, rules-oriented morality which ignored the ambiguity, poetry and high rhetoric of the Qur'an. Hanif's love for language, recitation and ritual coexisted in a tenuous balance with the hard Salafi piety of his adopted community.[13] Deep friendships were formed, but over a few years Hanif grew unsettled. He slowly realized that his sexual orientation would be highly problematic in his new community:

> I was very much in denial, but I was aware of my attractions that were problematic to the orientation of the Islamic community that I was a part of ... I was a part of this community for a good three years before I really came out to anybody ... being closeted like that became spiritually suffocating – trying to fit myself into this very strict interpretation of what I was supposed to be.

Hanif admits that he fell into a strategy of repression, avoiding the moral problem of being gay by concentrating on being 'a good Muslim.' The Qur'an was both solace and provocation in his spiritual growth:

> There were those verses that I kept stumbling upon, the verses referring to Prophet Lot and Sodom and Gomorrah. That was a constant hang-up for me. But at the same time there was such a sense of spirituality to just sit with the Qur'an and recite it, to memorize it and recite it during prayers. Pushing the Qur'an aside was never something that I considered, because it gave me peace. But there were still these verses that I stumbled over ... [Yet] there are verses that occur

---

[13] Salafi refers to the modern Islamic conservative reformist movement that rejects medieval interpretation, mystical tradition, and progressive understandings; the Salafi movement accepts only literalist understandings of the Quran and unquestioning conformity to hadith as true and authentic Islam. The Wahhabi movement represents a militant and extreme form of Salafi belief.

several times which say that God created the heavens and the earth and everything in between them, or which show the ambiguity between daytime and night-time. There are those parts of the Qur'an that gave me peace, as if there is a place for me somewhere in the Qur'an, a place of ambiguity even if I do not fit in these boxes that I'm supposed to fit in.

His cognitive dissonance built up to the point that Hanif decided to speak with a respected elder who occasionally gave Friday sermons: 'I thought he would be more open and compassionate, but he said, "This is a disease and this is not natural. There are people you can go to talk about this and try to fix whatever is wrong with you." ' The elder said that some sort of 'ex-gay' therapy was required, using a strategy that many Islamic leaders adopt from fundamentalist Christian churches in the USA:

We met a few times to talk, but when it became clear that I was not going down that route then he felt that my presence in the mosque was going to be a problem for everybody . . . Through him, a lot of members of the community found out about me and it was really no longer comfortable for me to go there . . . He did not keep confidentiality because he thought that the safety of the community was at stake.

As rumor about Hanif's sexuality spread through his mosque community, some members organized an intervention, silencing the elder while confronting Hanif. They argued that his homosexuality was a test and trial for him by God, and that he must struggle to change his psyche through prayer and fasting. In his gut, Hanif knew that this 'cure' was unrealistic:

I felt very much alone, because the community was so very important to me. There were a few friends who stuck by me . . . But it still felt lonely . . . I was wanting to be there and pray with everyone and hear the Qur'an, but not wanting to talk with anyone because I knew that people just wanted to corner me. I was really afraid that people would corner me in the hallway and say, 'Well, I heard this about you – is it true?'

From these depths of alienation, Hanif began to write and to reach out to others. He started a blog in which he posted his reflections and poetry. Poetry he found to be 'a genre of expression that really helped me more creatively deal with faith in a way that journal writing or talking with people just didn't. I began [my blog] about a year after the fiasco of being outed.' His poetry often incorporates images or quotations from the Qur'an (a rhetorical style called *iqtibas* in Arabic literature):[14]

> Often, I'm surprised how a certain verse will come to me when I'm writing. I don't sit down to explain what I think about a certain verse – it is not a self-conscious *tafsir*. Rather I have a thought or feeling that I'm writing about and then a verse will just come to me. I've been thinking about this embodied *tafsir*, or what Sa'diyya Shaikh calls 'tafsir of praxis.' I think embodied is the right word. I don't think many people in the West easily consider the embodied aspects of scripture. The first time I interacted with the text was in translation, but once I reverted [by this, Hanif means 'converted to Islam'] I was introduced into an entire tradition of relating to the text: reciting, memorization, the sound of the Arabic, how one prostrates at the end of some verses. The Qur'an is a text you touch with your hands – granted, you're in a state of purity – and recite on your tongue. This embodied experience becomes primary, and *tafsir* comes second. As a gay or queer man, this is also liberating. It allows me to feel my way into new ways of seeing a verse rather than taking someone else's interpretation based on their own experiences and biases.[15]

Writing poems helped Hanif appreciate how the Qur'an has deeper layers. By exploring these deeper levels, he hopes to get out of the dead-end interpretation offered by mainstream Muslim communities – especially the

---

[14] *Iqtibas* means weaving phrases from scripture into a literary composition in such a way that it plays a double signification: the phrase makes sense within the semantics of the composition while at the same time retaining its quality of being borrowed from scripture and pointing to divine presence in language. This literary device was common in medieval Arabic and Hebrew poetry, and is still used in American folk music.
[15] Shaikh, 'A Tafsir of Praxis.'

Salafi variety – to the verses about sexuality, gender identity and sexual orientation:

> Playing with language through poetry helped me to envision the possibility that the Qur'an has deeper and deeper layers of meaning. If I can play with language in this poetic way, then surely the Qur'an is poetic and there must be these deeper meanings. There are, even in unexpected places! Even with the story about Prophet Lot, one can imagine alternate possibilities and alternate readings of that story . . . I'm writing about whatever feelings or whatever experience I'm trying to describe and make sense of, like the feeling of anger at the idea that same-sex relationships are categorically *haram*, and being frustrated with that. [So I imagine] what would happen if I went on the *mi'raj*? What would I say to God? There is a hadith about Moses telling the Prophet Muhammad [during his *mi'raj*] to go back to his Lord and lessen the burden of prayers, requesting 'Not fifty times, please! Maybe just five?' How would I ask God to lessen the burden? It helps me to rethink my own struggle with those problematic verses. Even Moses was saying that fifty prayers are just too much – we are just human beings here! At the same time, queer people are just people and we should be given an equal playing field when it comes to sexuality and relationships and marriage and intimacy.

Hanif wonders, where is the Moses of today who can ask Muslim leaders if their assessment of human nature is realistic? If all human beings were created with desire for intimacy and sexual pleasure – which is both a weakness and a strength impelling us to live close to others in care and concern – then why can't Queer people also have the chance to live, love, partner and marry? This is Hanif's persistent question.

Hamida

Although Hamida comes from a family with roots in Nigeria and Liberia, her early experiences of Islam were similar to Hanif's. She also converted to Islam during university studies in the USA. She self-identifies as a black American Muslim queer woman, and is quick to add – 'I'm very happy with that.' Now in her forties, Hamida is a writer and theater artist, with training in conflict resolution and an advanced degree in counseling psychology and global mental health. She worked as a teacher in public school, at the UN, with GLSEN (the Gay Lesbian and Straight Education Network) and the Anti-Defamation League.[16] She recently married her partner: they now live together as a legally wedded same-sex couple and look forward to raising children together. Hamida also belongs to a Sufi order and leads *zikr*, which is Islamic meditation based on concentration through reciting the names of God.

In all these facets of her life, the Qur'an is the touchstone, motivator and constant friend. Her keen introspection, deep faith and spiritual reflection shine through the twinkle in her eye and her luminous smile. Many in the wider Queer Muslim community look to her as an advisor, guide and healer. She counsels Queer Muslims to put aside their fear of the Qur'an and engage with it as a kind of therapy:

> It is really important for Queer Muslims who are aiming to have a new relationship with the Qur'an to do that in community, to do that with others and not alone in your room. Because that multiplicity of perspectives adds some possibilities that would otherwise not be there. I think that is true for everyone, but especially so if you are trying to generate a new understanding.[17]

In her view, the Qur'an is not a rule book but rather a gathering place where people come together to improve themselves, increase in integrity, deepen in faith, and learn to care for each other more than just for oneself. It is not surprising, then, that the Qur'an first came to Hamida through friendships:

> I came to Islam when I was eighteen . . . through a friend of mine who was my boss at the college library. He had studied in Yemen. I

---

[16] The Gay Lesbian and Straight Education Network (GLSEN) is a national organization that strives to make K–12 schools safe and supportive for all with regard to sexual orientation, gender identity and gender expression (see www.glsen.org).

[17] All quotations of Hamida are from a personal interview on November 26, 2016.

met him just after he had come back and he had just such a glow about him . . . I began to learn the Qur'an through him. We would meet in the prayer room in the basement of the library where we worked . . . I remember getting my first Qur'an at the bookstore on campus . . . I wrote my name on the inside cover with the date and everything. I remember that as a very precious moment – a moment filled with awe.

As she adopted Islam, Hamida joined the campus MSA (Muslim Students Association). Despite its conservative and patriarchal leanings, she learned from her MSA community and its study circles:

We started with 'the Earthquake' [*Surat al-Zalzala*] . . . It touched me deeply, especially thinking about 'whosoever has done an atom's weight of good will see it' (Q 99:7). There is something about that which has continued to stay with me as I think about what it means in life to do even just an atom's weight of good. There are so many beautiful passages that stuck with me from that time. It was the first time I read all the way through the Qur'an, and I remember reading the beginning of the chapter called 'the Thunder' [*Surat al-Ra'd*] and its description of the earth and all the way that Allah directs the rain, the earth, the seed in the earth, everything at every level (Q 13:1– 10). Those first ten lines just stayed with me and really moved me quite a lot.

In the image of a diversity of plants growing from the earth, each bearing its distinctive fruits but all being nourished 'from one single water,' she found an awesome signifier for unity in diversity (Q 13:1–3). Those verses end with the Qur'anic endorsement of social activism: 'Surely God does not change the condition of a people until they change the relations between themselves within themselves' (Q 13:11).[18]

Hamida eventually left the MSA, whose understanding of the Qur'an was too shallow for her. She was aware of herself as a lesbian woman and a

---

[18] Wadud, *Qur'an and Woman*, p. 36.

Muslim, integral without division, and undertook to change her condition in life in hopes that God would bless her by changing the condition of society around her as a result. After college, Hamida found a Sufi community that nurtured a more open-ended understanding of the Qur'an – one linked much more to personal development and spiritual quest. She perceived that the Qur'an's every word has many levels of meaning limited only by one's egoistic distraction:

> What I've learned from being a *derwish* is that . . . the Qur'an has a multitude of layers to it that are in fact infinite . . . There is a mechanism in the depth of our vision that actually opens the Qur'an for us. That message is really powerful for me. The way that I hold the Qur'an now is that it is not an external book that I merely read and take in; rather, it is a quest to peel away the layers of my own self so that I can actually see it and receive it at a deeper level. That is the conversation that I am in with the Qur'an, asking how do I live in such a way that the depth of my seeing grows?

Hamida found a supportive community in her Sufi order where she is fully equal as a woman and quietly accepted as queer. The order does not court publicity about these mores of acceptance and has no formal policy about sexual orientation and gender identity.[19] It is about soul training rather than social norms: in soul training, everyone is equal and equally vulnerable to egoism. It gives Hamida a path to integrate the disparate elements of her life and her multiple identities – as a black woman in America, as a Muslim, as a lesbian, and as a healer.[20]

Not all queer Muslims find such a supportive community. It took strength of character for Hamida to search out such a community and she helped build it into the accepting community that it now is. Many queer

---

[19] Not all Sufi orders are accepting of LGBTQ members. Even those orders active in Europe and North America often uphold patriarchal values, sometimes in defensive mode so as not to attract criticism from mainstream Muslim communities.

[20] Hancock, *Intersectionality*, highlights how 'intersectionality' as an activist-intellectual concept emerged among black women feminists. To understand 'intersectionality' among queer Muslims, see Khalid and Yip, 'Looking for Allah.'

Muslims are desperate to find a Muslim community that is accepting and nurturing. Many feel abandoned or wounded by the Qur'an that is used against them as a weapon, not just by Islamic leaders but often by loved ones in their family.

For women, especially young women and gender queer or non-binary folks, the way that the Qur'an has been used to hurt them is very real – that is a very real experience. I don't have that experience so there is no way that at this point someone is going to take certain verses of the Qur'an and try to beat me with it . . . I don't experience any sort of the struggles that I think other people expect. I am not wrestling with the idea that 'there is no space for me here in this Qur'an.' I don't wrestle with any of that because I know that that is not the case. Being queer and Muslim means that I feel compelled to really stand with my face in relationship to the Qur'an with a certain strength that maybe other people [who are not queer] don't have to. Other people are constantly telling me that I don't have the right and because of that, the strength and the confidence with which I hold on to it must be more intense . . . I do think that queer people generally have to have a certain determination, if one is to do more than just survive or even just to survive. There is not much that one can take for granted when you're queer . . . because all of it is something that you've had to stand for. So I think that is an advantage in relationship to the Qur'an, because it means for me that I am willing and able – *inshallah* to some limited extent – to see with depth that not everyone necessarily has if they take things in life for granted. I cannot just say, 'Oh well, so and so told me that that is what it means – that is how it has been for generations in my family – we just believe that.' No, I have to decide for myself! . . . This Qur'an is in me and therefore I need to understand it for my own self – the self that other people tell me is wrong, but I know it's not wrong. So how do I understand myself in a true way? I can say that I chose Islam, even though I don't believe that on a finer level of things. But at a certain level, yes, that is the case. Because I chose it and because at the end of the day, every day I choose it again and again, I become free of the baggage that [burdens] people who take that choice for granted or feel that it was chosen for them. I don't have that. It allows me to be with Qur'an in a way that is a lot lighter than it is for other people.

As Hamida draws queer Muslims into a supportive community, she encounters many who are injured by family, community and religious leaders who justify their aggression through the Qur'an. It is very difficult to heal such psychic wounds, but Hamida is convinced that the Qur'an was revealed to heal and not to harm. For her, textual and experiential approaches to the Qur'an are integral.

Some queer Muslims avoid the Qur'an, based on traumas they have from betrayal and condemnation. Hamida encourages them to re-engage with it through an 'indirect approach'. The direct approach is to read the verses that address sexual morality (such as those about the prophet Lot, or fornication, or gender segregation) which are used against queer Muslims; even reading them to critique mainstream understandings and generate alternative interpretations can be traumatic for many. The indirect approach is to think 'Who is Allah?' and encounter God through the divine names (asma' allah al-husna), which are qualities of God such as 'the merciful One' or 'the forgiving One' or 'the wise One'. The Qur'an articulates these names which are woven into its discourse.

> I really believe that the names are a beautiful way to approach the Qur'an ... If you've had a wound that's come to you when people have hurt you with the Qur'an then you have to wonder, 'Who is Allah because I can't believe that Allah is this other thing that people have told me and have been using to hurt me – I don't believe that!' So the names are a way to begin to answer that question for yourself in a new and more tender way.[21]

---

[21] Lawrence, *Who is Allah?*, pp. 175–6. Hamida also refers to and advocates the book, Meyer, Hyde, Kahn, et al., *Physicians of the Heart*.

She recommends pondering God's names as an empowering way to think about one's relationship to God and how this relationship is activated through the Qur'an. She combines her professional expertise in social work and therapy with her talent for prayer, which together she calls 'energy work.'

In addition to helping individuals, she put her skills into a conscious-ness-raising project which reaches a much broader audience.[22] That project was a theater piece entitled 'Coming Out Muslim: Radical Acts of Love.' It is a two-woman show, co-written by Hamida and her colleague Wazina. Since 2011, the duo has performed all over the USA, telling stories about other people's theories of why LGBTQ people exist, about the gift of being queer and Muslim, about tensions between culture and religion, and about searching for love – both romantic and spiritual.

> I wanted the audience to actually hear the Qur'an in the show, so there is a moment when *Surat al-Zalzala* is recited. That is always a wonderful moment for me. Also, I really wanted to bring in the names, particularly for people who are in a conversation in which they hear, 'Oh well, God didn't make you queer so you must have chosen it yourself.' I really wanted to bring in the names that indicate creation – *Ya Bari, Ya Musawwir, Ya Khaliq* – the Fashioner, the Shaper, the Creator – even if the audience did not understand them.[23]

The judgments of others do not affect her intimate relation with the Qur'an, and through the Qur'an with God. We will be asked on Judgment Day, she concludes, about our own faith, sincerity and integrity – 'How does one hold one's own truth for oneself?' Hamida is content to hold her own vision of the Qur'an's healing power and not be swayed by those who are quick to judge based on shallow social distinctions.

---

[22] Hamida's co-author and co-star is Wazina, an Afghani-American lesbian who is a performer and educator. See the performance website: www.comingoutmuslim.com. A short feature on the piece is posted online: www.youtube.com/watch?v=htNGYJE6X84.

[23] Q 59:21.

Mehar

Mehar is a woman in her mid-forties, who grew up in a Pakistani family in the UK. She developed as a social worker with women who were victims of domestic abuse or rape. In midlife, she turned toward academic research and completed a PhD in Islamic Studies. Mehar is quiet and introverted with deep capacity for introspection and ethical insight.

Although she now values the Qur'an and how it deepens her capacity for creative faith, that piety came after a long internal struggle. In contrast to Hamida and Hanif, she did not choose the Qur'an – it was imposed upon her from childhood. Exclaiming, 'It was not my own choice at all!' she smiles and recollects:

> I was born into a beautifully conservative Muslim and culturally very traditional family. The Qur'an was always read in Arabic ... An immigrant teacher from our local community would teach children how to read [the Qur'an] with *qa'ida* [rules for recitation]. I learned how to read Arabic, but it was more by rote. I read the Qur'an in Arabic bit by bit by bit, but I had no connection with it. It was just something that you were expected to do.[24]

As a teenager, Mehar moved back to Pakistan just when she was maturing personally and sexually. There, Mehar's schooling included Islamic education in English, rather than rote memorization of Arabic, which gave the subject new depth to her:

> That is really when I opened up to a love of the divine and love of the Prophet. Initially there were discussions of different aspects of faith including how contexts of sacred revelations provide and shape meaning. But ultimately the way Islamic Studies was taught in Pakistan became appropriated by the state narrative – those were the days when General Zia ul-Haq was in power.[25] ... For women,

---

[24] All quotations of Mehar are from a personal interview on October 15, 2016.
[25] Saeed, *Politics of Desecularization*, pp. 145–50. General Zia ul-Haqq took power in 1978 in a coup, and then declared himself President of Pakistan, annulling the constitution and 'Islamizing' the legal and educational system; supported by the US government and Saudi

the state Islamic ideology was really about women being contained into particular forms of dress, modes of piety, and stipulated propriety . . . I did find it enlivening to be able to engage with the Qur'an on a personal basis, and to question whether this is the state's interpretation of religion or whether this is really what the Qur'an is telling me. That part was a bit of a wake-up call! Why is the state's narrative different from the one that I understand? Why is one man's witness considered equal to that of two women? How did that make logical sense in terms of the Qur'an's worldview? So for me, the most important part of studying in Pakistan was access to the Qur'an in ways that had not been available to me before. That was not the end of the story – in fact, it was actually the beginning of the story.

After finishing university in Pakistan, Mehar's family moved back to the UK. In her early thirties, she began to question her sexual orientation. Faced with the reality of being a lesbian in a Muslim family, she started to disengage from Islam. She constantly heard condemning messages from Islamic leaders, family members and religious texts:

I must admit that I was part of that belief system – I used to believe it was wrong to be gay! I thought, 'If I am who I am and the Qur'an tells us that it is wrong to be gay, then I need to disengage from recognizing myself as a Muslim.' That is the only logical conclusion I found myself reluctantly and fearfully arriving at, fearful because I was being confronted with letting go everything that held so much depth of meaning for me. My faith had been my existential scaffolding. I was very upset with God, angry and distressed. Yet I would constantly weep at the sound of the *azan*, and I was trying to figure out what that meant for me . . . I grew up listening to beautiful *na'at-khwans* (poems describing the virtuous beauty of Muhammad), beautiful *hamd* recitations (poems in praise of God), beautiful *tilawat* (cantillation of the Qur'an), beautiful *zikr* (melodious meditation by chanting

---

Arabia, he ruled for a decade until he died in a plane crash, the cause of which is yet unknown.

the names of God).[26] My family members are associated with beautiful Sufi *tariqas*.[27] I think my tears were really about me struggling with this disconnect between what I had been given to believe and what I felt just didn't fit for me . . . I mean that I was a very constricted, isolated, reclusive, internally contained being, and I did not quite know how to make sense of the world around me. I had come to a point where I had disassociated from recognizing or naming myself as a Muslim. Then one day, after many years, I heard the *azan* being called by a woman, it impacted my being and I simply fell apart. I was in tears. It felt as if my heart had immersed and bathed itself in the call to prayer. As much as I turned away from faith, I felt it constantly calling me back.

In this phase of despair and hopelessness, Mehar returned to the Qur'an. She engaged with it on an individual basis to make sense of her existence without relying on the interpretation of others.

Although I have a connection to the divine through my *namaz* [formal prayer] which I read in Arabic, and my *du'a* [informal petition to God] which I read in English, for me the pivotal starting point was the Qur'an in terms of attempting to access what I now understand by Islam or by the divine. Reading the Qur'an in English was an entry point into trying to create meaning for my life. For me,

---

[26] These are genres of devotional song, poetry and chant that are common in South Asian Sunni communities. *Na'at-khwani* means singing or reciting poems that extol the virtues of the Prophet in Urdu or Persian, while *Hamd* recitations are poems that praise God. *Tilawat* is recitation of the Qur'an with a melodious style, sometimes called 'cantillation.' *Zikr* is meditation by reciting the names of God, often in a group with melody or rhythm. Qureshi, 'Music in Islam.'

[27] By *tariqah*, Mehar means a Sufi order. The devotional orientation (one might call it 'sectarian allegiance') of Mehar's family would be Barelvi, a label applied to South Asian Muslims (in Pakistan, India and Bangladesh) who follow the popular practices of Sunni Islam in their region: loyalty to the Hanafi legal school, perpetuation of Sufi practices, accepting song and poetry in devotional life, and venerating saints and tombs. This might be called the 'vernacular' Islam of a majority of South Asian Muslims. It is called Barelvi because it was defended by Syed Ahmed Riza Khan of Bareilly, a Sufi scholar and jurist of the nineteenth century, against the condemnation of Muslims belonging to the less popular reformist Deobandi and Salafi movements. See Sanyal, *Ahmed Riza Khan*.

meaning turned out to be about the types of service, along with but beyond prayer and ritual, extending to the members of our direct and wider communities. What can I give, contribute and offer as part of my life for the duration that I am on this earth, in worship of the divine? Approaching or returning to the Qur'an through a call to prayer resonated deeply in my soul as if in that moment the divine was directly addressing and calling my spirit and being back to faith. At the time when I first turned towards the Qur'an, I did not have the formal education to read the Qur'an [in Arabic]. That deep call to prayer, and its shaking of my soul allowed my heart to open, to expand.

Mehar feels the limitation of not being a native Arabic speaker. Before deciding to do a PhD in Islamic Studies, her piety was formed by 'listening to the recitation without meaning' and letting the beauty of the sounds soften her heart:

I am not an Arabic speaker. I would listen to the recitation and it was more about a bodily response to the recitation rather than to specific verses. When I think of specific verses, I am usually reminded of those that say, 'Remember me so that I remember you' (Q 2:152) . . . Those are the kinds of verses that really struck me, because it wasn't about going publicly to the mosque or reading *namaz* in congregation. It was really about it giving me permission to have an individual, private, deeply personal connection with God . . . It was the little verses that express humility and urge one to recite and remember, so that God remembers you. I think my resonance for these verses is because I used to constantly think, 'How could God have forgotten a whole community?'[28] And then I would realize that perhaps I had forgotten God.

---

[28] In this phrase, Mehar is citing Q 59:18–19: 'Oh you who believe, stay aware of Allah and let each self be examined for what it presents for the future. Stay aware of Allah for Allah is cognizant of all that you do. Do not be like those who forget Allah and thus are themselves forgotten.'

When asked what gift the Qur'an gave her, she answers without hesitation 'expansion of my heart,' with a subtle indication of Surat al-Inshirah (Q 94:1–4). The Qur'an granted this gift once she had reached a point of maturity to receive it for herself as a lesbian:

> The Qur'an has helped me to access more deeply the capacity of expansion of my own heart, as well as the expansion of perspective in the way that I see my life. I mean, how I see my relationship with the Divine and with others . . . What I mean by the Qur'an as a gift in terms of my own expansion is that it allowed me to come out of the space of constricted lack of analytical spiritual loving engagement. It allowed me to engage in a way that let my heart and being breathe deeply and expand as it opened up to new possibilities of knowing and being. Previously I didn't feel that my heart was breathing! My heart was pumping but I was not living. I was not alive. Now I feel more and more alive, despite whatever challenges the world throws at me. My inner sense of my body flowing in resonance with what I understand as the Divine, I believe that to be the gift the Qur'an gave to me.

In this way, Mehar discovered a personal and intimate connection to the Qur'an, and through the Qur'an to God. She did this in a very individual manner without the mediation of a Sufi order, though she arrived at the same psychological goal that many Sufi orders aspire to reach: that is, to give their members a constant internal sense of the presence of God through meditating on the Qur'an as it reveals God's qualities.

Mehar's transformation was not merely internal but also manifested in her social and professional life. She aspired to earn a PhD in Islamic Studies, and generated the internal energy to pursue Islamic knowledge at 'secular' university institutions to which she had access. While she is aware of queer Muslim support groups active in the UK (like Imaan or the Safra Project) and has attended some of their programs, she shies away from overt LGBTQ community involvement or political activism. Instead, she participates in international networks of feminist and Islamic scholarship that are partly university-based, and partly devotional.

Javed

Javed is a young Muslim from South Africa whose family, like Mehar's, emigrated from South Asia. In South Africa under apartheid, Muslims and Hindus alike were categorized as racially 'Indian' and segregated into their own townships.[29] Though limited in mobility and rights, the 'Indians' excelled in business and education. Muslims from this community hold many positions in the new post-apartheid government and their scholars are recognized as leaders in international circuits. Javed is currently completing a PhD in Islamic Studies. He memorized the complete Qur'an at a young age in the Deobandi educational system.[30] As a *hafiz*, he is more interested in human rights than in sharia, but that is the result of a long journey.

In Javed's community, there is tremendous respect for those who memorize the Qur'an as he has.[31] He took several years off from secular school to memorize it through about twelve hours a day of reciting at madrasa:

> Up until that time when I finished memorizing it, my immediate experience of the Qur'an was more devotional. I was very young, but I did have an understanding that a lot of what Muslims consider to be Islam was not actually found in the Qur'an, or in some way has a tenuous relationship to the Qur'an. We learned a little Arabic, but we did not have sufficient Arabic to really navigate the meaning of the Qur'an to understand it. It was during the time when I was almost completing the Qur'an that I began to read translations. It was around that time, I began to experience the Qur'an not just as a devotional text, but as a text with a meaning that I can strive to understand. But I still held the Qur'an to be something sacred, something that held absolute truths. That would change later.

---

[29] Lemon, *Homes Apart*, pp. 1–25.

[30] In contrast, Mehar's Pakistani-UK background is called Barelwi; Javed's background as an Indian-South African is Deobandi. The Deoband movement is a reformist movement initiated in India in 1860, after the British abolished the symbolic leadership of the Mughal Empire. The movement was started by Sufis trained in jurisprudence, but has morphed over a century to become an extremely conservative (and in some places fundamentalist) movement. Metcalf, *Islamic Revival in British India*.

[31] All quotations of Javed are from a personal interview on October 16, 2016.

After the intense experience of memorizing the Qur'an full-time, Javed completed school and started university. His frame of reference broadened as he read more about history, law and social sciences. He began to see his life as rooted in the Qur'an, but not limited to it.

> There was this definition of piety [in the Qur'an] that I remember: 'Righteousness is not that you turn your faces toward the East or the West, but rather righteousness is that you believe in Allah and the Day of Judgment and the angels and book and prophets' (Q 2:177). Some of these verses stood out for me, crystalizing for me what my ideas of righteousness and piety were . . . but I became much more conscious of the limits of the text in a more critical way . . . Finding meaning exclusively in the Qur'an was, in a certain sense, no longer satisfactory.

Javed's exclusive immersion into the Qur'an broadened just as his 'Indian' community broke from its apartheid ghettoization. It was no longer sufficient to just follow ritual exactly in one small and isolated community – to 'turn your faces toward the East or the West,' as the Qur'an chides. The world changed around Javed as apartheid broke down amid violence and promise. A new multiracial and multireligious democracy took root, with the most progressive constitution in the world. Javed strove to find an ethical practice of Islam in a wider framework.

> I became skeptical about the tradition as a whole and about the Qur'an's place in the tradition. There were things that began to not sit well with me, that began to trouble me. I began to look for ways in which I could look at them through a more ethical framework . . . I was thinking about how things could be more just . . . Through that process, I became conscious that there were parts of the tradition that are just not so nice.

Javed understood then that the Islamic tradition was not divine as it was presented to him (in a conservative Deobandi, Hanafi, Sunni form). The tradition and its legal rulings were built by generations of scholars

– fallible human beings. He still held that the Qur'an is the sacred speech of God, but there were verses that troubled him morally and caused him to adopt a skeptical view.

> There is one verse that says 'Do not take Jews and Christians as your friends (Q 3:28) – or *awliya'*, the translation is an issue there – or some of the verses dealing with rules pertaining to gender and to women, or the Lot verses. All of these were problematic. Up until now, I feel that no amount of reinterpretation or acrobatics can take away what it is saying. For me, that's it: I have an Amina Wadud experience . . . to recognize what the scripture says and then to disagree with it in a particular way, not to reject it. Reject is too strong a word! Rather, to take a conscientious pause.

The verses about the prophet Lot's struggle with his people of Sodom and Gomorrah are often used to condemn queer Muslims, and especially gay men among them. Javed faces them with what Amina Wadud calls a 'conscientious pause.'[32] When faced with such a quandary, Javed cites a hadith that says, 'Take a fatwa from your heart.'[33] One must strive to the utmost to understand a verse and reflect profoundly on how it impacts oneself and others, and then take refuge with God and do what one's heart says is best.

> Simply put, I can say that they are not valid: the implication of the meaning of the verses is not valid. I recognize what it says, but I don't agree with the implementation of the principle in those verses as generally understood . . . For me, it went back to the issue of justice, how I thought about justice and how the Qur'an also spoke about

---

[32] For discussion of Amina Wadud's ethical response of saying 'no' to the sacred text, see Hammer, *American Muslim Women*, pp. 168–9; see also Abou El Fadl, *Speaking in God's Name*, pp. 213–28.

[33] According to a hadith report, the Prophet told the companion Wabisa ibn 'Ubayd (known as Wabisa ibn Ma'bad), 'Take a *fatwa* from your heart. Moral goodness is whatever your heart feels ease at doing, and sin is whatever brings discomfort to the heart even if people counsel you otherwise'; the hadith is recounted by Ahmad ibn Hanbal in his *Musnad*, and is report #27 in Ibrahim and Johnson-Davies, *An-Nawawi's Forty Hadith*.

justice. Any implementation of those verses in communities today led to a situation of injustice, in the ways that I see it being implemented or talked about.[34] ... The Lot verses went together with ... a general exclusion of a lot of people from salvation, from God's mercy, from holding equal human worth and dignity. These included non-Muslims, women in some respects, sinful Muslims, and also gay and lesbian Muslims ... For me, that was unjust to remove a whole people – all these kinds of people – from God's mercy and final salvation because of certain parts of your tradition and sacred text.[35]

Javed sees commonalities between Islamic jurisprudence and human rights law, as each seeks to systematize claims of justice and rights. However, Islamic jurisprudence has become captive in the hands of male elites, who erect boundaries around who is truly human with full dignity and rights. They refuse to countenance reforms that would uphold the dignity and full humanity of all. Elite male leaders ignore the egalitarian and universal voice of the Qur'an to instead create a system of domination out of its particular verses of compromise with a tribal, patriarchal society that is historically limited.

In this sense, democratic constitutions offer disempowered Muslims leverage to secure rights that are otherwise denied to them by their own community leaders. Living in South Africa, with its very new and exceptionally progressive constitution, Javed experiences the bifurcation between constitutional rights and religious loyalties with a heightened sensitivity.

Naseer

Naseer is an aspiring Islamic scholar on the island of Java. He does not identify as transgender but rather as a bisexual man. Unlike others interviewed here, Naseer comes from a Muslim-majority nation, rather than a

---

[34] Javed refers here to *maslaha mursala*, 'protecting the public good,' an accepted principle in Sunni legal methodology. By this principle, a scriptural injunction can be set aside if its implementation leads to injustice and harm to Muslims. On maslaha, see Duderija, *Maqasid al-Shari'a*, pp. 1–38, and Kamali, *Shari'ah Law*.

[35] Esack, *Qur'an, Liberation and Pluralism*, raises similar concerns and treats them systematically (also in the South African context but in ways universally applicable).

Muslim-minority community built through migration or conversion; Indonesia has the densest population of Muslims anywhere in the world, and is an emerging democracy. In his mid-twenties, Naseer plans to do a PhD in Islamic Studies. Like Javed, he is a *hafiz*, but comes from the Sufi-infused world of Indonesian popular Islam.[36] His father is a religious teacher in his home village and taught children the Qur'an. Naseer plans to return to his village one day to take over from his father, yet he will not have the same perception of the Qur'an as his father, since he memorized it guided by a woman.

> I learned the Qur'an from elementary school and how to recite it. I was taught how important the Qur'an is for my life and how central the Qur'an is in the Islamic tradition and to Islamic knowledge . . . I started memorizing the Qur'an when I was in high school. At that time, I went to my father's friend whose wife is a *hafiza*, a memorizer of the Qur'an, to memorize from her. I learned from a woman reciter. It is uncommon, but it was acceptable in my community.[37]

Naseer completed memorizing the Qur'an at age sixteen. Now, after finishing his BA in *tafsir* and currently doing his MA in hadith, he helps university students memorize it in informal night-time classes at the dorm. 'It is very hard to memorize the Qur'an. Memorizing the Qur'an is like tying a camel – if you control it every day and keep it tightly tied, then you can keep it, but if you loosen your control over it even for an hour then you can lose the camel forever. It is so hard to tie the camel again, once it is loosened!' Even while teaching and translating Islamic books from Arabic and English into Bahasa, he makes time to recite one-thirtieth of the Qur'an daily, so as not to forget.

---

[36] Naseer belongs to the community called *Nahdat al-Ulama* in modern times. Nahdat is comparable to the Barelvi school of thought in South Asian Islam, to which Mehar belongs, except that Nahdat is loyal to the Shafi'i school of law and the Barelvi school is loyal to the Hanafi school. Nahdat is defined against the reformist *Muhammadiyya* movement, just like the Barelvi school is defined against the reformist Deobandi movement, from which Javed comes. See Rumadi, *Islamic Post-Traditionalism in Indonesia*, and Bush, *Nahdlatul Ulama and the Struggle for Power*.

[37] All quotations of Naseer are from a personal interview on October 14, 2016.

He also teaches the Qur'an at an Islamic school for transgender Muslims, the first of its kind the world. In Indonesia, such a school is called a *pesantran* (in Arabic *madrasa*) and transgender people are called *waria* (specifically those ascribed 'male' identity but who identify as female).

> I teach reciting the Qur'an at a special *pesantran* for transgender people ... They try to understand the Qur'an in an interpretation that is friendly toward transgender people ... The most important phrase is 'those among your followers who are men having no desire for women' (Q 24:31).[38] We consider this to be the most important verse for transgender people because it was interpreted to refer to transgender people ... or *mukhannath*, meaning an effeminate man. We understand *mukhannath* to mean *waria* [Javanese for male-to-female transgender].[39] Some of them choose to dress like men when they are doing daily routines, but some of them are dressing like women ... We use only Qur'an and linguistic analysis to interpret the verses ... about justice and how to love everyone – human beings and the environment ... When we learn about the Qur'an, we look at the verses that relate to *mu'amalat* (social interactions) and how to do justice, about practical daily living.

Naseer conceives of his educational work with the transgender community as service: offering religious guidance to an oppressed group. The core of his teaching for transgender Muslims is: 'by reciting the Qur'an you can calm yourself down and feel more in touch with God and get closer to the supernatural powers like the angels.' He affirms inherent humanity and fundamental equality of transgender people with all other Muslims, with the Qur'an as the foundation of this belief.[40]

---

[38] Kugle, *Homosexuality in Islam*, pp. 67, 94.

[39] Ibid., pp. 241–2.

[40] There are several verses in the Qur'an that use the term 'pairing' with male and female in highly ambiguous ways, that could suggest two genders paired in one person rather than all people divided into a binary of either female or male. Two such verses are these: 'Was the human being not a spermazoid emitted? Then became a mucus and then was created then given form? Then God made the human being paired male with female' (Q 75:37–9) and 'Glory be to the one who created the pairs of every variety, from what the earth grows and from your selves and from that which you do not know' (Q 36:36). Ibid., Q 66 and 243–9.

This attitude is contested. Although *waria* people have inherited a special position from the premodern Islamic kingdoms in Java, in the present they are under threat. In 2016, Islamist vigilantes threatened the school where Naseer teaches.[41] The conflict was sparked by funerals: 'Some families refuse to bury a *waria* from their family so the [*waria*] community then does it, while some families agree to let the community do the burial for them.' The transgender community buries people according to their self-identified gender, so vigilantes accused the school of making new rules for transgender Muslims which deviated from sharia as they understand it, including funeral rites and prayer arrangements. Naseer insists that this was slander and incitement by the extremists – 'We just gather to do the religious rites, pray together, recite Qur'an, and discuss the religious teachings at the *pesantran*.' The elder transgender leader who runs the school used verse Q 24:31 to argue with traditional religious leaders who were convened to rule on the school's closure. Naseer explains that her interpretation 'was enough to make the religious leaders accept the *waria* people, because we don't do anything that disturbs the community.' However, Islamic vigilantes did not accept the authority of traditional leaders; police shied away from confronting vigilantes and insisted that, for public safety, the school should close. The transgender Muslim community was forced underground and lost its gathering place to meet, learn, study and pray together.

Naseer is very attentive to such subtle strategies for coping in a patriarchal society. His intimate life is a delicate negotiation with patriarchal expectations, which he has learned not to confront directly. He finished memorizing the Qur'an in the flush of adolescence and the challenges of high school. Of course, he fell in love.

I had a girlfriend but I was in love with a boy, so I told her that I was in love with a boy. It was very hard for me to say! . . . She was so disappointed because she saw that I was a *hafiz* of the Qur'an yet I loved a boy. So she left me, but after a year she came back to me and we started our relationship again. With the boy, I also had a relationship . . . You could call it a homoerotic friendship deeper than regular

---

[41] BBC Indonesia, 'Pesantran for Transgenders in Yogyakarta Closed.'

friendship. I had a very hard time because my girlfriend had left me for a year before she came back, and I had to pass my final exams as a senior in high school. It was a very hard time, so I used the Qur'an to calm myself down and keep all the things under control. It works!

Eventually his relationship with his girlfriend, which never involved sexual activity, evolved into a loving friendship. Her new boyfriend intuitively exempted Naseer from the competition of routine masculinity and jealousy, so she and Naseer are still close. Naseer's boyfriend went with him to university, where they live in the same dormitory.

When we hang out or have dinner, I grab his hand or he holds mine. When I visit him, we sleep together very close but we don't have sex. We know *fiqh* – we know it is *haram*. If it is intercourse then it is *haram*. Just touching, some people say it is sexual, but we don't think of it as sexual so we don't say that is *haram*. But no kissing – that is not allowed, because kissing will lead to something more! On the basis of *usul al-fiqh* there is a principle of *sadd al-dhari'a*, of not doing something that will lead to doing something that is *haram*.

Naseer is adamant that he and his boyfriend can sleep together in one bed without engaging in prohibited sexual acts, exclaiming, 'We have proved it!' They both share a style of piety, since his boyfriend has also memorized the Qur'an. Avoiding sexual pleasure is the compromise they are willing to make in exchange for the love, care, trust and intimacy that they need from each other.

Naseer is not sure where this love will lead him because it does not have a recognizable social form. He is hesitant to extend his innovative reading of the Qur'an outward toward a critical assessment of the *sharia* as both public law and private morality, even though a few scholars in Indonesia are doing so.[42] He plans to marry a woman and have children because that is

---

[42] For instance, Siti Musdah Mulia is a professor at Syarif Hidayatullah State Islamic University whose important interventions as a public intellectual and Islamic scholar are documented in Wee, 'Politicization of Women's Bodies in Indonesia'; Feillard and van Doorn-Harder, 'New Generation of Feminists.'

expected of him. How else could he return to his village and take up his father's post as religious teacher, when that time comes?

INTERPRETATION, THEORY, AND SUBJECT FORMATION

These interviews show how complex subject formation is for queer Muslims. They are subjects twice-formed: first, by being raised in a family to conform to certain religious, cultural and social norms, and second, by gaining self-awareness that being true to their inner disposition requires challenging those norms. Families perceive their expression of difference in sexual orientation and gender identity as rebellion; religious leaders who see homosexuality or transgender identity as a threat amplify and justify this misperception.

Queer Muslims find strength in intimate connection with each other, and solidarity with other marginalized groups within Muslim communities. They see their own struggles as linked with those of women for equality and respect, with those of racial minorities for justice and equal opportunity, with those of religious minorities for freedom of conscience and right to worship. By simply existing, queer Muslims prompt their communities to rethink how their norms came to be normative.

While there is no single method by which queer Muslims interpret the Qur'an, they assert that they are an integral part of God's diverse creation and not a perversion or deviation. They find their presence in creation and in Muslim society indicated by several Qur'anic verses referring to transgender people (Q 42:49–50), lesbian women (Q 24:60) and gay men (Q 24:31), based on the scriptures many metaphors about boundless diversity of natural and human types.

Queer Muslims highlight verses that insist that each individual stands before God for judgment, rather than before fallible human beings. They insist that homosexuality is not sodomy. They assert that God does not condemn them in the Qur'an on the basis of sexual orientation or gender identity, terms which are not found in the Qur'an attached to negative assessments or prohibitions. Islamic legal rulings condemn them through the terms sodomy (*liwat*) and tribadism (*sihaq*), but these terms are not found in the Qur'an; they were invented later by jurists.[43]

Queer Muslims argue that the Lot narrative depicts dominant males attempting to rape vulnerable men whom Lot tries to protect. The narrative does not apply to consensual sexual intercourse and does not condemn same-sex desire or orientation per se. This critique addresses the disparate verses that refer to the narrative (e.g. Q 29:28–9; 27:54–5; 26:165–6; 7:80–1). They assert that same-sex female desire and intercourse is not addressed specifically anywhere in the Qur'an (against several far-fetched interpretations by mainstream Islamic writers, addressing verses Q 4:15–16; 25:38 and 50:14 pertaining to the People of Rass).[44] Queer Muslims assert that the Qur'an should not be interpreted through hadith reports about homosexuality and transgender behavior, for these are of dubious authenticity and are not supported by Qur'anic verses.[45] They hold that critiquing hadith is not disrespecting the Prophet, but rather liberates him from statements wrongly ascribed to him in later generations.[46]

The queer Muslim community is both an actual and an interpretive community.[47] These systems of thought are intersubjective, meaning that

---

[43] Jahangir and Abdullatif, *Islamic Law and Muslim Same-Sex Unions*, pp. xx–xxi.

[44] Kugle, 'Strange Bedfellows.' See also Ali, *Sexual Ethics in Islam*, p. 81; Habib, *Female Homosexuality*, pp. 60–1.

[45] No hadith report condemning homosexuality or transgender behavior is *mutawatir*, meaning that none has multiple continuous and mutually confirming narration, which guarantees its reliability. The reports that condemn homosexual and transgender behavior are dubious because they have single chains of transmission (they are *hadith ahad*, meaning that at some point they are narrated by only one person to one person with no corroborating chain of narration to confirm it; this is true even if the hadith has been labeled *hadith sahih*, meaning that even if its chain of narration goes back to the Prophet himself, it still has a single uncorroborated link somewhere leaving it open to having been corrupted or falsified or invented). Despite this, jurists have accepted them and used them to formulate rulings.

[46] There is support in the Qur'an for radical skepticism regarding hadith reports collected in texts long after the Qur'an. 'These are the verses of God that we recite to you in truth, so then what saying will you believe in after God and God's verses?' (Q 45:6) is one of several verses that use the term 'hadith' to mean the Qur'an itself and to belittle the idea of following other kinds of speech as divine or normative; see also 68:44; 77:50; 53:59 and 56:81.

[47] 'Interpretive community' is a term from literary theory, coined by Stanley Fish. He asserted that 'the meaning of a literary text cannot be seen as separate from the reader's experience of it . . . [yet] totally subject responses are impossible since they cannot exist in isolation from sets of norms and systems of thought.' Newton, *Twentieth-Century Literary Theory*, p. 220.

they arise from dialogue in a community of shared assumptions and common experiences. The text is always constructed by the subject reading it, or more subtly by an 'interpretive community' that reads it in a particular way based upon their shared intentions. Fish and others build upon the philosophy of Gadamer and his concept of the fusion of horizons, in which 'a fusion takes place between the past experiences that are embodied in the text and the interests of its present-day readers.'[48]

This emphasis on the agency of present-day readers is crucial. Queer Muslims assert that they have authority to interpret scripture in the light of their subjective experiences in the present. Past interpretations are not relevant to the present if they conceive of gender as anatomical and lack a conception of sexual orientation. This traditional conceptual framework is impoverished and does not adequately capture the richness of contemporary life in which subjectivities are formed by citizenship, inalienable rights, individual autonomy and clinical psychology.

CONCLUSION

Over the last few decades, queer Muslims have emerged more into the public sphere, in places that enjoy civic rights, secular constitutions and the firm rule of law. They reject the basic assumptions of hegemonic patriarchy which have shaped almost every Muslim community of the past, whether Sunni, Shia or Sufi. But they do not reject the basic vocabulary of religion; rather, they strive for a community that is socially inclusive, theologically open-ended, and hopeful for salvation accessible to all within the wide gathering place of the basic religious vocabulary. This means with the Prophet Muhammad, the Qur'an, the essential beliefs it announces: 'The Prophet believes in what his Lord revealed to him and the faithful, all of them, believe in the one God, God's angels, God's books and God's messengers' (Q 2:285). Everything beyond the essential beliefs is open to interpretation, and that fact is a mercy from God.

---

[48] Ibid., p. 219.

BIBLIOGRAPHY

Abou El Fadl, Khaled. *Speaking in God's Name: Islamic Law, Authority and Women*. (Oxford: Oneworld, 2001)

Ahmed, Leila. *Women and Gender in Islam: Historical Roots of a Modern Debate*. (New Haven, CT: Yale University Press, 1993)

Ali, Kecia. *Sexual Ethics in Islam: Feminist Reflections on Qur'an, Hadith and Jurisprudence.* (Oxford: Oneworld, 2006)

Barlas, Asma. *Believing Women in Islam: Unreading Patriarchal Interpretations of the Qur'an.* (Austin: University of Texas, 2002)

BBC Indonesia (2016, February 26). 'Pesantran for Transgenders in Yogyakarta Closed.' [Online] (https://www.bbc.com/indonesia/berita_indonesia/2016/02/160225_indonesia_ponpes_waria_ditutup). (Accessed December 14, 2016)

Bush, Robin. *Nahdlatul Ulama and the Struggle for Power within Islam and Politics in Indonesia.* (Singapore: ISEAS, 2009)

Duderija, Adis (ed.) *Maqasid al-Shari'a and Contemporary Reformist Muslim Thought: An Examination.* (New York: Palgrave Macmillan, 2014)

Esack, Farid. *Qur'an, Liberation and Pluralism: An Islamic Perspective on Interreligious Solidarity Against Oppression.* (Oxford: Oneworld, 1997)

Feillard, Andrée and Pieternella van Doorn-Harder. 'A New Generation of Feminists Within Traditional Islam.' In *Islam in Indonesia: Contrasting Images and Interpretations.* Ed. Jajat Burhanudin and Kees van Dijk, 139–60. (Amsterdam: ICAS at Amsterdam University Press, 2013)

Habib, Samar. *Female Homosexuality in the Middle East: Histories and Representations.* (New York: Routledge, 2007)

Hammer, Juliane. *American Muslim Women, Religious Authority and Activism: More Than a Prayer.* (Austin: University of Texas, 2012)

Hamzic, Vanja. *Sexual and Gender Diversity in the Muslim World: History, Law and Vernacular Knowledge.* (London: I.B. Tauris, 2016)

Hancock, Ange-Marie. *Intersectionality: An Intellectual History.* (Oxford: Oxford University Press, 2016)

Hidayatullah, Aysha. *Feminist Edges of the Qur'an.* (London: Oxford University Press, 2014)

Ibrahim, Ezzeddin and Denys Johnson-Davies (trans.) *An-Nawawi's Forty Hadith.* (Delhi: Dar al-Islam, 1982)

Jahangir, Junaid and Hussein Abdullatif. *Islamic Law and Muslim Same-Sex Unions.* (Lanham, MD: Lexington Books, 2016)

Kamali, Mohammed Hashim. *Shari'ah Law: An Introduction.* (Oxford: Oneworld, 2008)

Khalid, Amma and Andrew Yip. 'Looking for Allah: Spiritual Quests of Queer Muslims.' In *Queer Spiritual Spaces: Sexuality and Sacred Places.* Ed. Kath Brown et al., 81–110. (London: Routledge, 2010)

Kugle, Scott. *Homosexuality in Islam: Critical Reflection on Gay, Lesbian, and Transgender Muslims.* (Oxford: Oneworld, 2010)

— *Living Out Islam: Voices of Gay, Lesbian, and Transgender Muslims.* (New York: New York University Press, 2014)

— 'Strange Bedfellows: Qur'an Interpretation Regarding Same-Sex Female Intercourse.' *Theology and Sexuality* 22:1–2 (2016): 9–24

— and Steven Hunt. 'Masculinity, Homosexuality and the Defense of Islam: A Case Study of Yusuf al-Qaradawi's Media Fatwa.' *Religion and Gender* 2:2 (2012): 254–79

Lawrence, Bruce. *Who is Allah?* (Chapel Hill: University of North Carolina Press, 2015)

Lemon, Anthony (ed.) *Homes Apart: South Africa's Segregated Cities.* (Bloomington: Indiana University Press, 1991)

Metcalf, Barbara Daly. *Islamic Revival in British India: Deoband, 1860–1900.* (New Delhi: Oxford University Press, 2005; first published 1982)

Meyer, Wali Ali, B. Hyde, S. Kahn et al. *Physicians of the Heart: A Sufi View of the Ninety-Nine Names of Allah.* (n.p.: New Leaf, 2011)

Newton, K.M. (ed.) *Twentieth-Century Literary Theory: A Reader.* (Basingstoke: Macmillan Publishers, 1988)

Qureshi, Regula. 'Music in Islam.' In *Sacred Sound: Experiencing Music in World Religions.* Ed. Guy Beck, 89–112. (Ontario: Wilfred Laurier University Press, 2006)

Rahemtulla, Shadaab. *Qur'an of the Oppressed: Liberation Theology and Gender Justice in Islam.* (New York: Oxford University Press, 2017)

Rumadi. *Islamic Post-Traditionalism in Indonesia.* Trans. Rebecca Lunnon. (Singapore: ISEAS, 2015)

Saeed, Sadia. *Politics of Desecularization: Law and the Minority Question in Pakistan.* (New York: Cambridge University Press, 2016)

Sanyal, Usha. *Ahmed Riza Khan Barelwi: In the Path of the Prophet.* (Oxford: Oneworld, 2005)

Shaikh, Sa'diyya. 'Islamic Feminism.' In *Progressive Muslims: On Gender, Justice and Pluralism.* Ed. Omid Safi, 147–63. (Oxford: Oneworld, 2003)

— 'A Tafsir of Praxis: Gender, Marital Violence and Resistance in a South African Muslim Community.' In *Violence Against Women in Contemporary World Religions: Roots and Cures.* Ed. Daniel Maguire and Sa'diyya Shaikh, 66–89. (Cleveland: Pilgrim Press, 2009)

Wadud, Amina. *Inside the Gender Jihad: Women's Reform in Islam.* (Oxford: Oneworld, 2006)

— *Qur'an and Woman.* (New York: Oxford University Press, 1999)

Wee, Vivienne. 'The Politicization of Women's Bodies in Indonesia: Sexual Scripts as Charters for Action.' In *Sexuality in Muslim Contexts: Restrictions and Resistance.* Ed. Anissa Hélie and Homa Hoodfar, 17–51. (London: Zed Books, 2012)

Part III

The Silent, Speaking and Living Word

Chapter 6

The Speaking Qur'an and the Praise of the Imam: the Memory and Practice of the Qur'an in the Twelver Shia Tradition

Sajjad Rizvi, University of Exeter

'Our teaching is difficult and arduous; the only ones who can bear it are a prophet sent to humanity, one of the cherubim, or an initiate whose heart has been tested in faith by God.' (Imam Muhammad al-Baqir [d. 114/733])[1]

'[E]verything we have figured in a manifest Imam (*imam mubin*)' (Q 36:12)[2]

S hia believers often hold that the Qur'an is a long poem in praise of the family of the Prophet in general and the imams in particu- lar. This is an expression of the famous narration (*hadith*) of the

---

[1] Al-Saffar, *Basa'ir*, p. 51.

[2] All translations of the Qur'an are my modifications of *The Qur'an with a Phrase-by-Phrase English translation*, tr. 'Ali Quli Qara'i (London: Islamic College for Advanced Studies Press, 2004). This is the best English translation from a Shia theological perspective available and far more readable than the translations more commonly found in Shia households, namely Mir Ahmed 'Ali (tr.), *The Holy Qur'an with notes of Mirza Mahdi Pooya* (New York: Tahrike Tarsile Qur'an, 1995), and *The Qur'an: Arabic Text and English Translation by M.H. Shakir* (New York: Tahrike Tarsile Qur'an, 1993).

'two weighty things' (*al-thaqalayn*) popular in early Shia sources; it also complements another early Shia hadith corpus that describes the Qur'an and the imam as so intimate that the former is silent unless the latter enunciates it for believers. Both the scripture of the Qur'an and the person of the imam are acts of the self-revelation of God. Throughout the life of a believer, punctuated with events of birth, coming of age, marriage, divorce and even death, this intimate complementarity of the Qur'an and the imam is seen in ritual commemorations that place the artifact and the lived reality of the Qur'an alongside the memorialization of the imams. The explicit absence of the particular names of the imams in the canonical text of the Qur'an arguably poses a challenge – or rather, an opportunity – to develop a hermeneutics that uncovers the real levels of meaning beyond the apparent word of the text. This is *ta'wil*, a tracing back to origins through layers of signification and an articulation to help believers understand the artifact and reality of the living Qur'an.

THE PURPOSES OF EXEGESIS: DISCLOSING WASAYA AND WALAYA

While the function of exegesis is to explain and gloss the revealed word, the manifestation of God and his plan in the form of scripture, the strategies of exegetes depend to a large extent on how they see the word of God and understand their authority to interpret it. In the Shia tradition, exegesis, like most other forms of Shia literature, is concerned with revealing and proclaiming the special status of the imams as heirs of the Prophet (the *wasaya*) and friends of God chosen to deploy their authority on the earth (the *walaya*).[3] Insofar as the imams are the heirs of the prophets, they inherit the key prophetic functions that are adumbrated in Q 62:2: 'to recite to them His signs, to purify them, and to teach them the Scripture and the wisdom.' This is indicated in many narrations concerning the imams' inheritance of the prophets which

---

[3] Amir-Moezzi, *Coran*.

they receive directly and pass on from one imam to another, and which is consistent with the Qur'an.[4]

The underlying reality of the cosmos and the totality of the divine revelation are both associated with proclaiming the *walaya* of the imams. Because the names of the historical imams are explicitly absent in the Qur'an, interpreters must go beyond the literal word of the text by recourse to the words of the imams themselves.[5] The sixth imam, Ja'far al-Sadiq (d. 148/765), is reported explaining the *walaya* of the imams as 'the very truth, that much is apparent, but also the very inner matter, the secret, the secret of secrets, the innermost secret that itself veils the secret.'[6] In this sense the imams possess the esoteric truth of the Qur'an. The ultimate truth of the status of the imams is, therefore, hidden, and remains a secret to be preserved by their adherents. Just as the Qur'an existed in pre-eternity, and God called all those who would come to be to the primordial pact (*mithaq*) to acknowledge his lordship, that covenant includes acknowledgment of the *walaya* of the imams who existed in pre-eternity. Q 7:172 states: 'When your Lord took from the children of Adam, from their loins their descendants, and made them bear witness over themselves, "Am I not your Lord?" They said, "Yes indeed! We bear witness."'[7] According to Twelver Shia tradition, most forgot this pledge as the following verse acknowledges, thereby explaining why the Shia cause remained a minority position. This oblivion of the testimony to the *walaya* of the imams explains why, in the earliest period, Shia exegesis is very much addressing a particular elect, and not appealing to a wide audience.[8]

---

[4] Al-Saffar, *Basa'ir*, pp. 219–27.

[5] Corbin, *Islam Iranien*, vol. 1.

[6] Al-Saffar, *Basa'ir*, p. 59.

[7] Ibid., p. 146.

[8] Steigerwald and Bar-Asher, following Goldziher, focus on the sectarian aspects of the early tradition, which, according to Lawson, is revived in the Safavid period when the classical tradition is consciously revived (Steigerwald, 'Twelver Shi'i *ta'wil*'; Bar-Asher, *Scripture*; Goldziher, *Die Richtungen*, pp. 263–309; Lawson, 'Akhbari Shi'i Aproaches to Tafsir'). Gleave argues that the authority of the imams means that their exegesis, as reported in early works, does not require any justification for esotericism (Gleave, 'Early Shi'i Hermeneutics'). Ayoub and Karimi-Nia argue for the development of the genre due to the diversity and periods of encounter and exchange, followed in this by Rippin who questions essentialist definitions of Shia exegesis (Ayoub, 'The Speaking Qur'an and the Silent Qur'an'; Karimi-Nia, 'al-Masabih' and *Chahar paradayim-i tafsir-i shi'a*; Rippin, 'What Defines a (Pre-modern) Shi'i Tafsir?').

Nevertheless, the relationship between the revelation and the imam necessitates a hermeneutics of *ta'wil* to bring forth the significance of the person of the imam. Fundamentally this exegetical strategy is predicated on the distinction between three levels of aspects of the experience of the Qur'an:

+ The Qur'an as textual artifact, an object of veneration or recitation and contemplation, a collection of inscribed words with a structure, syntactical arrangement, and strings of meanings as expressed in narrations that stress the importance of a venerable treatment of the artifact and reading it in a book (*mushaf*).[9]
+ The Qur'an as a primordial reality revealing the nature of the cosmos, the light and the guide that requires rehearsal and teaching among people, and as a mediating reality between God and humanity.[10]
+ The Qur'an as a recitation, the power of the uttered word of God, doubled in its potency when articulated on the tongue of the imam.[11]

What this esotericism, drawing out the implicit and immanent imam from the Qur'an, makes clear is that the classical tradition demands a clear epistemology and hermeneutics before an engagement with the scripture. For example, one of the earliest major hadith compilations, *al-Kafi* of Abu Ja'far al-Kulayni (d. 329/941), begins with chapters on the notion of the intellect and its absence as well as the excellence of knowledge, divine unicity and the need for a divinely ordained guide (*hujja*) before it shifts to the Qur'an and other theological topics.[12] Theologically, one cannot understand the Qur'an without a prior comprehension of the nature of monotheism and its expression in the *walaya* of the imams.

But the fundamental theme goes back to a central proof-text for the Shia tradition, namely the famous hadith *al-thaqalayn* narrated from the Prophet: 'I am leaving behind two weighty things, the book of God and my

---

[9] Al-Kulayni, *Usul al-kafi*, vol. II (*Fadl al-qur'an*), pp. 513, 619.
[10] Ibid., pp. 596–606.
[11] Ibid., pp. 614–19.
[12] Cf. Amir-Moezzi and Ansari, 'al-Kulayni.'

progeny; cleave to them as neither will forsake the other until they reach me at the pool (in the afterlife).'[13] Both the imam and the Qur'an are personal guides that have complementary roles in facilitating faith and understanding reality. Hence the person of the imam as manifest in this hadith is the basis for Shia exegesis. The Prophet's successors, the imams, inherit his special knowledge that includes his direct relationship to the revelation, and the *walaya* of the imams as succession to prophecy mirrors the relationship between the interpretation (*ta'wil*) of the text and its actual revelation (*tanzil*). The function of *ta'wil* is to reveal the *walaya* of the imams. Al-'Ayyashi (fl. tenth century) quotes from Imam Ja'far al-Sadiq: 'God made our *walaya* the pole of the Qur'an and the pole of all scriptures; through [*walaya*] scriptures were elucidated and through [*walaya*] faith becomes manifest.'[14] The notion of *ta'wil* is predicated on two principles. The first is the privileged knowledge (*'ilm*) of the imams that identifies the imams with those rooted in knowledge (*al-rasikhuna fi-l-'ilm*) (Q 3:7).[15] Another hadith cited in *Basa'ir al-darajat* expresses this relationship:

[Imam Muhammad] Al-Baqir was asked about the narration: every verse has a manifest and a hidden aspect . . . Manifest is clear and the hidden is its *ta'wil*, and what has happened and what will not, and the course of the sun and the moon, and the *ta'wil* of all that will happen to the dead just as it will happen to the living. As God says, 'No one knows its interpretation except Allah and those firmly rooted in knowledge'. (Q 3:7)[16]

The second principle is expressed in a hadith, narrated from the fifth imam, Muhammad al-Baqir, that each verse of the Qur'an has an apparent (*zahir*) and a hidden (*batin*) aspect, and that even the hidden aspect has further aspects which suggests a hierarchy or multiplicity of esoteric meanings.[17]

[13] *Sahih Muslim*, Hadith #4425; *Sunan al-Tirmidhi*, Hadith #3718; *Sunan al-Nisa'i*, vol. 5, 130; al-Qummi, *Tafsir*, vol. I, p. 3; al-'Ayyashi, *Tafsir*, vol. I, p. 4; al-Milani, *Hadith al-thaqalayn*; al-Hindi *'Abaqat al-anwar*.
[14] Al-'Ayyashi, *Tafsir*, vol. I, p. 5; Ayoub, 'The Speaking Qur'an and the Silent Qur'an,' p. 181.
[15] Al-Kulayni, *Usul al-kafi*, vol. I, pp. 153–4, 159–61; al-Saffar, *Basa'ir*, pp. 364–8.
[16] Al-Saffar, *Basa'ir*, p. 365.
[17] Al-'Ayyashi, *Tafsir*, vol. I, p. 12; al-Tustari, *Tafsir*, p. 16.

Al-Baqir states that none can claim to know the totality of the revelation – the apparent and the hidden meanings – except for the successors to the Prophet.[18]

For the Twelver Shia community then, the imam has a privileged role in articulating the Qur'an:

1) as light and guidance
2) as revelation or divinely ordained guide
3) as the 'bearer of the divine *amr*' going back to the following Qur'anic verses:
   a. 'O you who have faith! Obey Allah and obey the Apostle and those vested with authority among you' (Q 4:59)
   b. 'And amongst them we appointed imams who guide by our command when they had been patient and had convictions in our signs' (Q 32:24)
   c. 'We made them imams who guide by our command and we revealed to them the performance of good deeds, the maintenance of prayers, and the giving of *zakat*, and they worship us' (Q 21:73)
4) as privileged bearer of divine knowledge.

THE SPEAKING AND SILENT QUR'AN AND IMAM

Both the Qur'an and the imam are pre-existing and eternal manifestations of the divine: the text of the Qur'an is a historical expression of both the knowledge of the divine and of its heavenly exemplar in the 'preserved tablet' (*al-lawh al-mahfuz*), and the historical imam is an expression of the pre-existence in the heavens or at the Throne of God of the Prophet and the imams.[19] This relationship – whose initial formulation seems linked to the famous hadith, ''Ali is with the Qur'an and the Qur'an with 'Ali'[20]

---

[18] Al-Kulayni, *Usul al-kafi*, vol. I, p. 165.

[19] Amir-Moezzi, *Divine Guide*, pp. 29–59.

[20] Al-Hakim al-Nisaburi, *al-Mustadrak*, vol. III, p. 124 (Hadith #4628); Ibn al-Haythami, *Majma' al-zawa'id*, vol. IX, p. 134; al-Kulayni, *Usul al-kafi*, vol. I, p. 136; Majlisi, *Bihar al-anwar*,

– becomes the basis for an important Shia topos of exegesis: the Qur'an is the silent (*samit*) imam, and the imam is the speaking Qur'an (*al-kitab al-natiq huwa-l-wali*).[21] Many hadiths indicate this belief, including those that identify the imams with the speech, the words, and the spirit of God.[22] Similarly, another narration stresses that the Qur'an itself cannot speak (*laysa bi-natiq*) and hence requires those worthy of it – its folk (*ahl*, i.e. the imams) – to make it enunciate.[23]

The Qur'an as it is exists only with the imam. Al-Baqir is reported as saying: 'No one can claim to have the totality of the Qur'an both its manifest and its hidden except for the successors of the Prophet (*awsiya'*).'[24] The imam and the Qur'an reveal the hidden God, but most people fail to see it. Imam Ja'far al-Sadiq is reported to have said: 'God has disclosed himself to his creation in his book but they do not have the insight (to perceive him).'[25] The clearly polemical intent of such narrations, and the need to direct people seeking the Qur'an and its knowledge to the imams, is clear. Al-Sadiq is also quoted as stating that a quarter of the Qur'an directly relates to the imams and another quarter to their enemies. Amir-Moezzi describes this phase of exegesis as 'personalized commentary,' where commentators identify the figures – the good and righteous being the imams and the evil their enemies – who are 'hidden' beyond the letter of the scripture.[26]

Finally, the complementarity of the imam and the Qur'an is expressed by pointing to the meaning of the phrases 'imam mubin/kitab mubin' that occur at least six times in the Qur'an. In Sunni exegesis it is usually understood as the Qur'an, or its primordial status as the eternal speech of God. In Twelver Shia exegesis these verses are associated with the imam and his knowledge, which is received directly from God.

1) With Him are the treasures of the Unseen. No one knows them
   except Him. He knows whatever there is in the land and sea. No

---

vol. XXII, p. 222 and vol. XXXVIII, p. 38.

[21] Al-Bursi, *Mashariq anwar al-yaqin*, p. 135; Amir-Moezzi, *Coran silencieux.*

[22] Al-Kulayni, *Usul al-kafi*, vol. I, pp. 139, 149; al-Saffar, *Basa'ir*, pp. 94–102.

[23] Al-Kulayni, *Usul al-kafi*, vol. I, p. 176.

[24] Al-Saffar, *Basa'ir*, pp. 349–51.

[25] Ibn Abi Jumhur, *'Awali al-la'ali*, vol. V, p. 116; Amuli, *Al-Muhit al-a'zam*, vol. I, p. 207.

[26] Amir-Moezzi, 'Silent Qur'an,' p. 169.

leaf falls without his knowing it nor is there a grain in the darkness of the earth, nor anything fresh or withered but it is in the manifest book (Q 6:59).

2) You do not engage in any work, neither do you recite any part of the Qur'an, nor do you perform any deed without our being witness over you when you are engaged therein. Not an atom's weight escapes your Lord in the earth or in the sky, nor is there anything smaller than that or bigger but it is in a manifest book (Q 10:61).

3) There is no animal on the earth, but its sustenance lies with Allah and He knows its enduring abode and its temporary place of lodging. Everything is in a manifest book (Q 11:6).

4) There is no invisible thing in the heaven and the earth but it is in a manifest book (Q 27:75).

5) The faithless say, 'The Hour will never come to us.' Say, 'Yes indeed by my Lord it will surely come to you.' The knower of the unseen not even an atom's weight escapes him in the heavens or in the earth nor is anything smaller than that or bigger but it is in a manifest book (Q 34:3).

6) Indeed it is we who revive the dead and write what they have sent ahead and their effects and we have figured everything in a manifest imam (Q 36:12).

EARLY EXEGETICAL STRATEGIES: VINDICATING THE SHIA IMAMS

The narrations contrast the outward revelation of the Qur'an (*tanzil*) with the inner *ta'wil*.[27] Shia sources cite a hadith of the Prophet: 'There is one among you who will fight for the *ta'wil* of the Qur'an just as I myself fought for its revelation (*tanzil*) and he is 'Ali ibn Abi Talib.'[28] As inheritors of the Prophet, the imams know the totality of what was revealed and what the

---

[27] Al-Saffar, *Basa'ir*, p. 196.
[28] Al-'Ayyashi, *Tafsir*, vol. I, p. 15.

interpretation is.[29] The hadith compilations demonstrate a range of exegetical strategies in the words of the imams: explaining the words through 'meaning equivalence', explanatory glosses, linguistic explanations, and examples of the *ta'wil*.[30] To these, one could add the correction of the way in which the text is recited.

This is one way of making sense of the gradually revealed text and protecting it against the interference of the enemies of the faith. The *Kitab al-tanzil wa-t-tahrif* of Ahmad al-Sayyari (fl. fourth/tenth century) brings out the contrast between *tanzil* and *ta'wil* and presents a recitation/reading different from the 'Uthmanic recension and its recitations that were being codified in that Buyid period.[31] Al-Sayyari's work is not exegetical, but merely attempts to correct the *zahir* of the text by inserting the names of the imams and those of their enemies, and thus is distinct from most early Shia exegesis that purports to present the esoteric teachings and revelation of the Qur'an as transmitted from the imams to their followers: the late third-/ninth-century exegeses attributed to 'Ali b. Ibrahim al-Qummi, Abu-Nadr al-'Ayyashi al-Samarqandi, Furat al-Kufi, as well as the exegeses attributed to Imams 'Ali and Ja'far al-Sadiq in the recension of al-Nu'mani (d. 360/971), and the eleventh Imam al-Hasan al-'Askari (d. *c.*860/874 CE).[32] These early commentaries read the text to vindicate the Shia case and provide the counter-narrative to the Sunni version of the early history of Islam. Al-Qummi, for example, in a long introduction on the hermeneutics of the text, clarifies the need for an exegesis to vindicate the Shia position on *walaya* and to show how the Qur'an as it is before the people refutes the various non-Shia heresies of dualism, anthropomorphism, materialism, idolatry, determinism, the Mu'tazila, and so forth.[33] In particular, the

---

[29] Al-Saffar, *Basa'ir*, pp. 229–35.
[30] Gleave, 'Early Shi'i Hermeneutics', pp. 146–66.
[31] Al-Sayyari, *Revelation and Falsification*.
[32] The Shia *tafsir* attributed to Imam Ja'far al-Sadiq, which is different from the text cited in the Sufi exegesis of Abu 'Abd al-Rahman al-Sulami (d. 412/1021), remains in manuscript. There is a study: Ensieh Nasrollah Zadeh, *The Qur'an Commentary attributed to Imam Ja'far al-Sadiq (a.s.): A Study of its Dating and Interpretive Method* (unpublished PhD dissertation, University of Birmingham, 2003), although she did not examine the main manuscript tradition which is in India. This *tafsir* is narrated on the authority of Abu-l-Fadl 'Abbas b. Muhammad b. al-Qasim b. Hamza b. Musa b. Ja'far al-Sadiq, who is also the authority for the *tafsir* of al-Qummi.
[33] Al-Qummi, *Tafsir*, vol. I, pp. 5–6.

exegete must emphasize the *ta'wil* to demonstrate the rights of the imams and the usurpations of their enemies.[34]

In this early phase, Shia exegesis attempted to make the text speak and express the Shia truth about the role of the imams and their teachings about the divine that lie beyond the surface of the text. These works focus on major Shia theological issues: the *walaya* of the imams, the dissociation (*bara'a*) from their enemies sometimes discussed with code names stressing the *rafidi* (rejectionist, anti-Sunni) nature of early Shia Islam, the infallibility (*'isma*) of the prophets and, by implication, the imams, the notion of *bada'* or how it seems that God's decree changes as grasped by human minds, and intercession (*shafa'a*) of the imams with God to obtain paradise for their followers and extricate them from the hellfire.[35] Rippin has cautioned against essentializing early exegesis as esoteric.[36] However, as Muslim exegetical traditions developed, and Twelver Shia scholarly interactions with other Muslims increased, the major exegeses of the medieval period collated lexical and narrative as well as esoteric features. Esoteric commentary was thus woven into the fabric of texts in different disciplines.

A key feature of these works is supposed to be their adherence to the notion that the 'Uthmanic recension has been corrupted (*tahrif*). But what does *tahrif* mean? In what sense did the hadith suggest that the words of the Qur'an had been altered, omitted or supplemented? Some have suggested that the issue of what constituted the text of the Qur'an, famously exemplified in the debate over whether stoning was a mandated punishment in the text or not, was argued out in early hadith texts, whether Sunni or Shia.[37] The question of whether the Shia reject the 'Uthmanic recension has become a matter of modern anti-Shia polemics and still begs the question of what we understand the Qur'an as text to be, and how a text can be fixed and canonized around a series of 'recitations' and variants that in turn have been canonized in the classical 'Abbasid period.[38] On the

---

[34] Ibid., pp. 13–15.
[35] Bar-Asher, *Scripture and Exegesis*.
[36] Rippin, 'What Defines a (Pre-modern) Shi'i Tafsir?'
[37] Modarressi, 'Early Debates.'
[38] Brunner, 'La question,' pp. 29–38.

whole, the early Shia community – including the imams – were outside the process of the collation, redaction and then canonization of the inscribed text and its recitations, hence one might suggest that taking ownership of it would always have been under some duress; the Shia cause as an alternative sacred history makes it clear.[39] One could classify *tahrif* to entail the following types of variants: differences in vocalization or recitation, word substitution – usually significant ones such as using *umma* (community) instead of *a'imma* (imams) – rearrangement of word order, as well as omissions such as the name of 'Ali.[40] The exegeses show the imams speaking to define the revelation as privileged enunciators of the text whose relationship to the revelation authorized them to do so. Even if one assumes that the texts suggest that the imams possess the privileged and definition recension redacted by 'Ali (the so-called *mushaf 'Ali*), it is rare to see the exegeses attempt to define what that recension was, deferred as it is in a moment of messianism to its unveiling with the awaited Mahdi. Part of the process of being a believer whose heart has been tested for faith by God would entail accepting a silent Qur'an that was not fully sanctioned by the speaking Qur'an to enable membership of a wider community, precisely because the community of faith still had the revelation in the person of the imam.

SHIA EXEGESIS FOR NON-SHIA AUDIENCES

By the eleventh century, the Twelver Shia tradition moved to the task of systematic and comprehensive exegesis.[41] The theologians of Baghdad realized the importance of communicating in a more cosmopolitan context. They wrote important critiques of hadith-based studies on creedal matters and emphasized the significance of a rational hermeneutics of the text that

---

[39] Amir-Moezzi, 'Silent Qur'an.'

[40] Bar-Asher, *Scripture and Exegesis*, p. 47.

[41] Recently a comprehensive, albeit rather descriptive, work has been published in English on Shia exegesis with chapters on the major works from this period until the present translated on the whole from Persian originals – *Qur'anic Studies and Shi'a Exegesis*, ed. Abbas Bahmanpour, vol. 2 (London: Islamic College for Advanced Studies Press, 2013).

continued to vindicate the Shia case, but ignored issues such as the integrity of the Qur'anic text. Engagement with Mu'tazili thought had already begun with the *tradents*, although it is not evident in the earlier exegeses. Three major medieval exegeses – *al-Tibyan* of Abu Ja'far al-Tusi (d. 460/1067), *Majma' al-bayan* of al-Fadl b. al-Hasan al-Tabrisi (d. 548/1154), and *Ruh al-janan* of Abu-l-Futuh al-Razi (fl. twelfth century, the first major Persian Shia exegesis) – were influenced by Mu'tazili theology and some Avicennan philosophy. They represent the classical tradition and a standard structure: outward matters such as the lexical gloss and the reading (*qira'a*), followed by discussion of the relevant hadith and the meaning (*khabar, ma'na*), where the esoteric aspects come to the fore.[42] These comprehensive works deliberately played themselves within the wider genre of exegesis and directly appealed to a non-Shia audience, drawing upon Sunni hadith as well as explicitly citing a range of extra-Qur'anic and extra-Shia sources of authority, including lexicography, belles-lettres, rational theology and philosophy. Al-Tusi says that until his time, no one had written an exegesis that went beyond narrations and comprehensively discussed language, meanings and the whole range of religious disciplines that a scholar should master. He explicitly cited non-Shia sources approvingly, while insisting on the need to combat the heresies of the anthropomorphists, determinists and other groups.[43] Al-Tusi has an extensive discussion of how variants might arise in the text with the clear implication of denying *tahrif*, but also of rejecting the established notion of seven canonical recitations reflecting seven dialects that were promoted by Sunni exegetes.[44]

---

[42] This required certain elements of the classical exegesis genre to be established: works based on hadith (*tafsir bi-l-ma'thur*), studies of lexical meaning, language and stylistics such as *Ma'ani al-Qur'an* of al-Farra' (d. 207/822) and *Majaz al-Qur'an* of al-Zajjaj (d. 311/923), and the development of theological discourse, especially in the works of Mu'tazili authors such as Abu 'Ali al-Jubba'i (d. 303/915), Abu Muslim al-Isfahani (d. 323/934) and 'Ali al-Rummani (d. 384/994) (Gimaret, *Une lecture mu'tazilite*; Ghiyasi Kirmani, *Barrasi-yi*; al-Isfahani, *Jami'al-ta'wil*; Kulinich, *Representing*). Recent research suggests that the works of these medieval Shia authors drew upon *al-Masabih fi tafsir al-Qur'an* of al-Wazir al-Maghribi (d. 418/1027) who lived around fifty years before al-Tusi – we know that *al-Masabih* was cited (Karimi-Nia, 'Al-Masabih').

[43] Al-Tusi, *Al-Tibyan*, vol. I, p. 1.

[44] Ibid., pp. 5–10.

This development in exegesis mirrors the development in other disciplines such as jurisprudence, in which one sees Shia authors forsaking their earlier isolationism and staunchly rejectionist approach to non-Shia traditions and following the rules of their structure, method and goals of other Muslim communities of interpretation. But the basic principle of understanding the text to elucidate the *walaya* of the imams remained a constant within this larger framework. Al-Tusi, like all Shia exegetes to that date, continues to insist on the primary authority of the *Hadith al-thaqalayn*.[45]

THE RETURN TO THE IMAMS: FAYD KASHANI

The early modern period saw two different tendencies. In the first, the sixteenth, seventeenth and eighteenth centuries saw a revival of traditional Shia exegesis based on the sayings of the imams and refocused on what constituted the authentic and original Shia message. This was within the context of the rise of the Akhbari movement that rejected the use of independent reason in law and theology and instead insisted upon authentic legal and theological reasoning based solely on the explicit sayings of the imams. Works such as *Manhaj al-sadiqayn fi ilzam al-mukhalifin* of Fathullah Kashani (d. 980/1570), *al-Safi* by Muhsin Fayd Kashani (d. 1090/1680), *Nur al-thaqalayn* by 'Abd 'Ali Huwayzi (d. 1104/1693), *al-Burhan* by Sayyid Hashim al-Bahrani (d. 1106/1695), *Tafsir* of Sharif-i Lahiji also known as Qutb al-Din Ashkivari (d. c. 1095/1684), and *Mir'at al-anwar* of Abu-l-Hasan al-'Amili (d. 1139/1727) restated the positions of the early period and presented exegesis as an exteriorization of the inner teachings of the imams in a triumphalist manner (against Sunni exegesis) through lists of hadith.[46] These works argued that one could understand the Qur'an only through the words of the imam – anything else was an arrogation that implied exegesis based on one's own (false) opinion. Shia exegetes went beyond the hadith-based approach of the early texts in which the Qur'anic revelation was glossed through the living revelation of

---

[45] Ibid., pp. 3, 5.
[46] Lawson, 'Akhbari Shi'i Approaches.'

the imam; they went a logical step further by denying any understanding of the Qur'an, either intratextuality or intertextuality, without the explicit gloss attributed to the imam in a deliberate polemic against the more rationally based and ecumenical exegeses of the middle period.

Fayd Kashani prefaces his exegesis with a numerically significant (for a Twelver Shia) set of twelve introductions designed to establish the need to turn to the hadith of the imams because they alone know what the Qur'an is.[47] The Qur'an informs its addressees about the imams and about their enemies.[48] Since the principle of the need for *ta'wil* to uncode all that is within the revelation requires the imams, it is imperative not to seek other sources, and even the seemingly innocent act of following the lexicography and stylistics of Sunni authors goes against the hadith of the imams because it involves following someone's (false) opinion (*ra'y*).[49] Kashani emphasizes the need for the hadith of the imams by citing a series of hadiths.[50] Most of these exegeses were written in Arabic for scholars by scholars and reflected an intellectual shift in making sense of the Shia tradition that, in the seventeenth century, took a turn away from the philosophical and mystical towards a recovery of the words and texts of the imams themselves. At the same time, there was a rise in Persian exegesis that was part of a Safavid project of the venularization of the faith for a wider readership in the Persianate East.

SHIA ENGAGEMENT WITH THE MYSTICAL TRADITION

Another strong tendency that overlaps with the revival of Shia exegesis was mystical and philosophical commentary influenced by the school of Ibn 'Arabi (d. 1240). The tradition of mystical commentary starts with the *Tafsir al-muhit al-a'zam wa-l-bahr al-khidam* of Sayyid Haydar Amuli (d. after 1385). Amuli's work is incomplete: only the tantalizing seven

---

[47] Kashani, *Manhaj*, vol. I, pp. 19–20.
[48] Ibid., p. 24.
[49] Ibid., pp. 29–37.
[50] Lawson, 'Akhbari Shi'i Approaches.'

introductions survive. Amuli makes his intent clear in the first introduction: to write a work of *ta'wil* according to the principles of the people of singular reality (the Sufis who adhere, like Ibn 'Arabi, to the notion of *wahdat al-wujud* or the unity of existence) and the principles of the *ahl al-bayt* (the family of the Prophet, i.e. the imams), elucidating the three levels of understanding open to all things: the level of the *sharia* (the outward practice of the faith), the *tariqa* (the spiritual path), and the *haqiqa* (the inner reality unveiled to mystics and to the imams).[51] Given Amuli's position on the complete identity and complementarity between Sufism and Shia Islam, this approach is not surprising. He cites four major exegetical influences: *Majma' al-bayan* of al-Tabrisi, which he describes as the best Shia commentary; *al-Kashshaf* of al-Zamakhshari (d. 538/1144), which he says is well respected and useful for polemics; and the two 'ta'wilat' works of Najm al-Din al-Razi (d. 617/1220) and 'Abd al-Razzaq Kashani (d. 736/1336), both major Sufi commentaries, the latter in some ways prefiguring Amuli as a Shia Sufi.[52] Mulla Sadra Shirazi's (d. 1045/1636) exegesis, also incomplete, exhibits the influence of Ibn 'Arabi, but it cannot be reduced to the metaphysics of the Sunni Sufi.[53] Mulla Sadra's exegesis is based on his own metaphysics and arises, as he says, from a desire to understand what it means to be human and how, on the spiritual path, one follows the imams to become a saint (*wali*) who is also a sage and whose exegesis and practice of philosophy are in complete harmony.[54] For Mulla Sadra, the study of philosophy and exegesis is geared towards the acquisition of wisdom and becoming a sage. This theme of becoming a Shia sage will be taken up in the modern period by Tabataba'i.

Later commentaries with a more marked Sufi taste fulfill the promise of these earlier works. The *Bayan al-sa'ada*, an extensive and scholarly exegesis in Arabic by the Ni'matullahi Gunabadi Sufi Shaykh Muhammad Sultan 'Ali Shah (d. 1327/1909) shows the influence of Mulla Sadra's philosophy; however, the versified Persian *Tafsir-i safi* of Mirza Hasan Isfahani, known as Safi 'Ali Shah (d. 1317/1899), is both Shia and also conciliatory towards

---

[51] Amuli, *Al-Muhit al-a'zam*, vol. I, p. 195.
[52] Ibid., p. 231.
[53] *contra* Rustom, *Triumph of Mercy*.
[54] Mulla Sadra, *Tafsir*, I, pp. 2–3.

other non-Shia Sufis, perhaps influenced by his engagements with wider circles beyond Iran.[55] Both of these works use the Qur'an to demonstrate the validity and spiritual superiority of the Shia Sufi path and continue the method of Amuli, albeit with an eye to the new realities of a Qajar Iran that was opening up to external influences from Europe and India in particular. These works share a view of the Qur'anic text as multivocal and open to a hierarchy of interpretations with a preference for the mystical and supra-rational, and put forward the claims of the exegete as a Shia sage (*hakim*).

EXEGETICAL METHODS FOR THE MODERN WORLD

In more recent times, we find a greater concern for the social context and a desire to engage with modernity, which is common to various exegetical approaches in the modern period. The desire to communicate to a wider audience, a feature of modern exegesis, means a turn towards the use of vernaculars and more accessible style and language, the appeal to science and reason, and the need to be socially relevant. Voluminous exegeses continue to be published, and the leading ones of the twentieth century arise out of a concern to make a Shia reading and vindication of the text relevant to the times: the teaching exegesis in Persian *Tafsir-i namuna* compiled by a team under the supervision of Ayatullah Nasir Makarim Shirazi (b. 1924), the socially engaged and ecumenical (and arguably barely Shia) Arabic exegesis *Min wahy al-Qur'an* of Sayyid Muhammad Husayn Fadlallah (d. 2010), the scholarly Arabic exegesis *al-Mizan fi tafsir al-Qur'an* of Sayyid Muhammad Husayn Tabataba'i (d. 1981), and socially engaged and philosophical Indian *Tafsir-i Fasl al-khitab* of Sayyid 'Ali Naqi Naqvi (d. 1988) in Urdu.[56] Other multivolume exegeses associated with leading

---

[55] Kumpani-Zari'i, *Gunabadi va tafsir-i*; Cancian, 'L'esegesi'; Sarvatiyan, *Safi 'Ali Shah*; Alessandro Cancian at the Institute of Ismaili Studies in London is currently writing a monograph on the exegesis of Sultan 'Ali Shah.

[56] A popular, more traditional Urdu exegesis that focuses on its Shia identity, with a strong denial of *tahrif* and of exaggerated doctrine (*ghuluw*), is *Tafsir anwar al-Najaf fi asrar al-mushaf* of Husayn Bakhsh Najafi (d. 1990, published in Lahore in 1993) that, in fifteen volumes, defends a range of Shia theological positions through the text. Another scholarly work coming from the subcontinent is the Persian *Lawami' al-tanzil wa-sawati' al-ta'wil* of Sayyid

jurists include *Ala' al-rahman fi tafsir al-Qur'an* of Muhammad Jawad al-Balaghi (d. 1933), *al-Sirat al-mustaqim* of Sayyid Husayn Burujirdi (d. 1962), and *Mawahib al-Rahman fi tafsir al-Qur'an* of Sayyid 'Abd al-A'la al-Sabzawari (d. 1998), all of which have been more or less published. These commentaries continue the classical tradition's atomistic method of organizing and of glossing verse by verse. The commentary of Tabataba'i stands apart from these by insisting on an intratextual method – i.e., one in which the Qur'an glosses the Qur'an (*tafsir al-qur'an bi-l-qur'an*) alongside the hadith. Tabataba'i advances a strong attack on those exegetes who impose their own preconceptions and learning upon the Qur'an.

A number of other modern works embrace 'topical exegesis' (*tafsir mawdu'i*), in which the exegete selects topics of social and intellectual relevance and does not follow the order of the Qur'an itself.[57]

Yet another development in modern exegesis has been the phenomenon of women writing exegeses, especially in Persian – although it would be misleading to define them necessarily as feminist. These works include, most famously, the extensive and scholarly fifteen-volume work of Nusrat Amin Isfahani (d. 1983) entitled *Makhzan al-'irfan*, the *Bayani az Qur'an* by Zahra Rusta (b. 1975), and *Tafsir-i ravan* of Sayyida Siddiqa Khurasani (b. 1959), all in Persian.[58] These still require further study, not least to make sense of an emerging female voice in Shia exegesis. Given their training in Islamic philosophy and mysticism, a comparison between the work of Nusrat Amin and Tabataba'i could be quite fruitful.

All of these modern commentaries demonstrate a desire to reach out and make connections with broader communal and national identities, and they address modern subjects such as rationalism, science, and the need to make religion compatible with, and relevant to, the contemporary world. With the advent of new media and ways of dissemination, exegesis is no

---

Abu-l-Qasim Rizvi (d. 1906) and his son Sayyid 'Ali al-Ha'iri (d. 1941), parts of which were published in lithograph early in the twentieth century in Kanpur and Lahore; it is a staunch defence of the Shia faith and reading of revelation, with the father responsible for the first part up to surat al-Yusuf and the son completing the work. Its credentials were much praised by leading seminary scholars.

[57] One famous example is the ongoing *Tafsir-i tasnim* of Ayatullah 'Abdullah Javadi Amuli (b. 1933).

[58] Mihrizi, 'Zan dar tafsir'; Bid-Hindi, *Banu-yi nimuna*; Kumpani-Zari'i, *Gunabadi va tafsir-i*.

longer confined to books: popular TV programs on the many satellite channels in numerous languages bring the processes of interpretation and debate into the homes of believers, who also engage with each other on social media and more generally online, making sense of the revelation and deploying it for their own ends to understand what it means to live authentically as a Shia believer today. Authority is centralized in the institutions of learning, but also distributed to the individuals themselves – the one constant that remains is the refrain of many an introduction of a Shia exegesis to revert back to the imams as privileged enunciators of the revelation.

In this chapter, I have examined how Twelver Shia communities of interpretation have engaged with the Qur'an and understood it on the horizon of the person of the imam who reveals its *ta'wil* and who embodies the revelation as much as the scripture does. The tradition of exegesis among the Shia has remained vibrant and dynamic; it has developed and changed over time as different approaches and methods of glossing the revelation were embraced in order to make sense of it for Shia believers, always with a strong central focus on how the Qur'an reveals the *walaya* of the imams – and hence the recourse to the sayings of the imams and the practice of exegesis reinforces the authority of the revelation. The context and the audience tend to define the extent to which the exegeses are open and outwards looking, or more narrowly focused and inward looking, which is partly expressed in how they negotiate the complementarity or binary opposition of the *zahir* and the *batin*. Thus the commonalities that various exegetical exemplars bear to other exegeses in the wider Muslim traditions – and since we know that the very act of commenting upon the text bestows authority on the word of God, as well as implies the authority of the exegete who has the privileged status of one who can explain the text – are balanced out with the particularities of Shia exegesis as a mode of exemplification designed to emphasize the central complementarity of authority in the tradition between the Qur'an as a text revealed to and through the Prophet and his family and successors, the imams who personify, define and explain the text. But above all, exegesis is a process of establishing authority – of the revelation, both the text and the person of the Prophet and the imams – and of course of the exegete himself, who seeks to define what it means to be Shia.

BIBLIOGRAPHY

Primary sources

Amuli, Haydar b. 'Ali (d. after 1385). *Al-Muhit al-a'zam wa-al-bahr al-khidam fi tawil Kitab Allah al-'aziz.* Ed. Muhsin Musawi al-Tabrizi. (Qum, 2002)

al-'Askari, al-Hasan b. 'Ali. *Al-Tafsir al-mansub ilá al-imam al-'askari.* Ed. Shaykh Muhammad al-Salihi al-Andimashki. (Qum, 2009)

al-'Ayyashi, Abu al-Nasr Muhammad b. Mas'ud. *Tafsir.* Ed. Sayyid Hashim Rasuli Mahallati. (Tehran, 1991)

al-Bahrani, Sayyid Hashim (d. 1695). *Al-Burhan fi tafsir al-Qur'an.* (Beirut, 1973)

al-Bursi, Rajab (d. c.1411). *Mashariq anwar al-yaqin fi asrar amir al-mu'minin.* (Beirut, 1978)

Burujirdi, Sayyid Husayn (d. 1962). *Al-Sirat al-mustaqim.* (Qum, 1995)

Fadlallah, Sayyid Muhammad Husayn (d. 2010). *Min wahy al-Qur'an.* (Beirut, 1998)

Fayi, Abu-l-Fay (d. 1595). *Sawati' al-ilham fi tafsir kalam al-malik al-'allam.* Ed. Murtada Shirazi. (Qum, 1996)

Huwayzi, 'Abd 'Ali. *Tafsir nur al-thaqalayn.* Ed. Sayyid Hashim Rasuli Mahallati. (Qum, 1965)

Ibn Abi Jumhur al-Ahsa'i (d. 1504). *'Awali al-la'ali.* Ed. Mujtaba 'Iraqi. (Qum, 1986)

Ibn al-Haythami. *Majma' al-zawa'id.* (Cairo, 1934)

al-Isfahani, Abu Muslim. *Jami' al-ta'wil li-muhkam al-tanzil.* Ed. Muhammad Hadi Ma'rifat and Mahmud Sarmadi. (Tehran, 1388 Sh/2009)

Kashani, Fathullah (d. 1580). *Manhaj al-sadiqayn fi ilzam al-mukhalifin.* Ed. Sayyid Abu-l-Hasan Sha'rani. (Tehran, 1965)

Kashani, Muhsin Fayd (d. 1680). *Tafsir al-safi.* Ed. Husayn al-A'lami. (Beirut, 1979)

al-Kufi, Furat (fl. tenth century). *Tafsir.* Ed. Muhammad al-Kazim. (Tehran, 1990)

al-Kulayni, Abu Ja'far (d. 941). *Usul al-kafi.* Ed. 'Ali-Akbar Ghaffari. (Reprint, Beirut, 2005)

Lahiji, Sharif-i. *Tafsir.* Ed. Sayyid Jalal al-Din Muhaddith Urmawi. (Tehran, 1961)

Majlisi, Muhammad Baqir (d. 1699). *Bihar al-anwar.* (Beirut, 1983)

Munajjimi, 'Ali-Rida. *Sharh-i jami'-yi tafsir-i 'irfani-yi safi 'ali shah.* (Tehran, 1385 Sh/2006)

Naqvi, Sayyid 'Ali Naqi (d. 1988). *Tafsir-i fasl al-khitab.* (Lahore, 1991)

al-Nisaburi, al-Hakim. *Al-Mustadrak 'ala l-sahihayn.* (Riyadh, 1997)

al-Qummi, 'Ali b. Ibrahim (attr.?) *Tafsir.* Ed. Sayyid Tayyib al-Jaza'iri. (Najaf, 1966)

al-Qummi, al-Saffar. *Basa'ir al-darajat.* Ed. Mirza Muhsin Kucha-baghi. (Reprint, Beirut, 2010)

al-Razi, Abu-l-Futuh (d. after 1131). *Rawz al-jinan wa-ruh al-janan fi tafsir al-Qur'an.* Ed. M.J. Yahaqqi and M.M. Nasih. (Mashhad, 1987–97)

Sabzawari, Sayyid 'Abd al-A'la (d. 1994). *Mawahib al-rahman fi tafsir al-Qur'an.* (Najaf, 1984)

al-Sayyari, Ahmad. *Revelation and Falsification: The Kitab al-qira'at of Ahmad b. Muhammad al-Sayyari.* Ed. Etan Kohlberg and Mohammad Ali Amir-Moezzi. (Leiden, 2009)

Shirazi, Mulla Sadra (d. 1636). *Tafsir al-Qur'an al-karim.* Gen. ed. Sayyid Muhammad Khamenei. (Tehran, 2010)

Shirazi, Nasir Makarim. *Tafsir-i namuna.* (Qum, 1998)

Tabataba'i, Sayyid Muhammad Husayn (d. 1981). *Al-Mizan fi tafsir al-Qur'an.* (Tehran, 1973)

al-Tabrisi, al-Fadl (d. 1153). *Majma' al-bayan fi tafsir al-Qur'an.* (Beirut, 1961)

'Tafsir Imam 'Ali bi-riwayat al-Nu'mani.' In Muhammad Baqir Majlisi, *Bihar al-anwar,* vol. XC, 1–97. (Beirut, 1982)

al-Thumali, Abu Hamza. *Tafsir abi hamza al-thumali.* Ed. 'Abd al-Razzaq Hirz al-Din. (Qum, 2000) al-Tusi, Abu Ja'far (d. 1067). *Al-Tibyan fi tafsir al-Qur'an*. Gen. ed. Aqa Buzurg al-Tihrani. (Najaf, 1963)

al-Tustari, Sahl b.'Abdullah (d. 896). *Tafsir al-Qur'an al-'azim*. Ed. M.B. al-Sud. (Beirut, 2002)

Secondary sources

Amir-Moezzi, M.A. *The Divine Guide in Early Shi'ism*. (Albany: State University of New York Press, 1994)

— *Le Coran silencieux et le coran parlant*. (Paris: CNRS, 2011)

— 'The Silent Qur'an and the Speaking Qur'an: History and Scripture through some Ancient Texts.' *Studia Islamica* 108 (2013): 143–74

— *The Spirituality of Shi'i Islam: Beliefs and Practices*. (London: I.B. Tauris, 2011)

— 'The *tafsir* of al-Hibari.' In *The Study of Shi'i Islam: History, Theology and Law*. Ed. Farhad Daftary and Gurdofarid Miskinzoda, 113–34. (London: I.B. Tauris, 2014)

— and H. Ansari. 'Muhammad b. Ya'qub al-Kulayni et son *Kitab al-Kafi*: Une introduction.' *Studia Iranica* 38 (2009): 191–247

Ayoub, Mahmoud.'The Speaking Qur'an and the Silent Qur'an: A Study of the Principles and Development of Imami Shi'i Tafsir.' In *Approaches to the History of the Interpretation of the Qur'an*. Ed. Andrew Rippin, 177–98. (Oxford: Clarendon Press, 1988)

Bahir, Muhammad. *Abu al-Futuh al-Razi va tafsir-i rawz al-jinan*. (Tehran: Khanah-i Kitab, 2009)

Bar-Asher, Meir. 'The Qur'anic Commentary Ascribed to Imam Hasan al-'Askari.' *Jerusalem Studies in Arabic and Islam* 24 (2000): 358–79

— *Scripture and Exegesis in Early Imami Shi'ism*. (Leiden/Jerusalem: Brill, 1999)

Bid-Hindi, Nasir Baqiri. *Banu-yi nimuna: jilva-ha-yi az hayat-i banu-yi mujtahida Amin Isfahani*. (Qum: Bustan-i Kitab-i Qom, 1382 Sh/2003)

Boylston, Nicholas.'Speaking the Secrets of Sanctity in the *tafsir* of Safi'Ali Shah.' In *Approaches to the Qur'an in Contemporary Iran*. Ed. Alessandro Cancian. (London: Oxford University Press in Association with the Institute of Ismaili Studies, forthcoming)

Brunner, Rainer.'La question de la falsification du coran dans l'exégèse chiite duodécimaine.' *Arabica* 52 (2005): 1–42

Cancian, Alessandro.'L'esegesi dell'acqua nel sufismo sciita: il caso del *tafsir* di Sultan'Ali Shah Gonabadi.' *Indoasiatica* 6 (2009): 69–103

— 'Translation, Authority and Exegesis in Modern Iranian Sufism: Two Iranian Sufi Masters in Dialogue.' *Journal of Persianate Studies* 7:1 (2014): 88–106

Corbin, Henry. *En Islam Iranien*. 4 vols. (Paris: Gallimard, 1971–2)

Eliash, Joseph.'The Shi'ite Qur'an: A Reconsideration of Goldziher's Interpretation.' *Arabica* 16 (1969): 15–24

Fudge, Bruce. *Qur'anic Hermeneutics: al-Tabrisi and the Craft of Commentary*. (London: Routledge, 2011)

Ghiyasi Kirmani, Muhammad Riza. *Barrasi-yi ara' va nazarat-i tafsiri-yi Abu Muslim Muhammad ibn Bahr al-Isfahani*. (Qum: Huzur, 1378 Sh/1999)

Gimaret, Daniel. *Une lecture mu'tazilite du Coran: le tafsir d'Abu 'Ali al-Jubba'i*. (Louvain: Peeters, 1994)

Gleave, Robert.'Early Shi'i Hermeneutics: Some Exegetical Techniques Attributed to the Shi'i Imams.' In *Aims, Methods and Contexts of Qur'anic Exegesis (2nd/8th – 9th/15th c.)*. Ed. Karen Bauer, 141–72. (Oxford: Oxford University Press, 2013)

Goldziher, Ignaz. *Die Richtungen der islamischen Koransauslegung*. (Leiden: Brill, 1920)

al-Hindi, Sayyid Hamid Husayn. '*Abaqat al-anwar*. Ed. Sayyid 'Ali al-Milani. 11 vols. (Qum: Mu'assasah-i Naba', 1993)

Kariman, Husayn. *Tabrisi va majma' al-bayan*. (Tehran: Chapkhanah-i Danishgahaf, 1962)

Karimi-Nia, Murtada. *'Al-Masabih fi tafsir al-Qur'an: kanz min turath al-tafsir al-shi'i.' Turathuna* 113 and 114 (Jumada II 1434/April 2013): 55–100

— '*Chahar paradayim-i tafsir-i shi'a: muqaddima-yi dar tarikh-i tafsir-i Shi'i bar Qur'an-i karim.'* In *Jashn-nama-yi Ustad Muhammad 'Ali Mahdavi-rad*. Ed. Rasul Ja'fariyan, 425–43. (Tehran: Nashr-i Mo'arekh, 1391 Sh/2012)

al-Khu'i, Sayyid Abu-l-Qasim. *Al-Bayan fi tafsir al-Qur'an*. (Qom: Mu'assasat Ihya' Athar al-Imam al-Khu'i, 1997)

Kulinich, Alena. *Representing a 'Blameworthy tafsir': Mu'tazilite Exegetical Tradition in al-Jami' fi tafsir al-Qur'an of 'Ali ibn 'Isa al-Rummani*. (Unpublished PhD diss., School of Oriental and African Studies, 2012)

Kumpani-Zari'i, Muhammad. *Gunabadi va tafsir-i Bayan al-sa'ada*. (Tehran: Khanah-i Kitab, 1390 Sh/2011)

Künkler, Mirjam and Roja Fazaeli. 'The Life of Two Mujtahidahs: Female Religious Authority in Twentieth-Century Iran.' In *Women, Leadership, and Mosques: Changes in Contemporary Islamic Authority*. Ed. Masooda Bano and Hilary Kalmbach, 127–60. (Leiden: Brill, 2012)

Lawson, Todd. 'Akhbari Shi'i Approaches to Tafsir.' In *Approaches to the Qur'an*. Ed. G. Hawting and A. Shareef, 173–210. (London: Routledge, 1993)

— 'Notes for the Study of a "Shi'i Qur'an."' *Journal of Semitic Studies* 36 (1991): 279–95

Ma'rifat, Muhammad Hadi. *Al-Tafsir wa-l-mufassirun fi thawbihi-l-qashib*. (Mashhad: al-Jami'ah al-Radawiyah lil-' Ulum al-Islamiyah, 1997)

Mihrizi, Mahdi. 'Zan dar tafsir *Makhzan al-'irfan*-i Banu Amin Isfahani.' *Ayina-yi pazhuhish* 98 and 99 (Khurdad ta Shahrivar 1385 Sh/May to September 2006): 16–23

al-Milani, Sayyid 'Ali. *Hadith al-thaqalayn: tawaturuhu, fiqhuhu*. (Qum: n.p., 1992)

Modarressi, Hossein. 'Early Debates on the Integrity of the Qur'an: A Brief Survey.' *Studia Islamica* 77 (1993): 5–39

Rippin, Andrew. 'What Defines a (Pre-modern) Shi'i Tafsir?' In *The Study of Shi'i Islam: History, Theology and Law*. Ed. Farhad Daftary and Gurdofarid Miskinzoda, 95–112. (London: I.B. Tauris, 2014)

Rustom, Mohammed. *The Triumph of Mercy: Philosophy and Scripture in Mulla Sadra*. (Albany: State University of New York Press, 2012)

Sander, Paul. *Zwischen Charisma und Ratio: Entwicklungen in der frühen imamitischen Theologie*. (Berlin: K. Schwarz, 1994)

Sarvatiyan, Bihruz. *Safi 'Ali Shah va tafsirash*. (Tehran: Khanah-i Kitab, 1389 Sh/2010)

Steigerwald, Diana. 'Twelver Shi'i ta'wil.' In *The Blackwell Companion to the Qur'an*. Ed. Andrew Rippin, 373–85. (Oxford: Wiley, 2006)

Tisdall, W. St Clair. 'Shi'ah Additions to the Koran.' *Muslim World* 3 (1913): 227–41

Zaydi, Kasid. *Manhaj al-Shaykh Abu Ja'far al-Tusi fi tafsir al-Qur'an al-karim*. (Baghdad: Bayt al-Hikmah, 2004)

Chapter 7

The Qur'an and the Baha'i Faith

Todd Lawson, University of Toronto

And if all the trees on earth were pens, and the sea were ink, with seven more seas yet added to it, the words of God would not be exhausted: for, verily, God is almighty, wise.

(Q 31:27, Asad)

The Baha'i faith was born in Iran and for this reason it trails many Iranian clouds of glory. One of these is the high degree to which Islam and the Qur'an have had a great impact on the form and contents of the Baha'i revelation and the Baha'i religion. The Baha'i writings are steeped in the Qur'an and, to a lesser degree, also steeped in hadith – a topic not pursued here. Qur'anic quotations in Baha'i scripture are indicated in published works and manuscripts. However, Qur'anic diction and vocabulary is such a pervasive element of the Baha'i writings that it would be impossible to indicate every instance of influence or presence. The Qur'an has had, down the centuries, an unparalleled influence on Muslim culture in general and, from the earliest times, on Irano-Islamic culture in general, and an even more intense impact upon specifically religious works, whether mystical, philosophical, theological, or poetic, written by Iranians in both Persian and Arabic.[1] The Qur'anic content of the Baha'i writings is a source

---

[1] Lewis, 'Persian Literature and the Qur'an.'

of pride and inspiration among Baha'is as it obviously was among the central founding figures of the Baha'i faith: The Bab (d. 1850), Baha'ullah (d. 1892), Abdulbaha' (d. 1921) and Shoghi Effendi (d. 1957). Although, as long ago as 1938, Shoghi Effendi had instructed the Baha'i community to study the Qur'an thoroughly, it has not yet been completely and systematically tracked and indexed throughout all Baha'i publications, even though some steps in this direction have been made. One of the biggest factors in this comparatively slow progress has to do with the pervasiveness of the Qur'an throughout the Baha'i writings, the numerous different contexts and functions involved and, perhaps, most definitively, the truly vast literary terrain involved. The literary output of the founding figures mentioned above, in addition to a vast secondary literature in hundreds of languages, constitutes a textual base for such a study that is daunting in every way. Much of the Baha'i corpus has been published, but much more remains in manuscript form. However, it is possible to gauge the importance of the Qur'an in Baha'i scripture by taking account of its influence and presence in the two earliest major compositions of the Bab. As we will see in what follows, these two works are in fact *tafsirs*, or Qur'an commentaries. One of these is considered the inaugural work of the Baha'i era.

From one point of view, the depth of the Qur'anic roots of the Baha'i faith is perfectly natural and unsurprising for, despite laughable attempts to cast the Babi and Baha'i religions as tools of foreign intervention and manipulation (British, Russian, American), no compelling evidence has been bought to bear to counter the clear and quite reasonable assumption that the Baha'i faith is an indigenous Islamicate development. In the course of its genesis it relied solely on the inner resources of Islamic intellectual and religious culture to configure its own distinctive religious identity. Obviously, the nineteenth century was a time of intense and burgeoning globalism, and this also figured in the process. But the Bab – an Arabic word meaning 'gate' or 'door', and the title by which a sayyid from the Iranian merchant class, Ali Muhammad Shirazi, has come to be most widely known – and Baha'ullah – an Arabic title meaning 'the glory or splendor of God' and the honorific of Mirza Husayn Ali Nuri – both engaged with the Qur'an at the deepest levels of their writing. They adduced it as proof of their respective visions and claims, they commented upon it in both traditional and modernist modes, and they clearly considered it an inviolable and sacred record of divine revelation.

Abdulbaha', the son of Baha'ullah, also clearly knew the Qur'an very well and quoted it frequently in his talks and writings, as did Shoghi Effendi.[2] The Universal House of Justice, the administrative and spiritual authority for Baha'is today, also engages the Qur'an in its various communications and publications. The basic doctrinal position is that the Prophet Muhammad, the Qur'an and Islam represent essential, holy communication from God to humanity and that the Qur'an, apart from Baha'i sacred writings, represents the only fully authentic scripture to which humanity might turn. As mentioned above, Shoghi Effendi unambiguously instructed the Baha'is to study it with the aid of sources that are fair and unbiased, and to deepen their understanding of the similarities and differences between Islam and the Baha'i faith:

> [The Baha'is] must strive to obtain, from sources that are authoritative and unbiased, a sound knowledge of the history and tenets of Islam – the source and background of their Faith – and approach reverently and with a mind purged from preconceived ideas the study of the Qur'an which, apart from the sacred scriptures of the Babi and Baha'i Revelations, constitutes the only Book which can be regarded as an absolutely authenticated Repository of the Word of God.[3]

It may be speculated that the young Baha'i community of the West had been at least partly attracted to the Baha'i message, either wittingly or unwittingly, by its significant and compelling Qur'anic content. This content gave that message a distinctive voice and doctrinal shape and caused it to distinguish itself as a new religion in the West, where, for example, what might be thought the Islamicate 'epic of humanity' was being

---

[2] While Shoghi Effendi was still a baby, his grandfather Abdulbaha', the head of the Baha'i faith at the time, arranged for weekly visits from a local Qur'an reciter to chant to the future Guardian of the Cause of God. Rabbani, *Priceless Pearl*, p. 9.

[3] Shoghi Effendi, *Advent of Divine Justice*, p. 49.

heard with new ears.[4] It is possible that Shoghi Effendi, in making the study of the Qur'an obligatory for the Baha'is, wanted them to come to terms with this fact, to study the genetic, umbilical relation between the Qur'an and the Baha'i scripture in order for them to be able to distinguish, precisely, what was Islamic from what was Baha'i.

The distinguishing watchword of the Baha'i message, from the beginning, has been: *One God, One Religion and One Humanity*. To a Muslim, such a statement is unremarkable and unexceptionable. However, during the last decades of the nineteenth century and the first few decades of the twentieth, in the major centers of Europe and North America where this Baha'i message was being actively promulgated, it was received as a refreshing and much-needed religious orientation for the new, burgeoning and quite heady modernity that was rapidly transforming the planet into a global village. To those who became followers of the religion of Baha'u'llah, this watchword had the metaphysical heft of a perfectly timed divine intervention which some saw as a metaphor for the return of Christ and others saw, less figuratively, as simply *the* return of Christ in the person of Baha'u'llah or, in some cases, his son Abdulbaha'. Other Baha'i teachings promoted at this time, especially by Abdulbaha' during his travels to Europe and North America during the pre-World War I years, 1911–13, were: the abolition of war, including 'holy war'; the equality of men and women; the independent investigation of truth, and the condemnation of *taqlid* – 'blind imitation' in matters of religion; the abolition of the clergy; the establishment of a universal auxiliary language; that religious truth is not absolute but relative; that there have been messengers from God since the beginning of creation and there will always be messengers from God; the purpose of divine revelation is the promotion of an 'ever-advancing civilization'; the centrality of consultation (*shura*) for problem-solving; compulsory education; and, the harmony of science and religion. All these ideas and principles (and many others) were presented by Abdulbaha' as spiritually mandated religious law about which there could be no

---

[4] Recent scholarship on the early growth of the Baha'i community in the West, from the last decade of the nineteenth century onward, tends to support this. See Osborn, *Religion and Relevance*; Stockman, *'Abdu'l-Baha in America*; Stockman, *Thornton Chase*. On the Islamic 'epic of humanity,' see Lawson, *Qur'an, Epic and Apocalypse*, pp. 1–26.

disagreement. Thus, unity of belief and practice was also a key teaching of the Baha'i faith, and continues to be so. Disagreement among the Baha'is has always been forbidden, and so we see another example of how the Islamic doctrine of *tawhid* has truly irradiated and given a distinct identity to the Baha'i faith. Those who became Baha'is did so, and those who continue to become Baha'is do so, because they are convinced that God had spoken to humanity once again through Baha'ullah and because they see in such a God-given spiritual regime great potential for healing the ills that beset humanity.

Those familiar with the Qur'an, Islam and the history of Islamic thought (especially theology, philosophy and mysticism) will immediately see the many connections and derivations from Islam these principles indicate. And, in many cases, such as the equality of the sexes and the importance of consultation, many could immediately cite specific Qur'anic verses which first suggested such religious verities. One could say that the Qur'an provides much of the DNA and molecular structure of the Baha'i vision and to fully understand the Baha'i reception of the Qur'an therefore requires tools and methods that are in some ways analogous to those recently developed for use in physics, biology and even archeology. The suggestion here is that the Baha'i faith presents itself as both problem and tool in such an investigation.

The connection between the Qur'an and the Baha'i faith is literary (for lack of a better word) and so it is a living one. There can be no question of arriving at some immovable, permanent conclusion for the question because the question itself is in motion. The Qur'anic molecules are Suras, Ayas, words and ideas connected to other concepts that shape culture and behavior and are in turn shaped by culture and usage. Ultimately, the Baha'i faith represents a striking example of how it is possible to be a community of the Qur'an and not be Muslim – in short, it demonstrates how the Qur'an is the property of humanity.[5]

The Baha'i faith came to be in two major phases: the first was the Babi phase (1844–63); the second, the Baha'i phase (from 1863). In both phases the engagement with the Qur'an was key. In the Babi phase the first two

---

[5] On the Qur'an as the property of humanity, see Buck, 'Discovering.'

major works of the Bab were Qur'an commentaries, the second of which is considered the first work of the Baha'i era or dispensation. In the Baha'i phase, the first major doctrinal work by Baha'ullah, the *Kitab-i Iqan*, was a Qur'an commentary in the sense that the author explained various Qur'an verses that spoke of Judgment Day, the Hour and the Afterlife. In this work, written in both Persian and Arabic, Baha'ullah also explained numerous prophetic, messianic or apocalyptic hadiths and also engaged in some Bible interpretation. Whether from the point of view of Qur'anic exegesis or from the point of view of hadith commentary, the purpose was two-fold. First, it was to demonstrate to the reader that the Qur'an and hadith had fully predicted the appearance (*zuhur*) of the Bab, his proclamation (*da'wa*), claims and the activities of his followers. The second purpose of the book was to establish the credentials of Baha'ullah, then a follower of the Bab, in preparation for his eventual claims to be a divine manifestation (*mazhar-i ilahi*).[6] This book, known in English as *The Book of Certitude*, has been translated into countless languages and it is primary scripture for the global Baha'i community. One scholar has called it the world's most widely read non-Muslim Qur'an commentary.

Both in principle and in practice, *The Book of Certitude* helped crystallize Baha'i identity and lent considerable impetus to its missionary expansion. By virtue of its diffusion in 205 or more sovereign and non-sovereign countries and territories, the *Kitab-i Iqan* emerges as the most influential work of Qur'anic exegesis outside of the Muslim world. Though the Qur'an is not, strictly speaking, part of the Baha'i scriptural corpus, the importance of this fact of non-Muslim Qur'anic exegesis may be instanced in the parallel diffusion of Jewish scriptures (the so-called Old Testament) at the hands of Christian missionaries. What began as a Babi text has ended up to be the principal doctrinal work of a nascent world religion.[7]

What Christopher Buck says here about the relationship between the Qur'an and what has been described as Baha'ullah's most important doctrinal work could – with some necessary adjustment and nuance – apply to the entire corpus of all his published works. These works may be thought

---

[6] Buck, *Symbol and Secret*, esp. pp. 257–74 on the 'messianic secret' the text conceals.
[7] Buck, 'Kitab-i-Iqan.'

to culminate, at least theologically and doctrinally, with his book of laws, *al-Kitab al-Aqdas* / *Kitab-i Aqdas: The Most Holy Book*, composed in the prison city of Akka (Acco), Ottoman Palestine, 1873. As mentioned, research on the second phase of the Baha'i reception of the Qur'an is in the early stages, but already it is obvious that it holds much promise for a deeper understanding of the relation between the Baha'i faith and its parent, Islam. This has become quite clear in Buck's pioneering and innovative book referred to above and the work of others, such as Franklin D. Lewis, whose lucid and deeply informed discussion of this and related problems in several academic articles is essential reading for the question at hand.[8]

The role the Qur'an played in the birth of the Baha'i faith during the first phase of its development is noteworthy for several reasons. This phase is represented by the two earliest extended written works by the Bab: the *Tafsir surat al-baqara* (hereafter Baqara) and the *Tafsir surat yusuf*, also known widely as the *Qayyum al-asma'* (hereafter QA). The QA has been characterized by Baha'ullah as the most important book of the new dispensation, and the greatest ... of all books.'[9] Shoghi Effendi described it as having been universally regarded 'the Qur'an of the Babis' during the Bab's lifetime.[10] Some insight into the relationship between the Qur'an and Baha'i scripture is to be gained by observing here the interesting literary phenomenon of a commentary acquiring primary importance over the object of the commentary.[11]

The Bab was born in 1817 in Shiraz into a sayyid family of merchants. His childhood is marked by an extraordinary interest in the religious life, the reading of the Qur'an, his devotion to prayer and to the sacred examples of the lives of those he refers to as The Family of God (*Al allah*): the Prophet Muhammad, his daughter Fatima and the remaining members of the group known in Persian as the Fourteen Pure Ones (*chehardeh ma'sum*),

---

[8] Beginning with Lewis,'Scripture as Literature.'

[9] Baha'ullah, *Kitab-i mustatab-i Iqan*, p. 180.'In His Book, which He hath entitled "'Qayyumu'l-Asma" – the first, the greatest and mightiest of all books – He prophesied His own martyrdom,' Baha'ullah, *Kitáb-I-Íqán*, 231.

[10] Shoghi Effendi, *God Passes By*, p. 23.

[11] Lawson,'Interpretation as Revelation.'

the Twelve Imams recognized by Ithna-'ashari Shi'ism. His formal education was minimal, but as an extraordinarily pious young man he was
attracted to a recent development in Iranian intellectual circles known
widely as the Shaykhi school.[12]

The Bab, who studied briefly in Karbala with the second leader of this
school, Sayyid Kazem Rashti, wrote an astonishing number of works in
both Persian and Arabic. His literary activity dates from at least his teen-
age years and carried on until his tragic death in 1850 when he was killed
in front of a firing squad by the combined order of equally inimical state
and religious officials, at the age of thirty. He wrote prayers, letters,
responses to questions, books of spiritual meditation and instruction,
books of law for the new dispensation, commentaries on prayers, Qur'an
and hadith.[13] Emblematically for the general question of this discussion, it
is the composition of a Qur'an commentary that officially marks the beginning of the Babi *zuhur* or dispensation *and* the Baha'i era. The commentary
was on the twelfth Sura of the Qur'an, the Sura on Joseph referred to above
by its distinctive title, *Qayyum al-asma'* (QA). Before describing this work
in detail, it will be important to discuss briefly the writings of the Bab
which were composed prior to this epoch-making commentary, what has
been referred to by Baha'ullah as 'the first, the mightiest and the greatest of
books.'

We do not know exactly how many works the Bab wrote before he
composed the QA, which he began on the evening of May 22, 1844/5
Jumada al-Awwal, 1260. Two works stand out because they are datable
from internal information. The older of these two, 'The Epistle on Spiritual
Wayfaring' (*Risalat al-suluk*) is a relatively brief presentation of the crucial
elements of living a godly life. It contains numerous quotations from the
Qur'an in support of its main argument and also numerous hadiths, largely

---

[12] In fact, this is a term of *odium theologicum* coined by their opponents. The school itself prefers
Kashfiyya as a designation. *Kashf* is a Qur'anic term that means disclosure and is meant to
convey a method of knowing that combines reason and suprarational modes. One may translate
it as 'the Intuitionists.' The derisive intent of the term *Shaykhiyya* depends upon the mistrust of
Sufism and its shaykhs in the immediate milieu and implicitly charges that the Imam has been
replaced by a mere shaykh by the 'Shaykhyis.' Nonetheless, scholars continue to refer to the
Shaykhis, the *Shaykhiyya* and so on instead of the *Kashfiyya*.
[13] MacEoin, *Sources for Early Babi Doctrine*.

from the Shia-*akhbar* corpus. Thus, the various speakers of the text are: God, through the Qur'an, the Prophet and the imams, through the hadith, and the Bab, as author of the brief epistle. Another voice is also referred to and possibly evoked in the process – that of the aforementioned Sayyid Kazim Rashti. The author, the Bab, counsels his reader to look to the writings of his 'dear teacher' for a more complete discussion of the matters at hand.[14]

In the next work, Baqara, the method is quite traditional.[15] And its traditional structure, form and content will stand out in marked contrast later when we describe the Bab's next major work, the QA, a work that could not be more different from the standard works of tafsir. Baqara represents a distinctively Shia version of the category known as *tafsir bi'l-ma'thur*.[16]

Three central themes of the work have been identified: (1) religious authority – *walaya*; (2) divine self-manifestation – *tajjali*; (3) resurrection and the Day of Judgment – *qiyama*. Each of these themes is discussed in the tafsir by seizing upon key Qur'anic terms. Frequently, the explications of the Qur'an are ranged over a series of hierarchies, both ontological and sacerdotal – if one may use such a word. The hierarchies may consist of seven, four or three stages in most cases, with a few exceptions. Not every verse produces a commentary that contains a hierarchy, but virtually every verse is read to speak to *walaya* in some way or another. The work also preserves a certain degree of Shia/Sunni communalism, a feature that is largely absent from the second work of interest here – the QA. A central concern in both works, however, is the covenant, the *Day of Alastu*, and its renewal. Even though the *locus classicus* for this important Islamic teaching is not encountered until Q 7:172, the Bab makes sure here in his tafsir on Sura two that the reader never loses sight of its essential and non-negotiable importance.

---

[14] Lawson, 'The Bab's Epistle.'

[15] What follows is a brief, very general summary of this important pre-advent work by the Bab. For a more complete discussion of this unpublished Arabic work, including a description of the manuscripts, see Todd Lawson, *Intimacy and Ecstasy in Tafsir: The Earliest Qur'an Commentary of Sayyid 'Ali Muhammad Shirazi, the Bab (1819–1950)*, Leiden: Brill, in press.

[16] Lawson, 'Akhbari Shi'i Approaches to Tafsir.'

In support of the Bab's own words, which carry something of the expressive style of the Shaykhi school, he quotes numerous hadiths or Akhbar which are seen to bear directly upon the Qur'anic verse at hand. Occasionally, he provides the *isnad*, but more frequently he does not. However, a thorough study of the tafsir discloses that virtually all of the traditions adduced in it are found in widely known books of tafsir, especially those composed in Safavid times, or in other standard works of Shi'ism. Some hadiths, such as those found in the works of Rajab Bursi (1411), became a cause for later condemnation by critics on the charge of 'extremism' (*ghuluw*). This charge was also leveled at the founders of the Shaykhi school on similar grounds.

The key Qur'anic term *walaya* is as good a place as any to begin to understand such condemnation. It is a word uniquely suited to the religious (spiritual and administrative) program of Twelver Shi'ism. It stands for loyalty to the original covenant, which the Bab says was re-enacted on the *Day of al-Ghadir* when Ali was appointed *mawla* of the Muslim community by Muhammad. It is also useful in articulating the nature of the relation between the individual or common believer and the imam, as well as the relation of the imam to God. And, as the Qur'an itself says, it also characterizes to a very high degree the basic relation between God and humanity: God is the *wali* of the believers *par excellence*. *Walaya* has a simultaneously rich and restricted semantic field. It stands for allegiance and loyalty; it is glossed as 'love', pure and simple, in Shia works. It denotes, moreover, intimacy and mutual yearning in the playing out of the more purely devotional and mystical aspects of the religion. The mutuality of the word is of great significance because it guarantees that the true religious or devotional attitude depends upon acknowledging love from a higher source and returning the same love in gratitude and yearning. One of the basic meanings of the term is also 'friendship' and this, again, highlights and emphasizes the mutuality inherent in the religious duty indicated in the term *walaya*. This religious duty, furthermore, helps to limit the structure of sanctity and prophetic intimacy it houses.

A Qur'anic trope that is very much at home in the Babi and later Baha'i scripture is the poetic use of water to stand for divine love, knowledge, mercy and revelation. In Baqara, the Bab loses no opportunity to speak about the inestimable value of *walaya* by identifying it with water through a series of images expressive of life-giving, restorative and overwhelming qualities. The word has simultaneously consoling, nurturing, purifying and protective connotations.[17] Thus, according to the Bab, *walaya* is spiritual water; it circulates through the cosmos the way water circulates through 'heaven and earth.' The other two themes most frequently encountered require some mention, however limited, to form a picture of this work which may be thought a harbinger for what would ultimately be recognized as the Baha'i faith. In turn, the Baha'i faith may be thought to continue a distinctive exegetical conversation on the meaning of such key Qur'anic lexical items as *walaya*, *tajalli*, *qiyama* and *'ahd/mithaq* (covenant).

The Babi reception or reading of the Qur'an is apocalyptic and eschatological. In this, the Qur'anically derived term *tajalli* plays a dramatic role. The term is frequently translated as 'divine self-manifestation,' but considering its etymology, usage and attendant philological richness, this is a fairly bland rendering. It leaves unstated and unremarked the all-important notion of divine glory that the term obviously carries in its original Qur'anic context in *Surat al-A'raf*, Q 7:143, as is captured in the Yusuf Ali translation (slightly revised):

> When Moses came to the place appointed by Us, and his Lord addressed him, he said: 'O my Lord! Show (Thyself) to me, That I may look upon Thee.' God said, 'By no means canst thou see Me (direct); but look upon the mount; if it abide in its place, then shalt thou see Me.' When his Lord manifested His glory on the Mount, He made it as dust, and Moses fell down in a swoon. When he recovered his senses he said: 'Glory be to Thee! To Thee I turn in repentance, and I am the first to believe.'

If we consider the spectrum of Qur'anic usages of the triliteral root *J-L-L* (cf. Q 7:143, 187; 55:67–8; 91:3; 92:2), we note that it combines the ideas

---

[17] Lawson, *Intimacy*. On water and *walaya*, see Lawson, 'Friendship.' On *walaya* in general, see Hermann Landolt, 'Walayah'; Amir-Moezzi, 'Notes'; Dakake, *Charismatic Community*.

of luminosity, brightness, greatness, strength, beauty and power, as in the divine name al-Jalal. Thus, we might even be so bold as to translate the above verse as: 'When the Lord caused His glory to overwhelm the mountain.' We dwell on this idea because it is an important element in the specific religiosity of Shi'ism, in the religion of the Bab more pertinently, and perhaps most obviously in the tonality of the religious ethos of the Baha'i faith, whose founder, after all, is called, the Glory of God, even though a different, and as it happens non-Qur'anic word is used in the Arabic title Baha'ullah.[18] It also helps us to understand the nature of the Babi/Baha'i apocalypse, especially when we bear in mind that among the several distinguishing characteristics of the genre of apocalypse isolated by contemporary scholarship, glory, whether as event or object of contemplation, is a standard feature and as such may be traced as a significant motif in the Qur'an itself.[19]

The imminence of qiyama (a frequent Qur'anic word), or perhaps even its presence, was conjured in this tafsir through the use – whether conscious or not – of the venerable exegetical tool known as typological figuration. This is the process whereby current or recent events are seen as the repetition of ancient sacred history in which, for example, spiritual or political and cultural heroes are seen to reappear, along with their friends and supporters on the one hand, and their enemies on the other.[20] Indeed, in a work composed later in his short life, the Persian Bayan, the Bab explicitly states that his earliest followers, the sodality of eighteen persons known as the Letters of the Living (huruf al-hayy) were actually the return (ruju') of the Fourteen Immaculate Ones mentioned above and the four Gates (abwab) or Deputies (nuwab) who collectively formed a link between the hidden imam and his community during the period known as the Lesser

---

[18] Other frequent markers of glory as light in Baha'i writings, near-synonyms of tajalli, are derived from these roots: L-M-', L-W-H, N-W-R, SH-R-Q.

[19] Lawson, Qur'an, pp. 19, 27, 37–41. 'Glory – Herrlichkeit – theology' is also a central feature of contemporary Roman Catholic thought through the influential work of Hans Urs von Balthasar (d. 1988). A comparative study of the 'sacramental value' of glory in the two traditions, Islam and Christianity, might disclose previously unsuspected channels of communication, mutual understanding and commonality.

[20] Typological figuration, long recognized as an important factor in biblical interpretation, begins with the Qur'an for Islam. See Lawson, Qur'an, esp. chs. 3 and 4.

Occultation from (874–941).[21] Here we see a kind of Shia variation on the well-known Sufi institution of the 'substitutes' (abdal). Thus does the spiritual reality of the original friends of God (awliya'ullah) recur throughout history in subsequent generations in worthy individuals who are then enabled to carry on the promulgation (tabligh) of the cause of God (amr allah).[22]

THE *TAFSIR SURAT YUSUF*, KNOWN AS THE *QAYYUM AL-ASMA'* (QA)

To call the QA a 'swerve' may be something of an understatement; but in the present context it is at least accurate. It may be that the spiritual visions and encounters experienced by the Bab around this time account for the profound shift. This is especially the case with the powerful vision said to have occurred in April 1844 that may have diverted his attention from completing the full tafsir he had been contemplating, leaving us with Baqara as fragmentary evidence of an original desire to write a commentary on the entire Qur'an. This is one swerve. Another swerve, and a more significant one, is indicated by the way in which this later work simultaneously maintains and breaks with the tradition of tafsir, most specifically Shia tafsir. It should be noted, however, that even though this work nominally concerns the twelfth Sura, it actually represents a commentary on the entire Qur'an due to its innovative structure.[23]

The overwhelming import of this work, which must be thought of as disguised in tafsir, is to call attention to a new cycle of history. Accordingly, the long-awaited resurrection (qiyama) was now at hand, and this book represents the 'True Qur'an' expected to be in the possession of the Qa'im upon his return (ruju'). It focuses on the Qur'anic Sura on the biblical patriarch Joseph, and is divided into 111 Suras, each with 42 verses, the abjad value of the word bala, 'Indeed!' which was the response of humanity

---

[21] MacEoin, *Messiah*, p. 171.

[22] On the Sufi phenomenon, see Chodkiewicz, *Seal of the Saints*.

[23] For details, see Lawson, *Gnostic*, pp. 4, 6 and 39.

to the question posed by God on the Day of the Covenant, before the creation of the universe: 'Am I not your Lord?' The most frequent exegetical device encountered is paraphrase and the typological figuration introduced in the earlier commentary. The overall effect, the composition being entirely in rhymed prose (saj'), is somewhat hypnotic and calls to mind *dhikr* sessions with the added overlay of a definite, non-negotiable – if at times bewilderingly multivocal – messianic discourse of mission and summons.[24]

The following excerpt is from chapter 108 of QA.[25] It is written as a commentary on Q 12:109. As in the other 110 Suras of the Bab's composition, it is structured according to four sections. First is the opening and title of the Sura, the Qur'an verse as lemma for this Sura of the commentary introduced with the standard *basmala*. The second part is the actual composition, which is almost always introduced with a distinctive set of disconnected letters as the first verse. Some of these disconnected letters – as in the present case – spell a word when joined (here 'Muhammad'), while others are more along the lines of the Qur'anic exemplar.[26] The third section of the Sura includes this second verse of the Bab's versified commentary. It continues for the majority of the verses and represents the main substance of a given Sura. The final or fourth section is usually marked by a reiteration of the lemma, only this time paraphrased to emphasize the main message of the third section. In this example, however, such reiteration and paraphrase of the lemma is sparse. We have attempted to distinguish the Bab's words from words of the Qur'an by casting the latter in SMALL CAPS.

The Sura of the Servant

IN THE NAME OF GOD THE MERCIFUL THE COMPASSIONATE

NOR DID WE SEND BEFORE THEE [AS MESSENGERS] ANY BUT MEN WHOM WE DID INSPIRE – MEN LIVING IN HUMAN HABITATIONS. DO THEY NOT TRAVEL THROUGH THE EARTH AND SEE WHAT WAS THE END OF THOSE BEFORE THEM? BUT THE HOME OF THE HEREAFTER IS BEST, FOR THOSE WHO DO RIGHT, WILL YE NOT THEN UNDERSTAND?

---

[24] Ibid.

[25] The following is excerpted and adapted from Lawson, 'Súrat al-'Abd.' The opening Qur'an translation is that of Yusuf Ali.

[26] A chart of these disconnected letters is in Lawson, *Qur'an*, pp. 144–5.

Verse 1

Mim Ha Mim Dal

Verse 2

O People of the THRONE![27] Listen to the CALL[28] of your Lord, THE MERCIFUL,[29] He who THERE IS NO GOD EXCEPT HIM (*huwa*),[30] from the tongue of the REMEMBRANCE,[31] this YOUTH (*al-fata*),[32] son of the SUBLIME (*al-ʿaliy*)[33], the Arab to whom [God has] in the MOTHER BOOK[34] testified.[35]

Verse 3

Then LISTEN[36] to WHAT IS BEING REVEALED TO YOU FROM YOUR LORD:[37] VERILY VERILY I AM GOD[38] of WHOM THERE IS NO GOD BUT HIM.[39] NOTHING IS LIKE UNTO HIM[40] while He is God, LOFTY (*ʿaliyan*) GREAT (*kabiran*).[41]

Verse 4

O People of the Earth! HEARKEN[42] to the CALL[43] of the BIRDS[44] upon the TREES[45] leafy and perfumed[46] with the CAMPHOR[47] of Manifestation

---

[27] Q 27:2 and *passim*.

[28] Cf. Q 19:3.

[29] Q 20:90.

[30] Q 2:163 and *passim*.

[31] Q 15:9 *passim*.

[32] Cf. Q 21:60.

[33] Q 2:255 and *passim*. A frequent instance of paronomasia in QA associating the Bab with ʿAli and God which derives from a cognate theme in Ithna-ʿashari Shiʿism.

[34] Q 3:7; 13:9; 43:4.

[35] Cf. Q 17:78.

[36] Q 20:13.

[37] Q 33:2

[38] Q 28:30: *innî anâ 'llâh* is frequent in QA. It suggests that the Bab is claiming revelation.

[39] Q 2:163 and *passim*.

[40] Q 42:11. See Lawson, 'Súrat al-ʿAbd,' p. 137 for the identification of the hadith evoked here.

[41] Q 4:34.

[42] Q 2:93 and *passim*.

[43] Cf. Q 19:3.

[44] Cf. Q 27:16 and *passim*.

[45] Cf. Q 7:19; 24:35; 28:30.

[46] Cf. Q 6:59; 7:22; 20:12.

[47] Cf. Q 76:5.

(*kafur al-zuhur*) describing this YOUNG MAN (*ghulam*)[48] descended from the Arabs, from MUHAMMAD,[49] from 'Ali, from Fatima, from Mekka, from Medina, from Batha,'[50] from 'Iraq with what the MERCIFUL[51] HAS MANIFESTED (*tajalla*)[52] upon their leaves, namely that he is THE SUBLIME (*al-'aliy*)[53] and he is God, MIGHTY,[54] PRAISED.[55]

Verse 36

O People of the Cloud! LISTEN[56] to my call from the LAMP[57] in this whitened LAMP,[58] this is the GLASS[59] in this reddened GLASS[60] who was spoken to (*mantuqan*) in truth by the sea of the Earth of Saffron[61] in the HOUSE OF THE GATE.[62]

Verse 37

VERILY VERILY I AM GOD,[63] HE WHOM THERE IS NO GOD EXCEPT HIM.[64] INDEED, I HAVE ESTABLISHED THE HEAVENS AND THE EARTH around this Word[65] through a single letter LIKE IT. So obey My Word. FOR VERILY VERILY I AM THE TRUTH. There is no god except Me, the EXALTED (*al-'aliy*)[66] who am by God the comprehender of all the worlds.[67]

---

[48] Q 12:19.

[49] Q 3:144; 33:40; 47:2; 48:29.

[50] Name of the hollow or center of Mecca where the Ka'ba is located.

[51] Q 1:1 and *passim*.

[52] Q 7:143.

[53] Q 2:255 and *passim*.

[54] Q 48:19.

[55] Q 4:131.

[56] Q 2:93 and *passim*.

[57] Q 24:35.

[58] Q 24:35.

[59] Q 24:35.

[60] Q 24:35.

[61] *Ard al-za'farán*, a spiritual realm referred to by, for example, Ibn Arabi in his major work the *Kitáb futúhát al-Makkiyya*. For further details, see Lawson, *Intimacy*.

[62] Cf. Q 2:58; 4:154; 5:23; 7:161; 9:25.

[63] Q 28:30.

[64] Q 59:22, 23 and *passim*.

[65] Cf. Q 3:39 and *passim*.

[66] Q 16:2; 20:14; 21:25. For variations in the mss. here, see Lawson, 'Súrat al-'Abd,' p. 144.

[67] Cf. Q 4:108 and 126.

Verse 38

AND LISTEN[68] to this Most Mighty INTERPRETATION[69] from the TONGUE[70] of this man made great, he whom I have brought up in My presence. NO HUMAN DESIRE TOUCHED HIM[71] in Reality. Verily, he is the Truth[72] upon the Truth.[73] And his significance, by the law of FIRE,[74] HAS BEEN FULLY RECORDED IN THE MOTHER BOOK.[75]

Verse 39

And Say, by the Truth, WE HAVE SENT BEFORE YOU NO MEN [AS MESSENGERS] EXCEPT WE INSPIRED THEM; be ye THE PEOPLE of that blessed TOWNSHIP,[76] and conceal yourselves IN THE EARTH of the heart (fu'ad) in order to help him. Know that for those who deny him (mushrikin bihi),[77] they will suffer the dire punishment of the HEREAFTER[78] over the Fire[79] in the Fire,[80] and this has been written[81] with Fire.[82]

Verse 40

And He is God, over all created things a Witness.[83]

Verse 41

And verily, God is Comprehender of all the worlds.[84]

---

[68] Q 7:204; 22:73.
[69] Ta'wil, cf. Q 3:7; 12:6 and passim.
[70] Cf. Q 20:27.
[71] Cf. Q 3:47; 3:174; 19:20; 24:35.
[72] Q 2:91 and passim.
[73] Q 27:79.
[74] Cf. Q 27:8; 2:24 and passim.
[75] Q 3:7; 13:39; 43:4.
[76] Cf. Q 12:109.
[77] Q 9:7 and passim.
[78] Q 11:103 and passim.
[79] Cf. Q 27:8; 2:24 and passim.
[80] Cf. Q 27:8; 2:24 and passim.
[81] Cf. Q 7:157.
[82] Cf. Q 27:8; 2:24 and passim.
[83] Q 4:33; 33:55.
[84] Cf. Q 4:108, 126.

Verse 42

And verily thou art, through God, SELF SUFFICIENT, able to dispense with ALL THE WORLDS.[85]

With this excerpt, we gain some appreciation of the manner in which the Bab mined the apocalyptic substrate in the rich metaphorical, figurative and tropic terrain of the Qur'an. He did this in order to generate, through metalepsis, a new scripture – a new apocalypse. Many of these tropes and metaphors, similes and allegories became symbols of the returned imam, and his retinue whose task was, among other things, to usher in the Day of Judgment. The symbolism and structure of this composition bespeaks a singular literary accomplishment in which the primordial Day of the Covenant and the Day of Judgment are understood to be joined in a single gesture of revelation as simultaneous events.

A NON-MUSLIM COMMUNITY OF THE QUR'AN

The Baha'i reception of the Qur'an disturbs the traditional, and some would say comforting 'us and them,' paradigm so common to much of post-Qur'anic Islamicate discourse, despite clear attempts on the part of the Prophet, the Qur'an and countless creative Muslim exponents to vitiate this age-old and deleterious tendency afflicting humanity. Indeed, the Qur'anic pronouncement in Q 7:172 would seem to trump all past, present and future attempts, and such othering. This is the much referred to and beloved controlling myth or metaphor of primordial unity in which all future generations of the Children of Adam – a Qur'anic synonymn for humanity – were brought forth from the loins of Adam and presented with the ultimate question from God, in whose divine and peaceful presence this same humanity was now gathered: 'Am I not your Lord?' The gathering immediately responded in unison with the strongest possible affirmation: 'Yes indeed!' In addition to this primordial and eschataologically charged event, during which both consciousness and history are born,

---

[85] Cf. Q 3:97; 29:6.

there are numerous other Qur'anic passages which insist upon the unity of humanity, the oneness of God and the oneness of what we, writing in English, are inclined to call 'religion.' These three unities have characterized what may be thought of as the Baha'i *da'wa* from its very inception. They remain, moreover, a prominent watchword in Baha'i self-identity, ethos and doctrine. Unity is the central ideational sacrament in the Baha'i faith, just as it is in Islam.

The Baha'i faith may be seen, then, as a non-Muslim community of the Qur'an. I venture to say that this is a unique identity found nowhere else on the planet but in the Baha'i community. Such uniqueness demands critical analysis and patient study. The anomaly has been explained in the Baha'i writings by comparing the relation of the Baha'i faith to Islam with a model provided by a specific understanding of the relationship between Christianity and Judaism. As with many communities of the Qur'an before them, the Babi/Baha'i reading of the Qur'an depends upon a figurative reading of the Qur'an. (One may well ask, can there be any other kind?) The result here, as with other communities, is an innovative and creative application of the Qur'an to specific concerns in a specific historical and cultural context. From the literary angle, this may be referred to as metalepsis in that the resulting reading carries the focus far beyond accepted boundaries by, for example, using existing metaphors in ever-new figurative constructions and transforming the habitual hermeneutic circle into a spiral. It seems that the guardian of the Baha'i faith, Shoghi Effendi, was referring to the effects of this metaleptic process in the introduction to his history of the first century of the Baha'i faith:

> I shall seek to represent and correlate, in however cursory a manner, those momentous happenings which have insensibly, relentlessly, and under the very eyes of successive generations, perverse, indifferent or hostile, transformed a heterodox and seemingly negligible offshoot of the Shaykhi school of the Ithna'ashariyyah sect of Shia Islam into a world religion.[86]

---

[86] Shoghi Effendi Rabbani, *God Passes By*, p. xii.

With the above examination of the place of the Qur'an in the Baha'i faith we have a clearer idea of the earliest stages of such a process and we see that the Qur'an plays a major role in it. Much work remains to be done to acquire a complete understanding of the Qur'an in the Baha'i faith. For example, one of the more interesting ways in which the faith venerates and promulgates the Qur'an is in prayer. Prayer comprises an enormous amount of Baha'i literature. This would appear to be a relatively untouched area of inquiry. The Baha'i celebration of the Qur'an as a non- or post-Islamic religious gesture says, among other things, that the Qur'an belongs to humanity. Perhaps, as the Baha'i community progresses in carrying out Shoghi Effendi's instruction to thoroughly study the Qur'an, the community itself will become more and more aware of its debt to the Islamic revelation and therefore be more and more able to seriously consider in which ways it is and is not an Islamic religion.

BIBLIOGRAPHY

Amir-Moezzi, Mohammad Ali. 'Notes on Imami-Shi'i Walaya.' In *Ishraq, Islamic Philosophy Yearbook 2*, 502–32. (Moscow: Vostochnaya Literatura Publishers, 2011)

Baha'u'llah (Mirza Husayn 'Ali Nuri). *Kitab-i mustatab-i Iqan*. (Hofheim-Langenhain: Baha'i-Verlag, 1980)

— *The Kitáb-I-Íqán: The Book of Certitude, Revealed by Bahá'u'lláh*. Trans. Shoghi Effendi. (Wilmette, IL: Baha'i Publishing Trust, 1974)

Buck, Christopher. 'Discovering.' In *The Wiley Blackwell Companion to the Qur'an*. Ed. A. Rippin and J.A. Mojaddedi, 23–42. 2nd edn. (Hoboken, NJ: John Wiley and Sons, 2017)

— 'Kitab-i-Iqan: An Introduction to Baha'u'llah's *Book of Certitude* with Two Digital Reprints of Early Lithographs' (1998) [Online] (https://Baha'i-library.com/buck_encyclopedia_kitab_iqan). (Accessed December 11, 2018)

— *Symbol and Secret: Qur'an Commentary in Baha'u'llah's Kitab-i Iqan*. (Los Angeles: Kalimat Press, 1997)

Chodkiewicz, Michel. *Seal of the Saints: Prophethood and Sainthood in the Doctrine of Ibn 'Arabi*. Trans. Liadain Sherrard. (Cambridge, UK: Islamic Texts Society, 1993)

Dakake, Maria Massi. *The Charismatic Community: Shi'ite Identity in Early Islam*. (Albany: State University of New York Press, 2007)

Landolt, Hermann. 'Walayah.' In *Encyclopedia of Religion*. Ed. Mircea Eliade et al., vol. 15, 316–23. (New York and London: Macmillan and Free Press, 1987)

Lawson, Todd. 'Akhbari Shi'i Approaches to Tafsir.' In *The Koran: Critical Concepts in Islamic Studies IV: Translation and Exegesis*. Ed. Colin Turner, 163–97. (New York and London: RoutledgeCurzon, 2006; first published 1993)

— 'The Bab's Epistle on the Spiritual Journey towards God.' In *The Baha'i Faith and the World Religions*. Ed. Moojan Momen, 231–47. (Oxford: George Ronald, 2005)

— 'Friendship, Illumination and the Water of Life.' *Journal of the Muhyiddin Ibn 'Arabi Society* 59 (2016): 17–56

— *Gnostic Apocalypse and Islam: Qur'an, Exegesis, Messianism and the Literary Origin of the Babi Religion*. (London; New York: Routledge Press, 2012)

— 'Interpretation as Revelation: The Qur'an Commentary of Sayyid 'Ali Muhammad Shirazi, the Bab.' In *Approaches to the History of the Interpretation of the Qur'an*. Ed. A. Rippin, 223–53. (Oxford: Oxford University Press, 1988)

— *The Qur'an, Epic and Apocalypse*. (London: Oneworld, 2017)

— 'The Súrat al-'Abd of the Qayyúm al-Asmá' (Chapter 108): A Provisional Translation and Commentary.' In *A Most Noble Pattern: Collected Essays on the Writings of the Báb, 'Alí Muhammad Shírází (1819–1850)*. Ed. Todd Lawson and Omid Ghaemmaghami, 116–45. (Oxford: George Ronald, 2012)

Lewis, Franklin D. 'Persian Literature and the Qur'an.' In *Encyclopaedia of the Qur'an*. Ed. Jane Dammen McAuliffe, vol. 4, 55–66. (Leiden: Brill Academic Publishers, 2004)

— 'Scripture as Literature.' In *Reason and Revelation: New Directions in Baha'i Thought*. Ed. Seena Fazel and John Danesh, 101–28. (Los Angeles: Kalimat Press, 2002)

MacEoin, Denis. *The Messiah of Shiraz: Studies in Early and Middle Babism*. (Leiden and Boston: Brill, 2009)

— *The Sources for Early Babi Doctrine and History: A Survey*. (Leiden: Brill, 1992)

Osborn, Lil. *Religion and Relevance: The Baha'is in Britain, 1899–1930*. (Los Angeles: Kalimat Press, 2014)

Rabbani, Ruhiyyih. *The Priceless Pearl*. (London: Baha'i Publishing Trust, 1969)

Shoghi Effendi Rabbani. *The Advent of Divine Justice*. (New York: Baha'i Publishing Committee, 1939)

— *God Passes By*. (Wilmette, IL: Bahá'í Publishing Trust, 1970)

Stockman, Robert H. *'Abdu 'l-Baha in America*. (Wilmette, IL: Baha'i Publishing Trust, 2012)

— *Thornton Chase: First American Baha'i*. (Wilmette, IL: Baha'i Publishing Trust, 2002)

Part IV

Communities of Text and Tradition

Chapter 8

How the Qur'an Shapes
the Sunni Community

Ingrid Mattson, Huron University College
at the University of Western Ontario

Many years ago, when I was living in Connecticut, a well-known Sunni traditionalist scholar and preacher came to my home for dinner. I placed dishes of rice and bread, and bowls of salad and beef stew on the dining-room table, buffet style. Everyone filled their plates and we sat together around the fire in the living room where we ate and chatted. After finishing his serving, the scholar stood up, held out his dish and said, *hal min mazid* ('Is there more?').

After all these years, I still remember his words, because I immediately responded to them on many levels – as the host of the dinner, as a fellow believer, and as a scholar of the Qur'an, who is particularly fascinated with the way in which Muslims engage the Qur'an in all different situations. This phrase – *hal min mazid* – is, of course, from the Qur'an. Phrasing his request for another serving in the words of the Qur'an had the immediate effect of elevating the food, the meal, and the gathering as a whole. More than anything else, the Qur'an brings holiness to our lives. Human beings are constantly pulled, as if by gravity, into a state of dull mindlessness – *ghafla* – as the Qur'an says. We are mostly clueless, like groggy teenagers bumping into walls, as we try to get to the kitchen for a late-night snack. The clues are there, says the Qur'an. Think, ponder, reflect – be aware. The *ayat* of the Qur'an – its signs – draw our attention to the fact that every part of creation is a wondrous sign of creation.

Yet what was striking to me about the shaykh's use of this particular Qur'anic phrase – *hal min mazid* – to request more food, was the jarring contrast between the context of the friendly dinner, in which it was articulated, and the context in which the phrase occurs in Q 50:30. The verse says, 'when on that day We shall say to the Hellfire, are you full, and it will say, "Is there any more?"' The Qur'anic verse the scholar cited gives voice to hellfire, ravenous for more iniquitous souls to consume.

Does the Qur'anic context matter? What is the added value, as it were, in citing the Qur'an here? Was it performative, to demonstrate his mastery of the text? Was it a joke, and should the Qur'an be used that way? Was he shy to ask for more food, and instead of articulating his own desire, he cloaked it in God's words? Or, if each letter, each word of the Qur'an is God's word, then as much as we turn to it for guidance, we can also bring any part of it to any situation, at any time, in any way; each and every bit is special.

And so, Muslims name their children not only after prophets and righteous people, or to indicate a relationship to God such as Abdullah or Amatullah – 'servant (male or female) of God' – but also, Taha and Yasin – names adopted by taking some of the disconnected letters which open a number of Suras in the Qur'an. If these are names, why not *Basal*, meaning 'onions,' a word found in Q 2:61, and that had been given by someone to an unfortunate Afghan girl I once encountered?

If each articulation of the Qur'an, no matter how small – even a single letter – yields sacred meaning, perhaps a solution to every problem, even the most mundane, can be found in it. In this regard, Sunni Muslims often cite the great early interpreter of the Qur'an, the Prophet Muhammad's cousin, 'Abd Allah ibn al-'Abbas, who is reported to have said, 'If I lost my camel's hobbles, I would look for it in the Book of God.' The benefit of this approach is that the chaos of our lives can be meaningfully knit together through the text of the Qur'an. A risk of this approach is that by looking for everything in the Qur'an, we can too easily impose ourselves upon it, using it to signal our virtue, to rationalize thoughtless actions, or to put an end to debate.

In an episode of the Canadian sitcom *Little Mosque on the Prairie*, the young imam's non-Muslim friend, after getting him in trouble through an irresponsible stunt, says, 'Doesn't the Qur'an say, "Should old acquaintance be forgot?"' The imam responds, 'That's "Auld Lang Syne".' Even many Muslims mistakenly attribute hadith or cultural aphorisms to the Qur'an. Some might find this ignorance of the text of the sacred book troubling, yet it also could be seen as a demonstration of faith – faith that God's book is the source of all goodness. And while 'Auld Lang Syne' is not in the Qur'an, the holy book does say that Paradise has been prepared for those 'who hold in check their anger, and pardon others because God loves the doers of good' (Q 3:133–4).

THE CLOSEST THING TO GOD

We created the human being and we know what his soul whispers to him,
for we are closer to him than his jugular vein. (Q 50:16)

In my book, *The Story of the Qur'an*, I relate an anecdote told to me by Reem Osman, a Syrian-American from the suburbs of Chicago who was, as a teenager, certified in *tajwid* by the late, great Sunni scholar of the Qur'an, Abu'l-Hasan Muhyi'l-Din al-Kurdi (who died in 2009 in Damascus, certainly a mercy for him, as he did not have to witness the horror that would overtake his country soon afterwards). Reem described her meeting with Shaykh al-Kurdi as the final stage in the certification process, after having undergone extensive testing by the Shaykh's senior female disciple, Da'd 'Ali al-Husayni, an accomplished scholar in her own right. On the day of the exam, Reem was brought to a waiting room where she sat with a dozen or so other young women, who, one by one, approached a privacy curtain behind which lay the physically frail, but mentally acute, scholar on a daybed. The Shaykh asked the women to recite from various sections of the Qur'an to affirm their mastery of recitation. Reem described her astonishment at witnessing one teenager who, after having successfully completed her exam, pulled open the drapes and said, 'O Sheikh, I just want to see you!'

When I heard this anecdote, I was struck by how it mirrors the Qur'anic description of Moses, who, having climbed Mount Sinai says, 'My Lord, show yourself to me so I can gaze upon you!' (Q 7:143). It seems eminently possible that, having studied the Qur'an so extensively, the young woman's intense emotions were now expressed in the form of this sacred discourse she had internalized. From Moses, to George Harrison who sang, 'I really want to see you Lord,' we all long to be close to God. This longing, I believe, prompted Reem's friend to want to see the person who was, for her in some way, the penultimate source of the Qur'an, because Shaykh Kurdi's *isnad* linked his knowledge of the Qur'an directly to God.

The Qur'an is the most charismatic presence in the Sunni community; all other claims of holiness are suspect and contingent. Despite the pervasiveness of textual renderings of the Qur'an – from printed *mushafs* and smartphone apps, it is the words of the Qur'an spoken out – naming a child from it, invoking a Qur'anic phrase, or saying, *bismillah al-rahman al-rahim* before an action, with which most Muslims have contact with the Qur'an. It is still the soundscape of holy space and time; it is the pious phrase to decorate a speech; it provides the primary content to *khutbas* and other religious talks. Sunnis believe the Qur'an is the living word of the living God; this feels most true when the words are animated with speech in real time.

Most Muslim communities – not just Sunni Muslims – share this cultural sound and landscape of the Qur'an. So what in particular characterizes the Sunni community, in distinction to other communities, in its relationship with the Qur'an? This is a difficult question to answer for many Sunnis who occupy the privileged position of the majority and so do not have to know much about the particularities of other Muslim communities. Additionally, the Sunni community has a remarkable capacity to appropriate ideas and practices from other Muslim or Abrahamic communities and to likewise deem acceptable innovative practices it initially condemned, when they have proven popular and apparently beneficial. Simple examples include printing the Qur'an, decorating walls with Qur'anic calligraphy, holding Qur'an recitation contests. More contentious examples include reading the Qur'an metaphorically, using writings from the Qur'an in healing rituals, and using logic to restrict the range of possible meanings of the Qur'an. Some of these practices are still condemned by factions who consider themselves Sunnis. If the Sunni community is a meaningful entity, it is vast, contradictory, and contentious, a nation of undefined borders and regular bickering over membership.

THE QUR'AN SHAPES RITUAL AND MUNDANE LIFE

As an adult convert to Islam I had the common experience of many that, for some time, I insisted I was 'just Muslim' and refused to accept any sectarian identity whatsoever. I became a Muslim because the Qur'an, or, to be more accurate, a translation of the last *juz'* of the Qur'an, cracked open my heart so the light of God could illuminate it. At first, I wasn't even convinced that I had to 'become a Muslim' in the sense of embracing this religious identity and affiliate with the Muslim community in order to relate to the Qur'an. I had left my childhood religious tradition years before. I had quietly walked out of that room and closed the door behind me, and was not eager to become 'religious' again. I knew it would be difficult to live as a Muslim and I didn't want the hassle in my life. As I was holding back on making a commitment to be a member of this religious community, I had a dream of the Prophet Muhammad. I saw him receiving revelations, and finding it stressful, almost painful. I woke up and thought to myself that it will not be easy to bring the Qur'an and all it means into my life, but the Prophet Muhammad will show me the way. From that time on, the Prophet Muhammad and his teachings became a foundation for my understanding of the Qur'an and for my ethical worldview in general. This conviction placed me squarely within the Sunni community.

My reading of the Qur'an further led me to the belief that I would have to make some lifestyle changes if I were not to deny what I knew now – that the Qur'an was a message to me from my Creator. This interpretation was encouraged by my Sunni friends, who believed the Qur'an to hold not just spiritual and theological truths, but to give guidance on many aspects of life. The Qur'an, they believed, tells us not just to worship God; it

provides much of the content and shape of that worship. And practical
Qur'anic guidance, the Sunnis assert, is not limited to 'acts of worship'
('ibadat), but also addresses social, political, economic and other transac-
tions (mu'amalat) central to our common life. A key feature of the Sunni
community, then, is its insistence that the Qur'an is the most important
normative source for all decision making; as a result, the Qur'an has influenced every significant sector of Muslim societies.

All Muslims take comfort in the conviction that the Qur'an has been
perfectly preserved, so they do not have to argue over the composition of
the text. Nevertheless, as the Prophet's cousin 'Ali ibn Abi Talib is reported
to have said to the Kharijites, a group of his former supporters who later
turned against him for accepting mediation to resolve a political dispute,
'This Qur'an is merely a scripture placed between two covers. It does not
speak; it is merely men who speak through it.'[1] The meaning is obvious:
the Qur'an needs to be interpreted. But the irony here is that it is not only
the words of the Qur'an that are subject to interpretation, but all statements, including this statement made by 'Ali. For while Sunni Muslims
understand 'Ali's words to indicate that the Qur'an needs a human interpreter, for Shia Muslims, these words indicate the need for an infallible
interpreter, specifically, 'Ali and his designated successors. Here, a clear
sectarian line between Shia and Sunni emerges. Indeed, Sunni identity
developed in large part in opposition to the claim that any person or groups
after the Prophet Muhammad have a unique and perfect ability to access
or implement the meaning of the Qur'an.

For the Sunnis, the Qur'an is both a source of norms in itself, having a
number of passages with detailed and enumerated directions about such
things as forbidden foods and inheritance shares, and it also points outward
to additional normative sources, among them: the Messenger of God (the
Prophet Muhammad),[2] reason ('aql),[3] community norms (ma'ruf),[4]

---

[1] Mattson, *Story of the Qur'an*, p. 191.
[2] Dozens of verses in the Qur'an, including Q 2:151, 3:132 and 4:13.
[3] Many places, including Q 2:73, 76, 164.
[4] Many places, including Q 3:104 and 9:71.

wisdom (*hikmah*),[5] scholars/people of knowledge (*'ulama'*),[6] people of remembrance (*ahl al-dhikr*)[7] and rulers (*ulu-l-amr*).[8] Identifying, engaging and reconciling all these authorities and sources shaped the Sunni community over time, and remains an ongoing enterprise. That diversity and disputativeness define this community is the result of the fact that Sunnis seek God's guidance by engaging with multiple texts, traditions, authorities, human capacities and communal values.

We can find a sectarian border (*hadd*) of the Sunni community, then, at the point where the existence of an interpretive gap is rejected. Those who call themselves Sunnis cannot explicitly reject the human element in interpretation, even if they try to ignore the gap between text and interpretation with statements such as 'Islam says.' Debate, dialogue, discussion and exposition characterize the Sunni community which is, above all else, a discursive space that can change in size and shape, but will always be mainly framed by four things: the Qur'an, reports about the Prophet, the authoritative opinions of scholars and community norms.

THE PROPHET MUHAMMAD AND THE QUR'AN

Whether the person being formed within the Sunni community is an adult convert or a child, religious education typically follows a certain pattern. The Arabic language is introduced, with a focus on reading and pronunciation. The short Suras of the Qur'an are memorized. Edifying stories about the Prophet Muhammad are related. The young or new Muslim is taught the fundamentals of purification and prayer, the main dietary restrictions, and traditional Islamic etiquette. These rites, rules and conventions are grounded in the Qur'an and detailed with reference to the Prophet Muhammad's instructions and behavior.

The Qur'an repeatedly emphasizes the limitations of Muhammad – that he is only a human being, not divine, and without supernatural

---

[5] Many places, including Q 2:269 and 3:164.
[6] Q 35:28.
[7] Q 16:43; 21:10.
[8] Q 4:59.

powers.[9] It is God, not Muhammad, who is the object of worship. But the Qur'an also orders obedience to the Messenger of God (Q 8:1) and establishes him as an exemplar (Q 33:21). The Sunni community has understood this authority and status granted to the Prophet by the Qur'an to continue after his death. For the Sunni Muslim, the life and example of the Prophet Muhammad is inexorably linked with the Qur'an. The Qur'an cannot be understood fully and accurately without grounding its principles, values, commands and prohibition in the teachings and example (Sunna), as well as the character (*akhlaq*), of the Prophet Muhammad.

In requiring obedience to and imitation of the Prophet Muhammad, the Qur'an inspired great spiritual and intellectual undertakings that shaped the Sunni community. In the first two centuries of Islam, knowledge about the Prophet was transmitted in a number of ways: through oral and written reports (*hadith*), related casually or with great deliberation, as well as through the living example of charismatic individuals who strove to mold their behavior and even their gestures according to the Prophet's example, as it had been passed on to them from pious exemplars. Scholars argued over the best means to uplift important teachings and filter out inauthentic reports attributed to the Prophet. Imam Malik and Abu Hanifa placed more trust in the living tradition, while their younger colleagues, al-Shafi'i and Ibn Hanbal, had more faith in textual reports to preserve the Sunna.[10] The compromise that has mostly held until the rise of radical Salafism is that both are necessary to transmit the Sunna. Textual reports, that is, hadith, ensured that the Prophet's teachings are preserved. But the dominant Sunni opinion has been that only people of knowledge – '*ulama*' – understand the language, context, and normative implications of these reports. Scholars have to interpret hadith, just as they have to interpret the Qur'an, and then reconcile these texts with reason and use prudence to take into account the sentiments and capacities of their communities.

Before the advent of modernity, ordinary Muslims were certainly aware of the major hadith collections, such as *Sahih al-Bukhari*, given that they were taught in mosque study circles and read out ritually on occasion.

---

[9] Q 3:144; 41:6; 7:188, etc.
[10] A good history of the Sunni approach to Sunna and *hadith* is Brown, *Hadith*.

Before widespread literacy, however, few people would have joined these circles in any community, or attended complete readings of the collections, much less qualified for a certificate of learning (*ijaza*) issued by recognized scholars. In contrast, there was wide dissemination of smaller booklets and collections focusing on the Prophet Muhammad's character and virtues, such as Al-Tirmidhi's *Shama'il*, Al-Jazuli's *Dala'il al-khayrat* and Al-Qadi 'Iyad's *al-Shifa'*.[11] These texts were designed to instill love and devotion of the Prophet Muhammad in those who read them. Sunnis believe this is just what the Qur'an requires of them (see Q 9:24). The image of the Prophet that is generated by these texts is of a beautiful, humble and, above all, merciful person. This perception of the Prophet is an important filter through which Sunnis interpret the Qur'an, as well as legal and more obscure hadith reports.

The manner in which Sunnis engage with hadith texts has, however, changed considerably in the modern period. In early modernity, the printing press and more widespread literacy made all texts more readily available. In our time, all texts are easily accessible online. Included in the major hadith collections are some reports ordinary Muslims find irrational, immoral, strange and shocking. This is not a new response. In premodern societies, many of these texts were challenged by scholarly elites on the basis of science, ethics and theology, and were discredited by accepted hadith verification practices.[12] Some troubling texts remained as archives and for reference, but were not shared publicly by scholars; others were contextualized and interpreted in more palatable ways. But since these texts have been easily accessed publicly, they have been used by radicals to justify aggression in the name of Islam, to attack Islam by those hostile to the religion, and they have undermined trust among Muslims in the whole hadith enterprise.

A crisis over the reliability of hadith in the modern era might have been averted if the only challenge was finding traditional scholars willing to

---

[11] The contemporary Syrian hadith scholar Sheikh Muhammad al-Ya'qubi, who has crossed the globe surveying manuscript collections in mosques and family libraries, told me in a personal communication that, after the Qur'an, these texts praising the Prophet are the most numerous, far outnumbering Bukhari and Muslim.

[12] Brown, *Hadith*, pp. 96–100.

reconsider the content and influence of classical hadith collections. Indeed, early modernist Sunni scholars such as Muhammad 'Abduh (1849–1905), Rashid Rida (1865–1935), Muhammad Taha ibn 'Ashur (1879–1973) and others, increasingly added the filter of ethical goals (maqasid) and values based on a holistic reading of the Qur'an and Sunna to review hadith collections, and argued against an overreliance on them. Ibn 'Ashur, for example, cites a report that 'Umar ibn al-Khattab forbade people from spreading hadith and says, 'There is indeed a wonderful wisdom behind this policy, for God has already and clearly mentioned what is prescribed and forbidden in His Book and warned against people raising unnecessary questions.'[13] Ibn 'Ashur never rejected the use of hadith to supplement and interpret the Qur'an, but he believed that authority rested with scholars to draw upon them when necessary, only in accordance with the clear goals and principles of the Qur'an. In fact, he says that this was the reason why the righteous Umayyad caliph 'Umar ibn 'Abd al-'Aziz ordered their collection in the first place, a century after the rise of Islam: 'I assume that he wanted those traditions to provide a guiding light for the scholars of the community in understanding the objectives [maqasid] of the Shari'ah.'[14] The successors to 'Abduh and Ibn 'Ashur, such as Yusuf al-Qaradawi and Taha Jabir Alalwani, have been keen to maintain a central role for hadith, yet each has written books enumerating many conditions to their acceptance and application, with a strong emphasis on the rule that no hadith can contradict or abrogate the Qur'an.

The good work these Sunni scholars have done in helping rebalance the use of hadith with the Qur'an has been counteracted, unfortunately, by the Wahhabi movement, whose views have spread rapidly since the mid-twentieth century by oil-enriched Saudi institutions. Wahhabism developed out of the Hanbali school which had the most extreme dependence on hadith over other sources of law among the classical Sunni schools. Ahmad ibn Hanbal's Musnad contains about 27,000 hadith transmissions, many of them rated weak, and Ibn Hanbal explicitly preferred a weak hadith to

---

[13] Ibn Ashur, Treatise, p. 219.
[14] Ibid., p. 141.

a strong analogy from the Qur'an.[15] The Wahhabis have not, therefore, been intellectually inclined to reduce the influence of hadith. More problematic until recently has been Wahhabism's interest in upholding Saudi monarchal rule and customary patriarchal authority, making them cling even more strongly to reprehensible reports, particularly those of a misogynistic nature. This in turn has led to a strong backlash from reformers and liberals, with the most compelling intellectual and spiritually sound defense, perhaps, coming from the scholar Khaled Abou El Fadl.

As we have mentioned previously, membership in the Sunni community has always been contested, and there are those who would argue that neither the Wahhabis nor the modernists, including those who may or may not consider themselves 'reformers,' are truly Sunnis. In particular, an increasingly influential group of traditionalist Sunnis, such as Nuh Ha Mim Keller, Gibril Haddad, Hisham Kabbani and others, argue that affiliating with one of the premodern schools of law, being certified through the *ijaza* system, and affiliating with a Sufi path, are all necessary practices of Sunnism. Ethical objections to any of the content of traditional hadith collections is met with an assertion that 'the masses' should not be reading hadith texts without the guidance of a certified scholar who knows how to interpret them. In general, traditionalists argue, ordinary Muslims should focus on traditional texts praising the Prophet, so they can develop good character, and they should leave legal texts and reasoning to the experts.

SCHOLARS, THE STATE AND THE COMMUNITY

For Sunnis, the interpretive move between words and their meaning must be justified according to evidence and a methodology that is ostensibly accessible to all rational Muslims who can understand the sources. No person after the Prophet is infallible, and no person, be they a descendant of the Prophet, a mystic or a political leader, can claim access to divine knowledge that is inaccessible to others and that contradicts the Qur'an and the Sunna as understood by the community of scholars. This position

---

[15] Brown, *Misquoting Muhammad*, p. 44.

on interpretive authority emerged over the first two centuries of Islam from a diverse set of groups and individuals who differed on many issues, but converged on a few key points. As Matthew Kuiper notes, the two 'monumental legacies' of these 'proto-Sunnis' were 'the elevation and widespread embrace of Prophetic hadith and the decisive shift from caliph to *'ulama'* as the primary locus of religious authority.'[16]

A scholar in Sunni Islam is one who has knowledge (*'ilm*) of the Qur'an and the Sunna and the proper means of interpreting them. As Sunnism coalesced between the second and the fourth centuries AH, the four legal schools (Hanafi, Maliki, Shafi'i and Hanbali) came to dominate due to a number of factors, including the interventions of rulers in various ways, as well as their patronage of institutions. Traditional Sunnism is characterized by this denominationalism as a means of managing diversity. The recognition that there is a core set of diverse, potentially authentic interpretive methods and schools within Sunni Islam is an aspirationally irenic solution to the rejection of the Shia Imamate on the one hand, and the need to establish parameters of orthodoxy – or the appearance thereof – on the other.

The Hanbalis have often had an uneasy relationship with other Sunni schools. We have already mentioned their extreme reliance on hadith, including preferring a weak hadith over a strong analogy from the Qur'an. In addition, they did not always accept, especially after Ibn Taymiyya (d. 1328), the claims of consensus (*ijma'*), invoked by other Sunni scholars to firm up pragmatic or traditional opinions they could not convincingly prove by the Qur'an or Sunna. Furthermore, Hanbalis were mostly hostile to rational theology and to metaphorical interpretations of the Qur'an, believing both impose flawed human thinking upon God's perfect word. It is unsurprising that this school of thought seems to be the most uncomfortable in modern societies where the development and liberation of human rational and creative capacities is exalted.

As Kuiper has noted, a separation between religious and political authority was a hallmark of classical Sunnism. Scholars asserted that both forms of authority are grounded in the Qur'an, Sunna, and in reason. But

---

[16] Kuiper, 'Early Proto-Sunni Movement,' p. 88.

while Sunnis have always agreed that political authority is necessary, they have vehemently disagreed about how this authority is acquired. Because of the political upheavals of the first century of Islam, Sunni scholars were keen to avoid anarchy and were typically wary of revolutions. In the premodern period, and even in many societies today, they have often urged a pragmatic concession to political power. That is to say, no matter how a ruler gains power, his authority is acknowledged, as long as he (or, for some, she) is a Muslim and does not interfere with the practice of Islam. In some cases, and increasingly in modern society, the requirement that a ruler is Muslim is waived; what is most important is that political power be exercised to protect the lives and religion of Muslims. Summarizing the Sunni position, Hayrettin Yücesoy writes:

> As long as the caliphate was a reality, the Sunnis defended it; when circumstances changed, they revised their thought to reflect contemporary developments. Their overriding concern was the promotion of social harmony and the welfare of the community, for they were worried about the consequences of civil strife. In elaborating their views – although they continued to use religious arguments from hadith and the Qur'an because of their attachment to Sunni epistemology and methodology ... they also sought ways to explain the rational, historical, and human bases of governance.[17]

By the middle of the Abbasid caliphate, Sunnism came into its own once scholars were successful in claiming the authority to interpret the Qur'an and Sunna according to their methods, while denying political rulers the authority to do so on the basis of their office. In order to maintain their authority, scholars were keen to demonstrate their intellectual and moral independence from political power, even as they relied on the rulers to enforce the law and limits they set as orthodox. This has been true even in modern Sunni nation states, where religious and educational institutions have mostly been overtaken by the state. Few objective observers would consider this latter development to be good for scholars, for the state, or for

---

[17] Yücesoy, 'Justification of Political Authority', p. 28.

the general population. Scholars are often deemed corrupt and lackeys because their livelihood is fully in the hands of the state. Rulers who claim to govern according to the Qur'an and Sunna engender unrealistic expectations and inevitably disappoint, sometimes leading to various degrees of revolt, as with Nimeiry in Sudan, in Afghanistan under the Taliban, and in Saudi Arabia. The general population suffers from a lack of moral buffers between themselves and the state.

Sunni Muslims draw upon the Qur'an's frequent critiques of tyranny and political oppression to claim their political rights. While Satan appears in the Qur'an as the spiritual enemy of humanity, the role of earthly super-villain is played by Pharaoh, and it is this figure which many Sunnis project onto the dictators who oppress them. With the perception that much of the scholarly sector has been corrupted and co-opted by dictators, many Sunni Muslims have increasingly believed it is their collective responsibility to establish a just political order. For while the Qur'an does not offer a description of an ideal ruler, it does describe the ideal community (Q 3:103–4) whose obligation is to cooperate to establish justice and prevent evil. Bypassing traditional scholars with the hadith, 'there is no clergy in Islam,' and denying the need for interpretation with the modern slogan 'the Qur'an is our constitution,' revolutionary figures and movements have disrupted Sunni traditionalism.

While some of these disruptions could be seen as positive, the orgy of terrorist violence birthed in some corners of political Islam have sent many Sunnis looking for more peaceful and ethical interpretations of the Qur'an and Sunna. Some look to international councils of scholars to guide the *umma*, while others see these councils as too patriarchal, paternalistic, and too close to power to offer meaningful moral guidance. While political Islam limps through today's world like a veteran with PTSD and amputated limbs, traditional forms of Islam sit in the corner like a grandfather, full of poignant stories, respected and loved, but often ignored and deemed out of touch. Traditional claims of consensus no longer hold fast. But there is hope for the Sunni community, I believe, if Sunnis shift from *ijma'* to *jama'a*, that is, from scholarly consensus to community cohesion. And indeed, we see ordinary Sunni Muslims growing in confidence in their ability to work together in their local or national communities to lift up the

Qur'anic ideals of justice, fairness, purity and human dignity. Scholars have a role to play in these communities, offering expert opinion on specialized topics, but they no longer run the show.

The reality is that for many Sunni Muslims, Islamic law and political theology are not significant concerns. Their social, economic and political lives are dominated by other powers. The Qur'an is, nevertheless, a force still shaping their lives. We can illustrate this influence by returning to my dinner party, where the influence of the Qur'an was pervasive. We did not consume alcohol with our meal (Q 5:90–1), nor pork, nor any other forbidden food (Q 2:173). The animal whose meat we consumed was kosher (Q 5:5). We made ablutions and prayed together (Q 9:71) when the time came. Most of the women wore headscarves and all the men and women socialized chastely (Q 24:30–1).

And while ordinary Muslims may or may not have occasion to be in much contact with scholars of the religious law, theology and Qur'an interpretation, every mosque and congregational setting needs a prayer leader (*imam*) whose main qualification is the ability to fluently recite the Qur'an from memory. Ibn Khaldun said that 'Instructing children in the Qur'an is a symbol of Islam' and that the Qur'an is 'the foundation for all habits that may be acquired later on.'[18] The Sunni community continues to be bound together by its universal commitment to the memorization and recitation of the Qur'an and by their conviction that the Qur'an is the only infallible guide for their lives, if they can only be sincere and devoted enough to grasp its meaning.

BIBLIOGRAPHY

Abdul Rauf, Feisal. *Defining Islamic Statehood: Measuring and Indexing Contemporary Muslim States.* (New York: Palgrave Macmillan, 2015)

Abou El Fadl, Khaled. *Speaking in God's Name: Islamic Law, Authority and Women.* (Oxford: Oneworld, 2001)

Alalwani, Taha Jabir. *Reviving the Balance: The Authority of the* Qur'an *and the Status of the* Sunna. (London: The International Institute of Islamic Thought, 2017)

Brown, Jonathan A.C. *Hadith: Muhammad's Legacy in the Medieval and Modern World.* (London: Oneworld, 2009)

---

[18] Mattson, *Story of the Qur'an*, p. 119.

— *Misquoting Muhammad: The Challenge and Choices of Interpreting the Prophet's Legacy.* (London: Oneworld, 2014)

Hallaq, Wael B. *Shari'a: Theory, Practice, Transformations.* (Cambridge: Cambridge University Press, 2009)

Ibn Ashur, Muhammad al-Tahir. *Treatise on Maqasid al-Shari'ah.* Trans. Mohamed El-Tahir El-Mesawi. (London: The International Institute of Islamic Thought, 2006)

Kuiper, Matthew. 'The Roots and Achievements of the Early Proto-Sunni Movement: A Profile and Interpretation.' *The Muslim World* 104 (January/April 2014): 71–88

Mattson, Ingrid. *The Story of the Qur'an: Its History and Place in Muslim Life.* 2nd edn. (Malden, MA: Wiley-Blackwell, 2013)

al-Qaradawi, Yusuf. *Approaching the Sunna: Comprehension and Controversy.* (London: The International Institute of Islamic Thought, 2006)

Yücesoy, Hayrettin. 'Justification of Political Authority in Medieval Sunni Thought.' In *Islam, the State, and Political Authority: Medieval Issues and Modern Concerns.* Ed. Asma Afsaruddin, 9–33. (New York: Palgrave Macmillan, 2011)

Chapter 9

The Qur'an and the Ahmadiyya Community: an Overview

Mujeeb Ur Rahman, Independent

This chapter presents a brief introduction of the Jama'at Ahmadiyya (also known as the Ahmadiyya Muslim community), its doctrines, understanding and insights into the Qur'an. I draw primarily on Ahmadiyya sources.[1] The chapter also demonstrates how the Qur'an impacts the daily life of the Ahmadiyya community, and how their world-view aims to contribute to interfaith tolerance and world peace. Finally, I will also engage the dialectical tradition of Ahmadiyya hermeneutics. The Qur'an is the most authoritative text of the community. To proclaim and establish its excellence and supremacy is the community's highest objective.

INTRODUCTION

According to their beliefs, the Ahmadiyya movement represents the essence of Islam; the movement does not depart from Islam in the very least, nor

---

[1] Works by Hazrat Mirza Ghulam Ahmad Qadiani (d. 1908) are my main source. This chapter counts Bismillah as the first verse of each chapter.

does it add one iota to the doctrines and teachings of Islam. Yet it is a fresh presentation of Islam. It sets forth only that which has been inherent in Islam from the very beginning, but which had been overlaid in the last few centuries or the need of which had not yet arisen. Some outside observers and research scholars consider the Ahmadiyya a liberal movement offering the attraction of a fresh start to those who had lost faith in older interpretations of Islam. Similarly, Mirza Ghulam Ahmad was considered by some to be a modernist who placed emphasis on the purification of Islam from corrupting influences and practices. Therefore, the Ahmadiyya movement combined the purifying spirit of orthodox reform with a tinge of modern liberalism. In short, the Ahmadiyya can be seen as a renaissance of Islam.

The Prophet Muhammad was not raised simply for the sake of seventh-century Makkans, nor was the message of the Qur'an meant for the Arabian peninsula alone. He was raised for all mankind. The message was universal and meant to be realized in all ages to come. Therefore, the Qur'an addresses mankind: 'Say, "Oh mankind! Truly I am a messenger to you all from Allah"' (Q 7:159). It states: 'And We have not sent thee but as a bearer of glad tidings and a warner, for all mankind' (Q 34:29), adding: 'Blessed is He who sent down the criterion to His servant, that he may be a warner to all the worlds' (Q 25:2), and: 'this Qur'an has been revealed to me so that I may warn you and whomsoever it reaches' (Q 6:20).

THE RENAISSANCE OF ISLAM

The Qur'an mentions two groups of believers described as the Awaleen, or 'former ones,' and the Akhireen, or 'later ones.' The verses, 'And others among them who have not yet joined them' (Q 62:4), and 'A large party from among the early [Muslims] and a large party from among the later ones' (Q 56:40–1), indicate two periods of Islam according to Ahmadiyya tradition. Also there are Qur'anic verses indicating the appearance of a divinely commissioned reformer among the later ones who is to usher in the renaissance of Islam. According to tradition as well, religion was perfected and the divine bounty was completed during the period of Awaleen, but it was divinely ordained that Islam would spread across the world in later times when the means of communications would make it possible to carry this message to the corners of the globe. Concerning this it states: 'He it is Who sent His messenger with guidance and the religion of truth, that He may make it prevail over every other religion' (Q 9:33). This likely relates to the later period.

A DIVINE PLAN

The renaissance of Islam is seen to come after a millennium of gradual decline within the Muslim world. According to this divine plan, the appearance of the Messiah and the Mehdi – his awaited helper – in the latter days was to revive Islam and re-establish order.

According to Ahmadiyya tradition, the verses pointing to the age of the divine reformer correspond to the appearance of the founder of the Ahmadiyya movement. References to this time can be found in the following verses: 'The duration of [the age] is a thousand years according to what you reckon' (Q 32:6), and 'And the moon when it becomes full' (Q 84:18–19). Muhammad is said to be the sun, while the Messiah, deriving light from the sun, is 'the full moon,' signifying his appearance in the fourteenth night corresponding to the fourteenth century of Islam.[2]

THE SECOND ADVENT

The Ahmadiyya movement was founded in 1889 by Mirza Ghulam Ahmad of Qadian (1835–1908). He claimed the dual status of the 'Mahdi' and 'Messiah' of the later days. This claim incensed mainstream Muslim

---

[2] While it is true that the phrase *khatam al-nabiyin* has usually been interpreted as the last prophet, Islamic exegetical traditions and other branches of classical Arabic literature preserve material which indicates that this now generally received understanding of the Qur'anic verse is not the only possible one, and had not necessarily been the earliest. Even in the third century of Islam it was possible to offer divergent interpretations of *khatam al-nabiyin*. These interpretations can be found in the hadith literature. It was only in the second part of the tenth century CE that the finality of the Prophet was included among the articles of faith. It appears that, till then, belief in the finality of Muhammad's Prophet-hood had not been of central importance in Islamic dogma. See Friedmann, *Prophecy Continuous*; Nanotvi, *Tahzirunnas*.

orthodox Muslims and engendered bitter opposition, even though his claim was interpreted out of the Quranic text itself.[3] On a different level, the advent of Mirza Ghulam Ahmad ushered in the new era of prophetic succession known as *Khilafa 'ala minhaj al-nubuwwa*. According to Ahmadiyya tradition, he fulfilled the Qur'anic promise: 'As He made successors from among those who were before them' (Q 24:56). The present supreme leader of the global Ahmadiyya community, Mirza Masroor Ahmad, is his fifth Khalifa.[4]

DIALECTICAL HERMENEUTICS

The appearance of Mirza Ghulam Ahmad on the plane of world religions marked a watershed moment within Islam in the Indian subcontinent, and soon gave birth to Ahmadiyya dialectical hermeneutics. This hermeneutics was reformist in nature and sought to provide a perennial source of guiding principles.

Within classical Qur'anic exegesis, three general standards are almost universally agreed upon by medieval and modern commentators: (1) interpreting the Qur'an through the Qur'an itself; (2) interpreting the Qur'an through the Sunna of the prophet; (3) interpreting the Qur'an through the Prophet's companions. Philology has also been accepted as an aid to Qur'anic interpretation. While these principles are accepted in Ahmadiyya hermeneutics, some adjustments were made.

---

[3] In the history of religions we note the idea of a 'second coming' in the Buddhist, Jewish, Christian and Islamic traditions. In all these traditions, the second coming could signify the appearance of someone in the likeness of a prophet. Therefore, the second coming of the Messiah prophesied in the Islamic tradition was meant to be metaphorical. According to the Ahmadiyya interpretation of Qur'anic verses (Q 3:56, 145; 5:76), the Messiah, son of Mary, escaped death on the cross, set out to reclaim the lost sheep of Israel and travelled to India, where he died a natural death and lies buried in Srinagar, Kashmir. The Gospels and the historical record preserved enough testimony of this fact. This belief reinforces the idea that the second coming of the Messiah is metaphorical in nature. See further Ahmad, *Jesus in India*; Faber-Kaiser, *Jesus Died in Kashmir*.

[4] The Ahmadiyya concept of *khilafa* does not conflate state and religion. The term does not refer to a political head. He is, rather, the spiritual mentor responsible for the moral and spiritual well-being of all believers, and the worldwide dissemination of the message of peace and glory.

THE EXALTED POSITION OF THE QUR'AN

Before embarking upon any hermeneutical exercise, we need to bear in mind the Qur'an's claim about itself. In other words, we have to see how the Qur'an presents itself to humanity. It calls itself a 'blessed reminder' (Q 21:51). According to Ahmadiyya tradition, the Qur'an does not set forth teachings new or alien to human nature or conscience. It is, rather, a reminder of what is imprinted in our human mind and conscience. God does not require human beings to accept anything that is beyond their intellectual capacity, and only sets forth such doctrines as are comprehensible by human beings, so that His directives should not impose upon mankind a burden beyond their capacity (Q 2:287). As such, none of the doctrines, principles or commandments are to be imposed by authority. It is, rather, 'a book wherein there is no doubt' (Q 2:3), 'consummate wisdom' (Q 54:6), 'true certainty' (Q 69:52) and 'a decisive word' (Q 86:14). 'Falsehood cannot approach it either from before or from behind it' (Q 41:43). 'It is a book to explain everything and a [source of] guidance' (Q 16:90).

It claims to possess a spiritual quality that enlightens the heart and calls itself a cure for its diseases, healing also that which afflicts the human mind (Q 10:58). It calls itself *maknun* – i.e. protected or preserved. It also calls itself as *mubin* – i.e. manifest or clear. The Qur'an further claims that it is an admonition for all mankind and that it contains lasting commandments, stating 'a Messenger from Allah, reciting unto them pure scriptures. Therein are lasting commandments' (Q 98:3–4). It also claims, 'falsehood cannot approach it, neither from before nor from behind it' (Q 41:43). According to Ahmadiyya tradition, this means that the verities of the Qur'an cannot be falsified by anything discovered in the past or that may be discovered in ages to come. In other words, it does not inculcate anything through compulsion. After all, 'there should be no compulsion in religion' (Q 2:257).

The Ahmadiyya community approach the Qur'an and its meaning with these attributes and qualities in mind. It is this wise, unwavering approach which can lead us all to its true understanding. This exalted position of the Qur'an should guide any attempt to understand the text.

FIRST PRINCIPLE – NO ABROGATION OR REPEAL

The principal goal of reform has been to restore the status of the Qur'an to its exalted position. It has been generally accepted as the first principal of Qur'anic interpretation that the Qur'an interprets itself. But the text of the Qur'an was also subjected to the bewildering concept of 'repealing' (*nasikh*) and 'repealed' (*mansukh*, also known as 'abrogated') verses, which in the final analysis rendered the whole body of the text open to serious problems. Historically, as many as five hundred verses of the Qur'an were categorized repealed. By the time of Shah Waliullah (d. 1762), efforts were made to reduce this number to as little as five. This gradual elimination of repealed verses indicates that the entire theoretical framework emanated from failure to properly reconcile verses of the Qur'an with our understanding. Those who believed in the theory of abrogation had insufficient theoretical support from within the Qur'an itself.

Mirza Ghulam Ahmad, categorically and emphatically repudiated the concept of abrogation and stated that there can be no real abrogation or repeal in the Qur'an itself, nor is it permissible to add anything to it. He supported this proposition through Qur'anic verses. Thus, for the first principle of interpretation, Ahmadiyya hermeneutics stands on a solid foundation insofar as every word of the Qur'anic text is preserved and handed down to us. Speaking of this rule of interpretation, the founder of the Ahmadiyya movement said that:

> The touchstone of a true interpretation is that it should be supported by a host of clear and supporting testimonies of the Holy Qur'an itself and that the Holy Qur'an is not like other books that are dependent upon extraneous sources for the proof or disclosure of their verities. The Holy Qur'an is like a perfectly balanced structure, the whole dynamics of which are disturbed by the displacement of a single block.[5]

---

[5] Ahmad, *Blessings*, p. 28.

SECOND PRINCIPLE – THE SUNNA

The second principle traditionally followed is that interpretation of the Qur'an should be sought from the bearer of the Qur'an himself – i.e. the Prophet Muhammad. This means that if any interpretation provided by the Prophet is available, then it should be followed. In this regard, hadith is sometimes taken as synonymous with Sunna, despite the fact that hadith is only a vehicle of transmitting the Sunna and not the Sunna itself. At the dawn of the twentieth century, the status of the Qur'an and Sunna were the subject of intense debate within Muslim schools of thought in India. As a divinely commissioned arbiter, the founder of the Ahmadiyya movement judged between the two extreme positions held on this particular subject. He states:

> We do not regard Hadith and Sunnah as one, as is the practice of formal scholars of Hadith. They are distinct; Hadith is one thing, Sunnah is another. By Sunnah we mean the practice of the holy prophet which is an unbroken chain adhered to and which appears contemporaneously with the holy Qur'an and will always remain so. In other words, the holy Qur'an is the word of God Almighty and the Sunnah is the action of the holy prophet.[6]

He adds elsewhere:

> The correct way therefore is neither to treat the Ahadith as having greater authority than the Qur'an as do the Ahl ul Hadith of this age, nor to prefer the statements in the Ahadith which are contradictory to the Qur'an; nor to regard the Ahadith as vain and false. The Qur'an and Sunnah should judge the Ahadith and those that are not opposed to them should certainly be accepted.[7]

---

[6] Ibid., p. 32.
[7] Ahmad, *Essence*, vol. II, p. 132.

THIRD PRINCIPLE – THE HADITH

The third principle of understanding the Qur'an is the interpretation of the companions of the Prophet. There is no doubt that they were the first to inherit his guidance and were, therefore, the foremost inheritors of his knowledge. Allah blessed them abundantly and helped them in their understanding, and they practiced what they preached. Ahmadiyya hermeneutics accepts and accords the interpretation of companions due respect insofar as they are not in conflict with the explicit text of the Qur'an.

FOURTH PRINCIPLE – THE PURITY OF THE SEEKER

Mirza Ghulam Ahmad drew repeated attention to the criterion of truth and purity. According to him, the fourth principle of interpretation is:

> To meditate upon the meanings of the Holy Qur'an with the purity of one's own self, because purity of the self has a certain affinity with the holy Qur'an, as Allah [revealed Q 56:80] which means that the verities of the holy Qur'an are disclosed only to a person of pure heart, for the two have an affinity with one another. Such a person recognizes these verities, and smells them, and his heart cries out that this indeed is the true way . . . One of the many characteristics of the Qur'an, which mark it as a word of God is that to arrive at the comprehension of its deeper meaning and significance the seeker must, in addition to a certain degree of knowledge of the language and the principles of interpretation, cultivate purity of thought and action. The greater the purity of a person's life, the deeper and wider will be his comprehension of the meaning of the Qur'an.[8]

According to Ahmadiyya tradition, approaching the Qur'an with a predetermined mind, therefore, is impertinent, and such an approach is strictly forbidden. The Qur'an should be approached with purity of heart and with an open mind, free from all prejudices and predilections.

---

[8] Ahmad, *Ruhani khazain*, vol. 9, pp. 150–2.

FIFTH PRINCIPLE – ARABIC LEXICON

Another aid to the interpretation of the Qur'an accepted by medieval commentators is philology and expertise in the Arabic lexicon. Ahmadiyya hermeneutics accepts this rule, but Mirza Ghulam Ahmad added his own unique insights into the Arabic language (see further discussion in 'deeper insights' below).

SIXTH PRINCIPLE – PHYSICAL AND SPIRITUAL ORDER OF THE UNIVERSE

Another important aid for understanding is the universe's spiritual order and its connection to the physical order. According to Ahmadiyya tradition, there is complete harmony between the two. The Qur'an repeatedly urges observation and reflection, as well as the exercise of reason and understanding. For example, it states: 'in the creation of the heavens and the earth and in the alternation of the night and the day there are indeed signs for people of understanding' (Q 3:191). The objective is to urge reflection upon the event or phenomenon cited, that we as reader of the Qur'an may draw lessons from it. This in turn would help us grasp the truth – i.e. how God's divine attributes and laws operate (Q 2:270). Ahmadiyya tradition also holds that the Qur'an brings full harmony between science and religion. This theory sees no contradiction between the Qur'an on the one hand and human reason on the other. Science is concerned with nature, which is seen as the handiwork of God. The Qur'an is seen as the word of God. Both His handiwork and His word are *His*. Therefore, there can be no contradiction between the two. The unfolding of the Qur'anic message in its human context is discussed by Mirza Ghulam Ahmad, who states:

> The verities and fine points which foster understanding are always disclosed according to need. New corruptions call for ever fresh meanings, which are full of wisdom. It is obvious that the holy Qur'an is a miracle in itself, and the greatness of its miracle is that it is comprehensive of unlimited verities, but they are manifested at

their due time. As the difficulties of the time demand, those hidden insights are disclosed.[9]

The Qur'an states, furthermore: 'there is not a thing but we have unlimited treasures thereof, and we send them down in regulated and known quantities' (Q 15:22); 'but man can encompass nothing of His knowledge except what He pleases' (Q 2:56). According to Ahmadiyya tradition, it is not for mankind to discover knowledge beyond his limits. Such knowledge can only come from God. Small wonder it is, therefore, that we find in scripture oceans of meaning, especially when we read with the help of guiding principles laid down by the promised Messiah – i.e. Mirza Ghulam Ahmad.

SEVENTH PRINCIPLE – DIVINE GUIDANCE

Another vital aid to interpreting the Qur'an is the revelation granted to saints and the visions of the *muhaddithun*:

> This criterion comprehends all the other criteria because he who is granted the revelation of *muhaddathiyyat* possesses all the qualities of the prophet he follows and the true teaching is certainly made manifest to him.[10]

According to Ahmadiyya tradition, the deeper meanings and significance of a revealed word can best be understood through divine guidance.

DEEPER INSIGHTS INTO QUR'ANIC VERITIES: AL-FATIHA: THE EXORDIUM

Mirza Ghulam Ahmad points to another key to achieving a comprehensive understanding of the Qur'an – namely the Surat al-Fatiha (Q 1), or the opening chapter of the Qur'an. This exordium represents the epitome

---

[9] Ahmad, *Essence*, vol. I, p. 373.
[10] Ahmad, *Blessings*, pp. 30–1.

of scripture, a kind of prologue or prolegomena, with the rest comprising the text and explanation. Everything that is dealt with in detail throughout scripture, be it doctrine, law or whatever, is presented in its essence in the Surat al-Fatiha. Ahmad wrote several commentaries on this short chapter, in which he presented lively themes. The exposition of Islam for the benefit of Muslims, as well as others, has been immeasurably facilitated by these commentaries. He argues that almost any subject can be deduced from this one short chapter. Attributes of God, important spiritual truths, important stages in spiritual advancement, are all to be found within this first chapter. These 'discoveries' are of a fundamental character. They are discoveries of principles which have proved indispensable in the exposition of Islam today.

QUR'ANIC OATHS

Mirza Ghulam Ahmad opened up avenues to insights into the understanding of the Qur'an and made its deeper meanings and verities accessible to the modern man. What appeared enigmatic was explained in a scientific and rational manner. One area which had baffled many people was the significance of Qur'anic oaths, whereby God Almighty swears by his creation.

Explaining the philosophy of the Qur'anic oaths, the founder of the Ahmadiyya movement pointed out that:

Divine manifestations are of two types. One, those that are obvious and concerning which there is no controversy. Secondly, there are those divine manifestations which are inferential concerning which people differ and can fall into error. By calling to witness the obvious phenomena, God Almighty's purpose is to establish by their evidence His inferential manifestations . . . It is obvious that the sun and the moon and the day and the night and the heaven and the earth, possess the respective characteristics that we have mentioned, but everyone is not aware of the characteristics possessed by the human soul. Thus, God has set forth His obvious manifestations as witnesses for the purpose of explaining His inferential manifestations.[11]

Man is a microcosm or a tiny representation of the pattern found in the universe. Since the great bodies of the universe possess these qualities and provide benefits for God's creatures, then how can man, who ranks above all those bodies, be without those qualities? Ahmad states:

> So in these oaths God Almighty draws attention to this firm and eternal law of nature and calls for reflection upon it that all the vegetation of the earth depends upon the water of heaven. Thus, for the hidden law that governs divine revelation, the obvious law of nature is a witness.[12]

The Qur'an demonstrates both the visible and the invisible, the physical and the metaphysical, the material and the spiritual, the macrocosm and the microcosm. Thus scenes of Qur'anic wisdom and verities were made clear, and new tools of argumentation to explain the relationship of science and religion were provided to show that there is no disparity between the word of God on the one hand, and the acts of God on the other. Each explains and complements the other. According to Ahmadiyya tradition, anyone who studies the Qur'an will find that, from beginning to end, it provides two kinds of testimony – the testimony of reason and the testimony of revelation. In the Qur'an, these two are like two great streams running in parallel and continuously shaping one another.

PROPHECIES ABOUT OUR TIMES

Drawing on these principles, the founder of the Ahmadiyya movement produced further insights into the Qur'an. And, according to Ahmadiyya tradition, he demonstrated that the Qur'an contains prophecies about our times. The text not only gives a general account of the progress we observe

---

[11] Ahmad, *Philosophy*, p. 182.
[12] Ibid., p. 188.

today, but also an account of specific developments which have taken place in our times. Earlier commentators and scholars could not visualize the conditions of modernity. Therefore, they could not comprehend the prophecies in the Qur'an which have been fulfilled in modern times. Instead, they interpreted these prophecies as descriptions of the Day of Judgment.

For example, according to Ahmadiyya tradition the opening of *Surat Al-Takwir* (Q 81:4–11) points to developments that have taken place during our times. Mountains have been moved, blown away by dynamite. New means of transport and communication have been developed. Transport on the backs of animals has become obsolete. The oceans now flow forth into one another through the digging of canals. The publication of scrolls and documents not only became possible with the printing press, but through print and electronic media it has become possible to share them across the globe in a matter of seconds.

Further reflection on the concluding verses of *Surat Al-Takwir* may shed light on developments in the physical world, as well as prophecies about the revival of Islam (esp. Q 81:18–19). According to Ahmadiyya tradition, the 'receding night of darkness' and the 'breathing morning light' are witnesses of the universal laws which equally apply to the spiritual world. The receding night symbolizes the decline of Islam and the breathing morning is the dawn of reformation. The link between the opening verses and the concluding verses indicate the time of the revival.

ORDER IN THE QUR'AN

Another insight the Ahmadiyya community has received from its founder is the discovery of a coherent order throughout scripture. The verses of each chapter and the chapters themselves have a rational sequence. Every chapter, verse and word is believed to be in its ideal place. According to Ahmadiyya tradition, so perfect is the arrangement of words, verses and chapters that the internal arrangement of other books appears lacking in comparison. Equipped with these insights, the interpretation of the Qur'an contributes to the harmonious development of society and individuals, ultimately leading to an enlightened worldview and liberated mind.

ARABIC: THE MOTHER OF ALL LANGUAGES

According to Ahmadiyya tradition, the founder of the movement was granted divine insight into a unique characteristic of the Arabic language. He affirmed the position of some classical Muslim scholars that Arabic is the mother of all languages.

In his celebrated lecture at the conference of world religions in 1896, Mirza Ghulam Ahmad made this statement:

> We have shown in our book *Minan ul rahman* that the Arabic language is the only language which can claim to be divine, the fountain from which all sorts of knowledge flow, the mother of all tongues and the first as well as the last medium of divine revelation. It is first, because Arabic was the word of God which was with God and was at last revealed to the world from which men learned to make their own languages, and the last, because the last divine book i.e. the Holy Quran is also in Arabic.[13]

This was a bold claim. He adds:

> The proposition that Arabic is the source of all languages runs counter to the prevailing linguistic notions. To some it may come as a surprise; others may receive it with mixed feelings ... Philology is a science full of surprises and often makes curious detours ... Therefore, hasty judgement should be avoided as far as possible ... The Arabic language may have been bypassed by the European scholars. [However] one cannot attribute partiality to eminent philologists whose honesty of purpose and broad mindedness in the quest of knowledge is absolutely above board ... There is a [right] time for every discovery to be made.[14]

The timeliness of such discoveries is supported by Q 15:22 in Ahmadiyya tradition. Ahmad adds about the Arabic language:

---

[13] Mazhar, *Arabic*, p. i.
[14] Ibid., p. ii.

It was revealed with the ten perfect circles, and its system of roots is in accord with its educative system, and every one of its ten circles is accompanied by its system of roots according to its natural quantity and values in which distinct roots are appointed for the manifestation of divine attributes, and for the explanation of four types that have been mentioned, and for every circle of teaching a perfect circle of roots is available.[15]

He also expounded upon the following five unique virtues of Arabic:

Firstly, it possesses a complete treasure of simple words befitting every human requirement, while other languages are devoid of this perfection . . . Secondly, it accurately describes the attributes of God. It is the facsimile of the book of nature as regards the names of elements, vegetables, animals, minerals and human limbs. All these names are based on supreme wisdom and philosophy. Other languages cannot stand comparison with Arabic in this virtue . . . Thirdly, there is a complete order of verbs and nouns in Arabic. Similar verbs are mutually related with similar nouns in a scientific way. This perfection is not found in other languages . . . Fourthly, Arabic expresses more meaning in few words by using mere signs like al or Tanween or changing the order of the words, Arabic conveys an idea which other languages have to express in many sentences . . . Fifthly, Arabic possesses a store of simple words which faithfully and completely depict most subtle thoughts and feelings of man.[16]

Ahmad also provided several guiding principles of etymology. Among them he states:

And Arabic is the original language given by God and all other languages are like its sons and daughters they receive outfit from the sacerdotal vestments of Arabic . . . And they (non-Arabic languages)

---

[15] Ahmad, *Essence*, vol. I, p. 464.
[16] Mazhar, *Arabic*, p. 38.

do not possess a single word which is not Arabic . . . And when you employ utmost effort and industry to retrace a word to its ultimate origin you will find it to be an Arabic word which has been disfigured like unto a goat which has been skinned.[17]

One of his disciples, Mohammad Ahmad Mazhar (d. 1993), argued that:

(a) There are definite phonetic laws by means of which the root words of all languages can be traced to their Arabic origin with precision and certainty.

(b) These laws are simple and obvious. They are also accepted principles of philology; but Western scholars never attempted to apply them to Arabic in order to find out the ultimate origin of languages.

(c) The laws apply equally well to all languages so much so that the root words of all the languages can be divided into ten main categories (see below).

Arguing from Q 30:22, Mazhar points out:

The diversity of tongue has been placed on the same footing as the diversity of the human race – white, yellow, black etc. This is as much as to say that just as climatic differences have brought about racial differences while the human genus is the same, similarity, differences of climate and habit has caused a diversity in the languages. Otherwise they belong to the same stock.[18]

According to Ahmadiyya tradition, one should study the structure of various languages and compare and contrast them on an ethnological basis. This is why the diversity of language is placed in juxtaposition to the diversity of the human race.

---

[17] Ibid., p. 74.
[18] Ibid., p. 14.

The Qur'an, furthermore, is the impetus behind philological research and investigation. Mazhar summarizes:

(i) The structure of Arabic roots is mathematical. Each root is as distinct as a thumb impression and is immune from the 'diseases of words.' Therefore, it is impossible that Arabic could have been derived from any other language.

(ii) The roots are symbols which depict the natural phenomenon with which they are linked up. The words denote the philosophy and reason. In the words of the holy founder of the Ahmadiyya community the Arabic language and universe are two mirrors which are placed opposite to each other. Hence, Arabic vocabulary meets with every human requirement with its inexhaustible treasure of simple words.

(iii) Arabic language was a perfect machine. Every part was fitted in its proper place, various parts were removed which passed into other languages without the order and system.

(iv) Arabic is self-sufficient and does not stand in need of any borrowing from other languages.

(v) Another important characteristic is the absence of homonyms in Arabic. The Arabic words are constructed in such a way that different words must remain apart like the thumb impression of different individuals and there is no question here of corruption and confusion by way of homonyms.[19]

Mazhar argues that the words of other languages can be traced to Arabic roots by means of ten formulas derived from phonetic laws. With the help of these formulas, he claimed that one could trace Chinese, Sanskrit, Hindi, Persian, Latin, Greek, German, Spanish, French, English and Russian to the Arabic language.

---

[19] Ibid., pp. 55–6.

THE QUR'AN: A LIVING BOOK

According to Ahmadiyya tradition, the limitless changes of progress give rise to limitless ideas and interpretations of scripture. It is necessary, therefore, for the Qur'an to manifest itself in ever new forms, to disclose ever new forms of knowledge to meet the challenges of a new age. The world is dynamic, and so is the Quran. It yields much-needed guidance in advance. This has been the case for more than thirteen centuries, and it will continue to be the case through the ages (Q 14:25–6). The Qur'an speaks at every level; it seeks to reach every type of understanding, through parables, similitudes, arguments, reasoning, observation, the study of natural phenomena, and through moral as well as spiritual laws (Q 59:22).

Mirza Ghulam Ahmad states:

> It is a characteristic of heavenly water that it pulls up the water of all the wells, whether it falls directly into a well or not. In the same way, when a recipient of divine revelation appears in the world then, reason is illumined and clarified to a degree not witnessed before. People begin to search for the truth and their faculty of reflection is stirred up from the unseen. Thus, all this upsurge of reason and of the heart is initiated by the blessed advent of the recipient of divine revelation and the waters of the earth are pulled up by it . . . So, when you find that everyone has started a search for religion and an upsurge has stirred earthly waters, then rise up and be warned and know for certain that heavy rain has fallen from heaven and that the water of divine revelation has fallen upon.[20]

He adds:

> Be sure that the source of perfect knowledge is divine revelation which is bestowed on the holy prophets of God. Therefore God, Who is the ocean of grace, did not design that divine revelation should be sealed up for the future and the world should thus be

---

[20] Ahmad, *Philosophy*, pp. 188–9.

destroyed. The doors of His revelation and converse are always open. If you seek them along their proper ways you will find them easily.[21]

GUIDANCE FOR INTERFAITH DIALOGUE

Religion is a major influence on human relations, and there is hope that it might gradually become more effective in promoting unity and accord, rather than continue to be a source of friction and conflict. It is important, therefore, to consider what attitude Islam adopts towards other faiths and their followers.

When Mirza Ghulam Ahmad appeared, the Muslim world was in complete disarray. India was a battleground between world religions. Even some members of the Muslim clergy converted to Christianity as a result of intense Christian missionary work. Ahmad took to defending Islam and soon became a well-known defender of the faith. 'He presented to the world a captivating picture of religion (Islam) cleansed of the bolts and dust that had collected upon it as a result of superstition and natural weakness of the ignorant.'[22] He completely changed the flow of the debate, and laid the foundation of a new literature in India. He set rules for interreligious debate for the Ahmadiyya community, and said that every claim or proof put forth by the followers of a particular religion must come from the scriptures of that particular faith.

Ahmad adds:

I consider it essential that everyone who follows a book, believing it to be revealed, should base his exposition upon that book and should not extend the scope of advocacy of his faith as if he were compiling a new book.[23]

Another rule put forth for interfaith dialogue by Mirza Ghulam Ahmad was the Qur'anic principle that prophets of God had been raised in every

---

[21] Ahmad, *Philosophy*, p. 208.
[22] Ali, *Founder*, p. 104.
[23] Ahmad, *Philosophy*, p. 2.

nation (Q 13:8; 35:25). Therefore the founder of each religion must be respected and divine origin of their scripture recognized. In other words, he argued that all religions had truth within them and should therefore be respected. Even the idols worshiped by the Meccans were not allowed to be reviled (Q 6:109). Based on these two Qur'anic principles, the Ahmadiyya community has constructed a complete code of peaceful interreligious dialogue and debate.

Interreligious dialogue should be such as to preclude the remotest suspicion of any pressure or coercion. To initiate a dialogue, the rule is to 'call unto the way of thy Lord, with wisdom and goodly exhortation' (Q 16:126). And while arguing and disputing a proposition, the rule is to 'argue with them in a way that is best' (Q 16:126). When an interlocutor is unjust then the rule is, 'do not argue at all with such of them as are unjust' (Q 29:47). When it comes to defending one's position, the rule is to 'repel evil with that which is best. And lo, he between whom and thyself was enmity will become as though he was a warm friend' (Q 41:35).

If these principles are fully accepted and acted upon, interreligious relations would be lifted from the plain of controversy and misunderstanding to a level of reasoned and respectful mutual appreciation. This approach allows followers of all religions to respect beneficent values, wherever they may be found.

The quintessence of the objectives set out by Mirza Ghulam Ahmad consist of two objectives. The first is establishing a living bond between man and God, along with compassion and kindness towards His creation. The second has been epitomized by the words of the third Khalifa of the Ahmadiyya: 'love for all, hatred for none.' The Jama'at is engaged in a relentless effort to put this slogan into practice in the service of humanity through its multiple humanitarian projects.

The Ahmadiyya community places great emphasis on the Qur'anic teachings of the communal, interreligious and global peace. Under the auspices of its present head, the community holds regular peace conferences and regularly promotes interfaith dialogue. The head of the community has expounded upon the subject, and the Ahmadiyya community around the world is engaged in promoting peace and harmony at various levels.

THE POWER OF THE PEN – DEFENDING FAITH AND CONSCIENCE

According to Ahmadiyya tradition, jihad is one of the doctrines of Islam which has suffered much distortion during the centuries of moral decline and political power under Muslims. The understanding of jihad that gained currency during the period was completely alien to Qur'anic teachings. Many Muslims came to believe that scripture made it obligatory for them to use force for the propagation of Islam, and that the killing of nonbelievers was jihad. The idea even found its way into channels of education. The *Encyclopedia of Islam* claims that 'the spread of Islam by arms is a religious duty upon Muslims in general.'[24] This distorted concept of jihad spread throughout the Muslim world in the nineteenth century.

Mirza Ghulam Ahmad expounded upon what he deemed the true Qur'anic concept of jihad as illustrated by the prophet in the Sunna. He pointed out that Islam guaranteed freedom of conscience and enjoined that there shall be no compulsion or coercion in matters of faith. The permission to take up arms had only been granted on certain terms and preconditions. Explaining this enlightened interpretation of jihad, Ahmad states:

Islam was spread on account of the inherent qualities of its teaching and its verities, insights, reasons, proofs and the living support and signs of God Almighty and its inherent attractions are the factors that have throughout contributed to its progress and its propagation.[25]

He also states:

The philosophy of Jihad and its true significance is so recondite and profound a matter that the people of this age and those of the middle ages have committed grave mistakes on account of their failure to understand it. This has rendered the teachings of Islam open to the criticism of its opponents.[26]

---

[24] Ali, *Founder*, p. 75.
[25] Ahmad, *Essence*, vol. II, p. 327.
[26] Ibid., p. 319.

Explaining the real purpose of jihad and the reasons why permission to fight was granted, Mirza Ghulam Ahmad points out that the original text of this commandment in the Qur'an is, 'permission to fight is granted to those against whom war is made, because they have been wronged and, Allah indeed has the power to help them. They are those who have been driven out of their homes unjustly' (Q 22:41). He explains further that the Prophet never mounted an armed attack for the propagation of religion. It was not the Prophet who drew the sword, but his opponents.[27] In short, in drawing attention to several verses of the Qur'an, Ahmad clarifies the purpose and goal of jihad. According to him, its original objective was to fight in self-defense, to establish freedom of conscience and liberty of thought. Another objective of jihad was to defend places of worship belonging to different religions, against either desecration or destruction. The Qur'an enjoins Muslims to protect all places of worship, even with their lives (Q 22:40). Ahmad also points out that the conditions for jihad with the sword are non-existent in our time. Therefore, jihad by sword is no more.[28]

Mirza Ghulam Ahmad teaches that in this age, jihad has assumed a spiritual role. In this age, jihad is to strive for propagating Islam, to counter the accusations of opponents and to disseminate the beauties of the faith. He emphasizes that the community has been commanded to prepare itself with the same kind of rigor which the disbeliever has adopted, and to treat them as they treat us, but not to raise the sword against them, unless they raise the sword against us. He states: 'today it is the pen which is employed against Islam. Can he who fights the pen with the sword be anything other than a fool or a tyrant?'[29] The advice of the founder of the Ahmadiyya movement was ignored by the Muslim world to its own peril. It has come to suffer the consequences and is now reaping the harvest of the crop of evil in the form of extremist groups.

According to Ahmadiyya tradition, the founder of the Ahmadiyya movement established a Jama'at of dedicated and sincere followers who have stayed clear of pernicious and distorted understandings of jihad and

---

[27] See generally ibid., pp. 319–33.
[28] Ali, *Founder*, pp. 78–9.
[29] Ahmad, *Lecture Ludhiana*, p. 34.

apostasy. The Jama'at is now spread over 202 countries of the world, and it is today a vibrant voice preaching interfaith understanding, tolerance and 'love for all, hatred for none.'

I conclude this chapter with a message from Mirza Ghulam Ahmad in his own words:

> I hold a lamp in my hand, he who comes to me shall surely partake of its light and he who runs away from me shall be cast into darkness. I am the impregnable fortified fortress of this age; he who enters me shall save his life from robbers, brigands and predators, but he who wants to stay away from my walls is confronted with death from all sides.[30]

BIBLIOGRAPHY

Ahmad, Mirza Ghulam. *Blessings of Prayer.* (London: Islam International Publications, 2007)
— *The Essence of Islam: Volume I.* (Surrey: Tilford, 2004)
— *The Essence of Islam: Volume II.* (Surrey: Tilford, 2004)
— *The Essence of Islam: Volume IV.* (Surrey: Tilford, 2004)
— *Jesus in India.* (Chippenham, UK: Third Millenium Press, 2018)
— *Lecture Ludhiana.* (London: Islam International Publications, 2003)
— *The Philosophy of the Teachings of Islam.* (London: Islam International Publications, 2010)
— *Ruhani khazain, Volume 9.* (Rabwah, Pakistan: Nazrat Ishaat, 2008)
Ali, Muhammad. *The Founder of the Ahmadiyya Movement: A Short Study by Maulana Muhammad Ali.* (Lahore: The Ahmadiyya Anjuman Isha'at-I-Islam, n.d.)
Bengalee, M.R. *Tomb of Jesus.* (Washington, DC: Ahmadiyya Movement in Islam, 1975)
Faber-Kaiser, Andreas. *Jesus Died in Kashmir.* (London: Abacus, 1978)
Friedmann, Yohanan. *Prophecy Continuous: Aspects of Ahmadi Religious Thought and Its Medieval Background.* (Oxford: Oxford University Press, 2003)
Mazhar, Mohammad Ahmad. *Arabic: The Source of All Languages.* (Lahore: Review of Religions, 1963)
Nanotvi, Muhammad Qasim. *Tahzirunnas.* (Karachi: Maktabah-yi Qasimul'ulūm, 1976)

---

[30] Ahmad, *Essence*, vol. IV, p. 276.

Chapter 10

Why the Qur'anists are the Solution: a Declaration

Ahmed Subhy Mansour, Independent

A fter being released from prison in Egypt, I began writing a series of articles in 1989 that were published in the Cairo-based state newspaper *Al-Akhbar*, as well as the opposition newspaper *Al-Ahrar*. I promoted the theme: 'The Qur'an is the solution.' In these articles, I used the Qur'an as the sole criterion to judge, debunk and refute what I saw were the lies, myths and falsehoods of the Sunni creed, the crimes of the Wahabis/Salafis and the terrorism of Muslim Brotherhood members in Egypt.

Now, three decades after 1977, when my call to Qur'anism[1] in Egypt first began, the crimes of the Sunnis and other Muhammadans[2] has

---

[1] The term Qur'anism refers to the modern school of Islam which accepts the 'Qur'an alone.' This school was founded by Ahmad Subhy Mansour and rejects the authenticity of classical Islamic tradition, including the body of literature known as the Sunna (especially hadith) and the doctrines of the founders' Infallibility (*'isma*), Shia imamate (*imama*), among other doctrines. For a brief overview, see Reynolds, *Emergence of Islam*, pp. 207–8.

[2] The term 'Muhammadan' here refers to the adherents of the traditional Sunni and Shia school of law and theology. The meaning of this term is conveyed in critical studies of classical Islamic tradition, both by Islamic modernists and non-Muslim orientalists alike. See, in this regard, Tyabji, *Muhammadan Law*; Wensinck, *Handbook*; al-Tizini, *Muqaddimat awwaliyya*.

spread and escalated into full-blown religious conflict, where suicide bombers shout 'God is the greatest' (*Allahu akbar*) while they commit massacres. Mosques are supposed to be houses of worship, but too many Muhammadans have turned them into centers for conspiracy and militarized ideology. Therefore, I remind readers of the message underlying this chapter and raised more than three decades ago: the Qur'an is the solution. This reminder is based on the reformism and Islamic call to peace within Qur'anism, adhered to by Qur'anists, and called for in the Qur'an itself. Despite persecution and poverty, Qur'anists managed to spread Qur'anism all over the world thanks to cyberspace.

FIRST: OUR MISSION IS TO SPREAD OUR UNDERSTANDING OF THE TRUTH, WHOLE AND COMPLETE, WITHOUT FEAR OR FLATTERY

(1) Human beings inherently believe in Allah's existence, from the people of Noah until now. True believers deny and refute the existence of all mortal deities being worshiped alongside with our Lord, Allah, and they demonstrate that there is no god but Allah. The challenge, therefore, is that the caller to the truth must refute and deny all other deities besides Allah, and confine divinity to our Creator alone. This is the inherent meaning of the testimony of Islam: 'There is no god but Allah.' This phrase begins with a negation: 'there is no god,' thereby refuting the existence of any and all deities; then it ends with a declaration of monotheism in the second half: 'but Allah.' Hence, a believer begins by negating, and thereby denying other deities who are mortal creatures, to affirm ultimately that divinity is confined exclusively to God the Creator.

(2) In the Qur'anic stories of prophets, all the prophet's people worshiped God Almighty, but their problem was the fact that they ascribed to Him other deities and gods as partners. Every messenger and prophet conveyed one clear message: 'O my people! Worship Allah; you have no god other than Him' (Q 11:84). Likewise, the Muhammadans of today consider themselves 'Muslims' and utter the Islamic testimony of faith, but with their voices and tongues only I am afraid, not with their hearts.

Because they too worship Allah, but simultaneously deify and even worship earthly partners as well. These include: Muhammad, his so-called companions and contemporaries, and the so-called saints, imams, scholars, theologians, and so on, both in the past and present. Hence, Muhammadans fall into the same trap of polytheism as ancient people did. Furthermore, Muhammadans are gravely offended when their teachings and tenets are criticized, such as: the so-called intercession of Muhammad in the Hereafter; the pilgrimage to his tomb/mausoleum; the worship of pre-Umayyad caliphs and the so-called companions; and the deification of so-called imams and authors of hadiths, including Al-Bukhari among many.

Upon such criticism, some Muhammadans consider their critics apostates who have forsaken 'Islam' and who deserve to be put to death as per Sunni laws. The 'crime' of these critics, in my estimation, is that they deny and disbelieve in these mortal deities, the same as those formerly worshiped by their ancestors before Islam. How is it possible that such deep-seated monotheism can be violated? To Muhammadans, they cannot see how Qur'anists adduce evidence from the Qur'an, as well as from the revered traditions of the Muhammadans, to prove this divine truth. To Muhammadans, their faith dictates that the worship of mortals is more effective than their worship of God alone.

Some extremists, bigots and fanatics among the Muhammadans would go as far as to demand the beheading of such critics; and certain flatterers and hypocrites among them demand Qur'anists to stop debunking and refuting their holy teachings which deify mortals, and resist committing themselves to the call for monotheism. Such attitudes are like those of ancient people when they demanded of their messengers and prophets to uphold their native gods and lesser deities, so long as they recognized the one God and worshiped Him at the same time.

(3) We, Qur'anists, are vociferous and outspoken in conveying what we see is the truth. We prove through Qur'anic verses that Muhammad was merely a mortal human being who conveyed divine revelation from God. Receiving divine revelation does *not* make him a deity. He was a mortal like the rest of us. He did not control his life or fate and could not keep harm away from himself or others. Nor did he bring good to himself or others, except by

the will of God. Muhammad never knew the hidden past or unknowable future, and he does not own the Day of Judgment and could never revoke God's judgment via the so-called intercession. On the contrary, the Qur'an asserts that he will be judged like all humans (Q 19:71). This includes all messengers and prophets, and the so-called imams, companions and saints.

(4) We, Qur'anists, do not resort to flattery and hypocrisy; we do not fall in the trap of using politically correct terms or intentionally convoluted and vague expressions. We call a spade a spade. We are outspoken and clear in conveying what we see is the truth, reinforced with clear evidence and proof. We affirm that the so-called holy companions of Muhammad – i.e. his contemporaries – included both hypocrites and sinners. We assert that the four pre-Umayyad caliphs are guilty of starting civil wars in Arabia, as well as the crimes of conquering and invading neighboring territories.

We assert that the imams, theologians and scholars of the Sunni, Shia and Sufi creeds, past and present, have been complicit in crimes against Islam through certain falsehoods they have spread in their books. Such falsehoods include the so-called hadiths, sayings and traditions ascribed to Muhammad after his death, and sometimes ascribed to God Himself. Such authors have fashioned a new man-made Sharia that contradicts the divine Sharia within the Qur'an. Their Sharia laws are being applied nowadays, among others by ISIS and similar terrorist organizations.

The history of the so-called companions, and especially their wars, contradicts the understanding of Islam in the Qur'an; their actions were in fact not unlike those of ISIS. The so-called companions used to shout *Allahu akbar* when they conquered, occupied and invaded the territories of neighboring peoples who never attacked them in Arabia. They shouted the same words while committing atrocities, at times including enslavement, rape, theft and wide-scale death and destruction. Such heinous crimes are condemned and strictly forbidden in the Qur'an. Many terrorists today commit the same crimes, shouting the same slogan, all the while committing grave sins against God.

(5) We, Qur'anists, regarding all of the above, say the following. We make a clear distinction between Islam, found exclusively in the Qur'an, followed by Muhammad during his lifetime, on the one hand, and the Muhammadans who consider themselves 'Muslims' through their

man-made creeds and volumes of traditional literature on the other. Whatever was written and attributed to Islam after the death of Muhammad are, in fact, man-made lies and falsehoods, ascribed *only* to those authors and so-called imams.

We denounce the lack of distinction between Islam (and its higher values in the Qur'an) and the Muhammadans who are mortal human beings committing both good and evil. We denounce and reject the label 'Islamist' given to those persons who use the name of Islam in their political endeavors, namely to reach authority and rule, or to those terrorists who commit atrocities in Islam's name. Both these types of people are criminals who abuse Islam and tarnish its image; Islam is supposed to be a religion of peace, justice, freedom and mercy. Both types are foes and enemies of Muhammad, who was sent as a 'mercy to humankind' (Q 21:107). Such people have turned Islam into a 'terror to humankind' in some parts of the world. Qur'anists deem all such people who use the name of Islam to acquire political status or commit acts of violence to be criminals according to civil law and sinners according to the Qur'an. In this respect there is no difference between theocratic governments and terrorist organizations, both of whom wrongfully appropriate the name of Islam. This is the message of Qur'anism and we Qur'anists declare it openly without flattery, hypocrisy or compromise. Our call for Qur'anism may be shocking to Muhammadans, but we are less concerned with their shock than with adhering to the will of God.

SECOND: IN OUR BRAVE ENDEAVOR, WE QUR'ANISTS ADHERE TO THE ISLAMIC RULES STEMMING SOLELY FROM THE QUR'AN AND ITS HIGHER VALUES

These rules include complete religious freedom for all human beings, the notion that each individual is responsible for their own guidance and that each individual has the right to choose their religion before God. The explanation of these rules is as follows.

(1) We Qur'anists convey what we deem is true without imposing our beliefs or school of thought on others. Anyone who seeks the truth should

understand that truth itself is a lifelong quest. In this respect, God says to Muhammad in the Qur'an:

'We did not reveal the Qur'an to you to make you suffer. But only as a reminder for he who fears.' (Q 20:2–3)

'So remind, if reminding helps.' (Q 87:9)

'And you are not a dictator over them. So remind by the Qur'an whoever fears My warning.' (Q 50:45)

'You are to warn those who fear their Lord inwardly, and perform the prayer. Those who purify themselves do that for their own good. To God is the ultimate return.' (Q 35:18)

'You warn only those who follow the Message and fear the Most Gracious inwardly. So give them good news of forgiveness, and a generous reward.' (Q 36:11)

In accordance with these verses, Qur'anists never coerce in religion those who reject our call for Qur'anism. God further says to Muhammad:

'Had your Lord willed, everyone on earth would have believed. Will you compel people to become believers?' (Q 10:99)

Qur'anists never feel sorry for the Muhammadans who reject their call for Qur'anism; for God says to Muhammad:

'Whoever disbelieves, let not their disbelief sadden you. To Us is their return. Then We will inform them of what they did. God knows what lies within the hearts.' (Q 31:23)

'And do not be saddened by those who rush into disbelief. They will not harm God in the least. God desires to give them no share in the Hereafter. A terrible torment awaits them.' (Q 3:176)

'Oh Messenger! Do not let those who are quick to disbelief grieve you among those who say with their mouths, "We believe," but their hearts they do not believe.' (Q 5:41)

'Perhaps you may destroy yourself in grief, chasing after them, if they do not believe in this teaching.' (Q 18:6)

'What of him whose evil deed was made attractive to him, and so he regards it as good? God leads astray whomever He wills, and He guides whomever He wills. Therefore, do not waste your time in sorrow over them. God knows exactly what they do.' (Q 35:8)

(2) Qur'anists convey what they deem is true, without assuming that they are in possession of the absolute 'Truth' in matters of religion, but rather they publicly proclaim their beliefs, citing proofs and evidence, thereafter awaiting God's judgment in the Day of Resurrection with the rest of human beings of different creeds and denominations. This was the practice of all messengers and prophets mentioned in the Qur'an, which states:

'Say "O my people! Work according to your ability; and so will I." Then you will know.' (Q 39:39–40)

'Say "Our God, Initiator of the heavens and the earth, Knower of all secrets and declarations. You will judge between your servants regarding what they had differed about."'(Q 39:46)

'Say: "O my people! Work according to your ability and so will I." You will come to know to whom will belong the celestial abode. The wrongdoers will not prevail.' (Q 6:135).

'Oh you who believe! You are responsible for your own souls. He who has strayed cannot harm you if you are guided. To God is your return, all of you, and He will inform you of what you used to do.' (Q 5:105)

'Oh my people, do as you may, and so will I. You will know to whom will come a punishment that will shame him, and he who is a liar. So look out. I am on the lookout with you.' (Q 11:93)

'And say to those who do not believe, "Act according to your station; and so will We." And wait; we too are waiting.' (Q 11:121–2)

When Muhammadan muftis and clergymen issue a fatwa (a religious edict or point of view), some claim that it is the absolute truth of Islam. To us Qur'anists, this is an ignorant and nonsensical position. As such, we readily declare that our views are personal opinions and open to questioning and discussion.

(3) Qur'anists convey what they deem is true while respecting the freedom of others in matters of religion (i.e. their tenets, faith, rituals, customs and so on). Qur'anists believe in the Last Day, and they believe that each human will dwell eternally either in Hell or in Paradise. Everyone is free in their choice, as guidance remains a personal and individual responsibility. It is *not* the mission of any Muslim majority country to guide people in matters of faith, nor is it their duty to make them enter Paradise. Their mission, rather, is to protect their citizens and grant them religious freedom so that each of them may be responsible for their choice on the Last Day. To demonstrate that guidance is a strictly individual and personal responsibility, consider the following verses:

'Say, "Oh people, the truth has come to you from your Lord. Whoever accepts guidance is guided for his own soul; and whoever strays only strays to its detriment. I am not a guardian over you."' (Q 10:108)

'And say, "The truth is from your Lord. Whoever wills, let him believe. And whoever wills, let him disbelieve." We have prepared for the unjust a Fire, whose curtains will hem them in. And when they cry for relief, they will be relieved with water like molten brass, which scalds the faces. What a miserable drink, and what a terrible place.' (Q 18:29)

'Whoever is guided is guided for his own good. And whoever goes astray goes astray to his detriment. No burdened soul carries the burden of another, nor do We ever punish until We have sent a messenger.' (Q 17:15)

'And to recite the Qur'an, whoever is guided is guided to his own advantage. And whoever goes astray, then say, "I am one of the warners."' (Q 27:92)

'We sent down upon you the Book for mankind in truth. He who follows guidance does so for the good of his soul. And he who strays in error does so to its detriment. You are not their overseer.' (Q 39:41)

'You cannot guide whom you love, but God guides whom He wills, and He knows best those who are guided.' (Q 28:56)

Hence, even Muhammad could never truly guide those whom he loved; God will guide only those who themselves seek guidance.

(4) Qur'anists convey what they deem is true and never ask for reward. This was the practice of all prophets and messengers mentioned in the Qur'an. God says to Muhammad:

'Say, "Whatever compensation I have asked of you, is yours. My compensation comes only from God, and He is Witness over all things."' (Q 34:47)

God says the following about preachers and the callers to truth, whom we are to follow:

'Follow those who ask of you no wage, and are themselves guided.' (Q 36:21)

The call for Qur'anism, which we see as preserving true Islam, is a peaceful and reformist kind of jihad (literally 'struggle'), that entails the toiling and sacrifice of one's self, time and money. Ours is not a path to deceive others by swindling or fraud, nor is it a path leading to political power, wealth or any form of authority. That is why Qur'anists are mostly of humble means and tread lightly upon the earth. Qur'anists' teachings may invoke the ire of certain unjust rulers, clergymen and more affluent members of society. We face all our detractors through our online publications, and our peaceful calling for Qur'anism, in hopes to save their souls in the Hereafter. Despite the harm done us by them, we forgive all those who trespass against us.

(5) Qur'anists forgive those who harm them as best they can. This is part of Qur'anic law. God says to Muhammad:

'The Hour is coming, so forgive with gracious forgiveness.' (Q 15:85)

'As for his statement "My Lord, these are a people who do not believe." Pardon them, and say, "Peace." They will come to know.' (Q 43:88–9)

God says of true believers:

'Tell those who believe to forgive those who do not hope for the Days of God. He will fully recompense people for whatever they have earned. Whoever does a good deed, it is for his soul; and whoever commits evil, it is against it; then to your Lord you will be returned.' (Q 45:14–15)

That is why Qur'anists forgive and pardon those who harm them, hoping to be included in those mentioned in the following:

'And who is better in speech than someone who calls to God, and acts with integrity, and says, "I am of those who submit to God?" Good and evil are not equal. Repel evil with good, and the person who was your enemy becomes like an intimate friend. But none will attain it except those who persevere, and none will attain it except the very fortunate.' (Q 41:33–5)

THIRD: WE SEE THAT OUR CALL FOR QUR'ANISM IS THE ONLY SOLUTION AT PRESENT TO PEACEFULLY REFORM THE RELIGION OF THE MUHAMMADANS

(1) Despite great suffering, I received the necessary knowledge, training and expertise to undertake this mission of peaceful religious reformation. Despite our modest means, our call for Qur'anism has spread across the world. We have a deeper appreciation of the Qur'an than our detractors; we read and understand it using its own terminology within its own context, and we use it as a yardstick against which to measure the man-made creeds of the Muhammadans, as well as their so-called holy traditions that they have accumulated in the name of Islam.

(2) In thirty years, we have demonstrated with clear evidence the contradiction between what we see is true Islam (the Qur'an alone, a religion of mercy, charity, tolerance, justice, human dignity, religious freedom, and political liberty based on democracy) and what we see are man-made creeds fabricated by the Muhammadans who consider themselves 'Muslims.' Especially problematic in this regard is the creed of Sunni Wahabism, which has spread across the world.

(3) Evidence and proofs of all of the matters discussed here may be found on our website.[3] We hope the reader will consider them carefully.

BIBLIOGRAPHY

Reynolds, Gabriel. *The Emergence of Islam: Classical Traditions in Contemporary Perspective.* (Minneapolis: Fortress Press, 2012)

al-Tizini, Tayyib. *Muqaddimat awwaliyyah fi al-islam al-muhammadi al-bakir nash'atan wa ta'sisan.* (Damascus: Dar Dimashq li al-Tiba'ah wa al-Sahafah wa al-Nashr, 1994)

Tyabji, Faiz. *Muhammadan Law: The Personal Law of Muslims.* (Bombay: N.M. Tripathi, 1940)

Wensinck, Arent J. *A Handbook of Early Muhammadan Tradition: Alphabetically Arranged.* (Leiden: Brill, 1971)

---

[3] http://thequranists.org/.

Afterword

Reuven Firestone

We have observed in this book a remarkable attestation to the fact that the act of reading and interpreting is a complex and variable enterprise. Humans find meaning in things subjectively, but not without reasoned judgment, rationality or logic. It has long been understood by literary theorists that reading is 'experiencing' a text, and experience is highly personal. The reader invests his or her life experience *into* what is being read, and therefore reacts to two sets of information: there are the words produced by the author on the one hand; then there are the words as absorbed and processed by the reader. A permeable border always exists between the two, so that whatever the particular 'intent' may be of the author, it is inevitably filtered through the particularities of personality and experience of the reader. No one can escape this feature of human cognition, no matter how educated, experienced or authoritative the reader may be.

This process of conveying and absorbing information is relativistic to a certain extent, because the chemistry between writer and reader works something like a dance or duet. The reader cannot help but respond faithfully to two forces simultaneously: the physical words on the page, and the personhood of the self who is processing those words. It is arguable, therefore, that readers respond faithfully, even if highly personally to the written production, even if their reading is 'mistaken' from the perspective of another reader. This complex duet is further complicated by the fact that individuals live within, and identify with, communities. We live among people, and we both influence and are influenced by them through formal and informal education, culture, language and history.

As a result, these chapters have offered perspectives and methodologies that are developed not merely by the individual authors who wrote them, but also with influence from the communities of which they form a part. They are the products of people who exist not as lonely islands, but as distinct individuals living in community, and to a certain extent agents or envoys of those communities. Stanley Fish popularized the concept of 'interpretive communities' as noted in the introduction to this volume. The notion of interpretive communities helps to unpack the complex interplay between literary production and the meaning(s) made of it by those who process it through reading. Such consideration is important for understanding the reception of art, for all art – whether literary or plastic, audial or sensual – is expected to evoke personal responses among those who perceive it.

But what about a different genre of words? What about scripture, which according to traditional and virtually universal common understanding is profoundly more significant than any other written form?

The adherents of the scriptural monotheisms all agree that God reveals, and that God's most important revelations have been collected and preserved in writing – 'scripted' or 'scribed' into what we commonly refer to as scripture. Scripture is, by its very essence, an official document; or perhaps better put, *the* official document that faithfully represents the will of God. Once written down and formalized into a canon, divine writ may never be physically altered because doing so would represent the extreme hubris of mortals amending, overruling or abrogating God's ultimate authority. Scripture thus represents the fixed and unchanging physical record of the Ultimate, which by definition articulates the perfect and complete will of God, the divine imperative.

Because God is presumed to be all-knowing of past and future as well as the present, then while the words of scripture may appear to represent only a moment in history – the 'moment' of the divine disclosure that is then recorded – they are nevertheless considered by traditional religious thinkers to be relevant for all time. There is no need for any 'new' revelation once the canonical revelation has been received and recorded because God is aware of the future, and via divine omniscience, reveals an eternally valid message. This is a common perspective among the various monotheist communities, each relating to its own record of divine disclosure. It is also a source of great tension between them because each presumes that its own scriptural revelation is complete, while simultaneously assuming that the scripture of the other is in one way or another inadequate, incomplete, abrogated or inaccurate.

But even within a single community of believers that agrees on the authenticity and reliability of its scripture, the static state of the unchanging canonized written word presents a profound challenge. That challenge is to make sense of the *meaning* of the ageless words of God, even as times change, as technology and language and culture and society develop through the generations and millennia.

People who reflect on the subject of words and language recognize that words carry nuances and varieties of meaning in normal human discourse. We note from our own experience that different people hear identical words in different ways. Sometimes skillful writers choose words in a judicious manner for their literary creations in order to convey different levels of meaning or in order to induce a deeper or more insightful response among those who might be sensitive or open to greater complexity and contemplation. How much the more so if God is the author!

As human beings, we interpret everything. We perceive and process our perceptions in ways that reflect the particularities of our character, personal history and temperament. This produces our comprehension, which as an individualized response to the world around us reflects all the particularities of our personal experience. As a consequence, multiple witnesses to a common occurrence testifying under oath in a court of law frequently describe what seem to be entirely different events. It should not be surprising then, when considering human responses to holy scriptures, to observe the broad array of scriptural interpretations throughout the centuries and millennia of human religious experience. Perhaps the traditional assumption of the scriptural monotheisms that humanity was created in God's 'image' or 'likeness' is an attempt to make sense of this seemingly unique quality of the human animal, which in its essential nature of reflective thought seems to differ significantly from the perceptive abilities of all other creatures.[1] In short, it is essential to our human nature to perceive the world in our uniquely individual ways. As such, we often disagree – about potentially anything – and in theory, everything.

Yet despite our tendency toward deeply individual and personal reflection, we humans tend to congregate with others among whom we share common assumptions, conventions and expectations. We form communities for many reasons, but one of them is to find comfort in a shared reality and perspective. Such communities can be defined (in part) as 'communities of interpretation.'

This seems to be the nature of the human sentient condition. We are pulled on the one hand toward realization of our human individuality and on the other toward a shared experience of perception. We want both the freedom to realize and articulate our own deeply personal perception, and the support and love and security that is found within a community with shared awareness and insights.

Another seemingly natural aspect of the human condition is the desire to find larger communities of shared experience, or to convince others to join our own interpretive community. Who does not enjoy the knowledge that many people agree with one's own view? Who would not feel good knowing that 'everyone' agrees? Certain people seem to have a greater ability than others to live with a certain level of tension between one's own views and the views of others. Some people, on the other hand, feel tension and insecurity knowing that others do not share their views, particularly on issues of great personal significance. Such people are more likely to impose their views and perceptions on others who do not share them, often through attempts at verbal persuasion, but also sometimes through power and force. The formation of 'orthodoxies' can be a result. Orthodoxies are often created with the most noble of intentions, though they tend to develop particularly when other forces are also at play, such as politics, issues of wealth or security and safety, or fear.

---

[1] Genesis 1:27; 5:1; Bukhari 6227.

Whenever orthodoxies attempt to impose their views on large populations, communities form that resist the impulse to conform to views imposed upon them. This response is also part of the independent, sentient nature of the human condition. But resistance tends to invite greater stringency on the part of the orthodoxy, which in turn invites more resistance. This cycle can be seen throughout human history, not only in relation to religion but all aspects of human perception.

One might agree with these basic observations of human nature. But what of Truth? Is it all a matter of personal perception? Is everything so relative that we must discard any semblance of absolute meaning in the words of scripture? Is the divine word only and always what *we* think it is? Does that mean that any interpretation is valid? Are there no limits to the freedom to create meaning?

A number of issues are at play here, but perhaps the most salient is the distinction between the Creator and the created. In short, the divine will is ultimately unknowable, but not because God does not reveal it. God discloses through revelation, some of which is recorded in scripture. But nobody has the capacity to truly understand the divine will fully, and anyone who claims to do so exhibits an astonishing level of arrogance. The proof of Truth's unknowability lies in the inability of the smartest and wisest humans to agree about it, not only between religious communities but also within them. Truth is elusive. The best we can do is to work towards getting closer to it, and that realization should produce patience, humility and surrender of (at least some of) our ego; that is a form of submission, of islam with a small 'i.'

But while Truth is ultimately unknowable with full certainty and in all its fullness, it remains a precious goal to aspire to through study and contemplation, and it is even accessible to the limited degree in which we can connect and make sense from it. Our individual efforts can bring us closer, but our human limitations render the task so much more difficult to do alone. Only through engagement with others can we pool the knowledge, experience and wisdom that can bring us closer to understanding. And this is only possible where a discourse of sharing is accepted or, better, encouraged.

Just as important, it is only in an environment in which individuals along with their communities of interpretation can freely articulate their perceptions without imposition that humanity can live together in true peace and justice. While no one can truly and fully know the divine will or the true and fullest meaning of divine writ, we nevertheless derive deep significance and meaning from the eternal flow of communication from the Ultimate. With the freedom to share our perceptions and the willingness to learn from others, we can deepen our understanding of the Transcendent, and therefore of the meaning in our own lives and struggles. This extraordinary conference, and the spirited and courageous volume that it has produced, have presented us with an excellent model for how we can do exactly this.

Reuven Firestone

Index

Locators in *italics* refer to information in the footnotes.